The Green Building Bible

3rd Edition, Volume 2

The low energy design technical reference

ISBN 1-898130-04-3

Principal author: Richard Nicholls

Publishing editor: Keith Hall

Publisher: Green Building Press

Green Building Press

www.greenbuildingbible.co.uk

www.greenbuildingpress.co.uk

the Green building bible

Copyright

Publishing editor: Keith Hall
Green Building Press, PO Box 32,
Llandysul, SA44 5ZA
Tel: 01559 370798
E-mail: keith@greenbuildingpress.co.uk
Web Site: www.greenbuildingpress.co.uk
Advertising: Jerry Clark 01208 895103
jerry@greenbuildingpress.co.uk

Disclaimer

Extra copies of this book or Volume 1 can be ordered on the gbp internet store at: www.newbuilder.co.uk/books or by post - send cheque or postal order, made payable to *Green Building Press,* for £9.95 (incl p&p) per copy. Send to *Green Building Press*, PO Box 32, Llandysul, SA44 5ZA.

Cover photo: Air 403 wind turbine and photovoltaic panels on a workshop roof at the home of the publisher.

3rd edition, Volume 2

Acknowledgements

This book would not have been possible without the willing help of numerous people. I am indebted to Richard Nicholls for all his comprehensive and clearly presented text and for producing it all to our very tight publishing timescale. Also thanks to contributing authors for this volume: Derek Taylor, Mike George and John Garbutt.

I would also like to extend my thanks to the advertisers who have supported this new additional volume to the Green Building Bible. Their input has enabled us to keep the cover price affordable, and because of our strict advertising policy, these businesses add to the usefulness of this book.

I am indebted to my wife Sally and our close friend Jerry Clark for their many hours of proof reading and correcting. My son Keith Hall Jnr. also deserves a mention for helping to enhance many of the illustrations and diagrams in this book.

Keith Hall - publishing editor
Green Building Press

The Green Building Press is a member of Green Ink.

The public lending rights (PLR) of this title have been assigned to the World Land Trust.

The World Land Trust identifies and conserves vital wilderness areas under threat. Its strategy is to purchase such land and then work with non-governmental organisations to manage it in the most environmentally sensitive way.

Contents

>>>

Contents

Printed on Era silk paper and board; an FSC product which contains 50% recycled fibre by Cambrian Printers, an FSC Accredited company (TT-COC-2200): 01970 627111 www.cambrian-printers.co.uk
No reproduction in any form without prior approval of the publisher.
Cover design © Green Building Press.

All web links in this book were checked and live as at September 2006.

FSC
TT-COC-2200

Welcome to the future part 2

Welcome to Volume 2 of the third edition of the Green Building Bible. The green building movement has many facets with promoters of many different styles and approaches. The need to construct sustainable homes, offices, towns and cities has never been as widely acknowledged as it is now. With environmental disasters and evidence of climate change increasing, even the sceptics are beginning to understand the urgency of the task ahead. We need buildings that use far less energy and, as far as possible, are able to withstand extremes of heat and cold without the need for mechanical assistance. Unlike previous generations, we can no longer expect, or rely on, a never ending flow of fossil fuels.

Creating greener buildings and cities is not a pipe dream. We have the knowledge and the ability to make far better use of the natural resources and adapt to the climate around us. We can turn around from our consumerist and throwaway society and incorporate sustainable measures into all new and existing buildings.

For this new addition to the Green Building Bible title, I invited long term acquaintance and highly respected academic, Richard Nicholls, to compile a comprehensive set of guidelines to help our readers put ideas into action. I have encouraged Richard to explain, in terms that most of us can understand, the technical aspects of low energy buildings. He has achieved this admirably and this book is a pragmatic approach to the subject. It adds to and builds upon the dialogue that is presented in Volume 1. It puts flesh on the skeleton of the ideas that are so broadly discussed.

Most in the industry will agree that there is no single blueprint for the perfect green building but I'm sure we all agree that through debate, discussion, and the sharing of practical and technical know-how, plus a strong desire to achieve the goal, we will succeed in creating a sustainable society.

Keith Hall

Keith Hall - Publishing Editor
keith@greenbuildingpress.co.uk

Gaia Architects

Ecological designers for 20 years
throughout the UK and Europe.
Projects include all building types,
plus research, community
consultation, masterplanning
and feasibility study services in
rural and urban contexts.

The Monastery
2 Hart Street Lane
Edinburgh
EH1 3RG

Tel: 0131 557 9191
Fax: 0131 557 9292
Email: architects@gaiagroup.org
Website: www.gaiagroup.org

1 Energy and environment

Introduction

All developed societies are dependent on energy for running homes, industry and transport infrastructures. Like most other societies the UK has three sectors that are the main consumers of this energy: industry, transportation and buildings. In 2004 these three sectors accounted for 21%, 35.7% and 43.3% of the total UK primary energy consumption respectively (Figure1.1). The consumption of energy is costly and has been proven to be highly damaging to the environment, therefore its use needs to be reduced. Unfortunately the reverse is the case. Over the period 1990 to 2001 there was a 19% increase in domestic energy consumption. This was due in part to a 10% increase in the number of homes and also due to the additional appliances and central heating added to existing buildings. Since buildings account for the largest proportion of UK energy consumption, those designing and building them are finding themselves ever more challenged in the quest to reduce this burden on the UK and global environment.

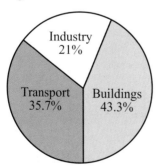

Figure 1.1. Breakdown of UK energy consumption. Energy is used by the building services installed within buildings to create a comfortable, safe, healthy and productive environment.

Types of energy

Chemical energy such as coal, oil or gas are often referred to as fuel. The energy component forms part of the fuel until it is released by combustion. Fuels are useful as they are a store of energy and can be used to move energy from one location to another simply by transporting the fuel. The amount of energy contained within an amount of fuel is known as its calorific value. The calorific values of gas, coal, fuel oil and wood are;

Natural gas = 10.5kWh/m³
Coal = 7.5kWh/kg
Fuel oil = 11.7kWh/litre
Wood chips = 4.67kWh/kg

Mechanical energy is the energy contained within an object due to it being in motion. One example is the energy in a rotating fan blade. Mechanical energy is useful for making other

> The basic scientific unit of energy is the joule (J). But this unit is too small for describing the quantities of energy used in buildings. Instead we normally use the unit, watt hour. This is still small so we tend to use thousands of watt hours ie kilowatt hours (kWh). 1kWh is equivalent to 36,000,000 joules!

things move in turn for example the fan blade gives up some of its energy to air next to the blade causing that to move. Hopefully the air movement goes to provide a useful function, such as extracting fumes or cooling.

Thermal energy is also known as heat. Heat can be put into objects and this increases their temperature. Examples are heating room air and domestic hot water. Heat can also be removed from objects and this decreases their temperature, such as removing heat from water to create chilled water. Human beings detect thermal energy as warmth. It is an essential requirement for human survival and comfort.

Electromagnetic energy is a form of radiant energy eminating from within the atomic structure of matter. One of the properties of electromagnetic energy is its wavelength. The wavelength varies depending on the energy content. Human beings are sensitive to some wavelengths. For example, the wavelengths known as infra red are felt as heat by the skin. Another shorter wavelength band is detected by the human eye as light.

Electrical energy is the energy contained within moving electrons. Moving electrons are detected as an electrical current in wires. The electrical current on its own is not much use but the effects of it are. These are; heating effect - can be used for space heating or creation of light, and electromagnetic effect - can be used in electric motors to create movement.

Renewable energy is simply energy in one of the forms described above which is obtained by tapping into the natural energy flows around us. For example, passive solar heating relies on the infra red part of the electromagnetic radiation from the sun, and wind power uses the kinetic energy embodied in moving air. Biomass is a form of chemical energy produced during the growth of plants following the absorption of sunlight. The main advantages of renewable energy are that it does not rely on a finite reserve of fuel and it does not emit CO_2 when used. However, whilst it is assumed biomass is carbon neutral, because new growth absorbs the CO_2 released during combustion of the old growth, there will in fact be some CO_2 released due to the processing (e.g. chipping) of the biomass and also from the transport from where it is grown to where it is needed.

Nuclear energy is energy derived from the splitting apart of large atoms (fission) or the joining together of two small atoms (fusion). In each case new atoms are formed and energy is released in the form of thermal, electromagnetic and kinetic energy. This energy is captured and used to produce steam which drives a turbine to generate electricity. Fission forms the basis of nuclear power in the UK. Research continues into fusion and the reactors that would contain it.

Nuclear power fell out of favour over the last two to three decades due to the problems of radiation, cost of decommissioning and probably most importantly, opposition from the public. However, as fossil fuels start to dwindle and old nuclear stations reach the end of their life, the UK is starting to rely on imported energy. Politicians are starting to prepare the ground for a resurgence of nuclear power to replace, and possibly add to, the current nuclear capacity. Nuclear power produces low carbon emissions but is unique in its production of large amounts of radioactive waste.

Energy efficiency and pollution

Energy cannot be created or destroyed but it can be converted from one form to another. For example chemical energy can be burned to produce heat, and mechanical energy can be used in a generator to produce electricity.

Energy for use in buildings can be described in two ways: primary energy or delivered energy.

Primary energy is that which is found within the unprocessed energy source, such as fossil fuels, biofuels or sunshine.

Delivered energy is that which is delivered to the building. For coal, oil and gas, delivered energy is very similar to primary energy as little is lost during extraction. However, the delivered value of electricity is provided by a much larger quantity of primary energy, as a great deal of

Pollutant gas output is quoted as a mass of gas, measured in kilograms(kg), per kilowatt hour (kWh) of delivered energy. Carbon dioxide output is also specified in terms of a weight of carbon per unit of delivered energy (kg/kWh). It is possible to convert between the two quoted values by considering the atomic weight of carbon and oxygen. Carbon has an atomic weight of 12, oxygen has an atomic weight of 16. So the molecular weight of CO_2 is (12+16+16) 44. Therefore the fraction of carbon in carbon dioxide is 12/44ths or 3/11ths. To convert a mass of carbon dioxide to a mass of carbon multiply it by 3/11. To convert a mass of carbon to a mass of carbon dioxide divide it by 3/11.

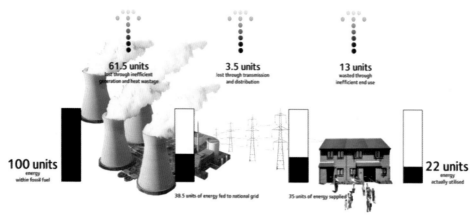

Figure 1.2. According to Greenpeace, centralised electricity supplies waste more than two thirds of the energy available from fossil fuels. This accounts for more than 20% of the UK's CO₂ emissions. Photo © Greenpeace

the energy in the coal, oil or gas is wasted in the power station during generation. For a typical coal fired power station, for every 100kWh of primary energy taken in as coal only 35kWh will be output as delivered electricity. The rest goes to waste.

The efficiency of all combustion devices is less than 100% since hot flue gases need to be exhausted. This means that not all of the input energy to a combustion device appears as thermal energy on the output side. For example a gas boiler may have an efficiency of 80%. This means that if an output of 100kWh is required, 125kWh of energy, in the form of gas, needs to be input to the boiler. The extra amount is to make up for the losses from the boiler.

The chemical reaction, (combustion), that takes place between fossil fuels and oxygen to release heat also produces a number of gaseous by-products. Typically these are carbon dioxide (CO_2), sulphur dioxide (SO_2), nitric oxide (NO) and nitrogen dioxide (NO_2). The latter two are collectively known as nitrous oxides (NO_x).

Different fuels have different pollution outputs per unit of energy. The pollutant gases given out depend on the elements present in the fuel before combustion, such as carbon and sulphur. Table 1.1 shows the output of carbon dioxide arising from the use of 1kWh of energy for various fuels. From the table it can be seen

that natural gas has the lowest carbon emission factor. Gas produces 53% less carbon than electricity and 28% and 38% less than from using oil and coal respectively.

The most polluting fuel, electricity, is generated from a mix of coal and oil fired power stations, nuclear power and a very small proportion of renewables. It can be seen that electricity has by far the greatest output of carbon per kWh. This is a direct result of inefficiencies in power generation from fossil fuels as mentioned earlier. In 2004 37% of UK emissions of CO_2 came from the energy industries (power stations), 21% from road transport, 18% from other industries and 16 % from residential fossil fuel use[1].

Many new combined cycle gas fired power stations were constructed. These power stations have an efficiency of 42 - 45% and

Delivered fuel	Carbon emission factor (kgC/kWh)
Natural gas	0.053
LPG	0.068
Biogas	0.000
Oil (all grades)	0.074
Coal	0.086
Biomass	0.000
Electricity	0.113
Waste heat	0.000

Table 1.1. Output of carbon per kWh of delivered fuel energy.

are therefore more efficient than coal fired stations. In addition the pollution output of the primary fuel, gas, is lower. For example, a coal fired power station produces between 64.9 and 76.2g of CO_2 per MJ of electricity generated. A combined cycle gas turbine power station produces between 28 and 33.3g of CO_2 per MJ of electricity[2].

Each of the gases arising from combustion is known to cause environmental damage. Carbon dioxide is a greenhouse gas, sulphur and carbon dioxide combine with moisture in the air to create acid rain, Nitric oxides add to poor air quality and ozone depletion.

Acid rain

Rain is naturally acidic due to the presence of dissolved carbon and sulphur dioxides from the atmosphere. However, the release of additional quantities of these gases from the burning of fossil fuels has made the rain more acidic.

The more accurate term is acid deposition since burning fossil fuels in buildings and power stations results in both wet and dry deposits. Dry deposition in the form of dust and gas generally occurs close to the source. The wet deposits, acid rain or snow, can be carried long distances in the atmosphere. Fuel combustion in one country can cause environmental damage in a neighbouring country.

Life forms have developed in an environment with a particular acidity level. Altering this natural state will distress the vegetation and freshwater life in those ecosystems. Acid rain also causes damage to buildings by reacting with the materials from which they are made. Historic buildings and statues made from certain types of stone are particularly vulnerable to attack.

The degree of acidity of a solution is indicated using the pH scale. pH7 is neutral, lower pH values represent increasing acidity down to pH1. pH values higher than 7 are more alkaline up to pH14. Table 1.2 shows examples of the range of acidities and alkalinities encountered in every day life.

PH	Example
13.0 strong alkaline	dilute sodium hydroxide
11.0	bathroom cleaner
7.0 neutral	distilled water
5.3 slightly acidic	normal rain
4.5	acid rain
3.0	Vinegar
1.0 strong acid	dilute nitric acid

Table 1.2. pH Values of some common liquids.

Research has shown that the acidity of lakes in some parts of Norway has increased from pH5.8 in 1940 to pH4.8 in 1990. Fish cannot live in lakes and rivers with water below pH4.5. Many north European deciduous forests are showing signs of leaf damage which is thought to be due to acid rain.

Global warming

The earth's atmosphere is transparent to short wave infra red (heat) radiation from the sun. This radiation is absorbed by the earth and is re-radiated at a longer wavelength. The atmosphere is not transparent to this long wave radiation and so the heat is trapped.

This warming effect is essential to life on earth. Without it the earth would be 30°C cooler. The degree to which heat is trapped in the atmosphere depends on its mixtures of gases. There are a number of greenhouse gases, natural ones such as methane and man made ones such as the chlorofluorocarbons (CFCs). The greenhouse gas which exists in the largest quantities is carbon dioxide (CO_2). This occurs both naturally and as a result of man's activities. Scientists have noted that the concentration of CO_2 is increasing in the atmosphere as a result of fossil fuel combustion and deforestation. It is now accepted by the scientific community that increased global warming is now occurring due to man's activities. The continuing disagreement amongst scientists is over the magnitude of the effects of global warming. It is predicted that atmospheric temperatures will increase, sea levels will rise, weather patterns will change and agriculture will be affected.

Estimates of the size of the temperature

increase and the likely consequences vary depending on the mathematical model of the climate being used. Various catastrophic scenarios have been detailed, such as melting of the ice caps and expansion of the oceans leading to widespread flooding and changes in weather patterns. However, there is a conflicting opinion that some of the worst effects may be limited by processes which arise due to global warming itself, resulting in negative feedback. The first factor is increased plankton growth in the warm oceans that would consume more CO_2. Plankton are tiny plants found in the upper layers of the sea. As they grow they consume carbon dioxide. The second factor is reflection of solar energy back into space from cloud cover which is predicted to increase as a consequence of global warming.

Models will continue to be refined to determine more accurately the consequences of global warming. What is known is that man made CO_2 increases are detrimental to climatic processes and all efforts should be made to limit unnecessary CO_2 output.

Air quality

The products of combustion from heating systems and power stations contribute to poor air quality. Nitrous oxides are known to be a lung irritant and as such they can cause breathing difficulties in adults and asthma problems in children.

Conserving finite fuels

One of the most difficult aspects of fossil fuel usage is to predict the longevity of supplies. Fossil fuels were created from prehistoric forests and so the amount is finite. It should be possible to predict how long reserves will last by dividing the quantities available by the rate of consumption. Various predictions have been made in this way. For example oil is estimated to last a further 40 years, gas 65 years and coal 300 years. These predictions vary due to a number of factors which are;
- new reserves being found due to exploration
- previously uneconomic reserves being brought into production due to increases in fuel costs

- variations in demand, for example, due to economic growth and recession
- increasing worldwide demand for fuel, especially from developing countries such as China and India.

These factors cause variation in the number of years before fossil fuel is estimated to become exhausted but the orders of magnitude remain the same. Fossil fuels will eventually run out. Energy conservation will slow down the rate of consumption which, being optimistic, will give society time to research, develop and implement alternative sustainable energy sources.

Better buildings

A number of research projects have shown that low energy buildings tend to be more desirable to the occupants than an equivalent standard building. In housing the effect is seen as an immediate reduction in gas and electricity bills. However, the reductions in bills are often not as large as predicted. This is because the building occupants use some of the potential savings to provide a warmer home. The home can be better heated but still have lower fuel bills. Improvements in temperatures also have an effect on health. In the UK many elderly people die each year due to hypothermia in poorly heated homes. In addition many accidents occur due to a reduction in mobility with low temperatures. Warmer homes can prevent much of this and also aid in respiratory illnesses by driving away the dampness that can lead to mould growth and dust mite infestations. The spores from the former and detritus from the latter can cause allergic reactions leading to asthma, especially in young children.

Many studies have shown that the workforce in low energy commercial buildings is more productive. This may be due to an overall corporate staff management system which not only values the environment but the employees too. It may also be due to the fact that many low energy office buildings are well daylit, naturally ventilated by openable windows and may incorporate planted atria and other spaces which inspire and add to occupant well-being.

14

Another benefit of low energy buildings is that maintenance costs are reduced since there will be less energy consuming plant installed, and that which is will run for fewer hours during a shorter heating season.

Reducing energy consumption

There are many benefits to be gained by reducing the energy consumption of buildings. A number of carrots and sticks are now in place to assist or encourage the saving of energy. The methods available can be broadly categorised as either fiscal, legislative or technical.

Fiscal

Taxation can be used to penalise the use of energy or reward the purchase of energy saving devices.

The climate change levy is a tax that has been added to energy costs incurred by industry, commerce, agriculture and public sector services. The aim is to discourage energy use by increasing the cost of fuels. It also makes purchases of energy saving devices and systems more cost effective by reducing the pay-back period. The tax is added to energy bills at a rate of 0.43p/kWh for electricity, 0.15p/kWh for gas, 1.17p/kWh for coal and 0.07p/kWh for LPG. It can be seen that these sums reflect the pollution output of the various fuels (Table 1.1). The more polluting the fuel the greater is the levy. Part of the revenue collected from this tax will go to reducing employers national insurance contributions, making it cheaper to employ staff. Part will also be used to fund energy efficiency schemes and renewable energy systems.

Some fuels are exempt from the levy, such as renewable energy and combined heat and power output. For some users the levy is being reduced, for example, energy intensive industries who are implementing energy reduction strategies. (see http://customs.hmrc.gov.uk)

Enhanced capital allowances. Taxation is a punitive method of encouraging energy efficiency but there are also enhanced capital

allowances available for energy efficiency equipment such as chp systems, efficient boilers, pipe insulation, variable speed drives and low energy lighting systems. These enhanced allowances allow the full cost of the devices to be written off over one year instead of over approximately eight years which is normal for most capital items. (see www.eca.gov.uk)

Legislative

Building Regulations. In recognition of the need to save energy the conservation of fuel and power is included within the Building Regulations which are enforceable by law. The Building Regulations are regularly reviewed. In the past the regulations have concentrated on reducing the space heating energy use of buildings. They now consider energy standards in both new and existing domestic (part L1a and L1b) and new and existing non-domestic (part L2a and L2b) buildings. The Building Regulations are considered in more detail throughout the book when relevant to the topic under discussion.

Energy Performance of Buildings Directive

The EPBD is a European Directive (2002/91/EC) which came into force in January 2006. Its aim is to improve the energy performance of buildings by increasing awareness of energy use in buildings. This, in turn, will lead to increased investment in energy efficiency measures. The objectives are:

Implement a method to calculate the energy performance of buildings. This must be holistic and consider all energy consuming aspects of the building. The calculation methods used in the UK are the Standard Assessment Procedure (SAP) for domestic buildings and the Standard Building Assessment Method (SBEM) for non-domestic buildings. The SAP method is freely available to download (www.bre.co.uk/sap2005)but accredited SAP software is only available for purchase. SBEM software, developed by the Building Research Establishment from a Dutch method, is available free to download from the website www.ncm. bre.co.uk

Energy certification of buildings, based on the above. All buildings occupied by a public authority or those visited by numerous people must exhibit an energy certificate for the building in a prominent place.

Setting of minimum energy requirements for new buildings over 1000m^2 of total useful floor area.

Minimum energy requirements for the renovation of non-domestic buildings over 1000m^2 total useful floor area.

Regular inspection of boilers and air conditioning systems. There are two methods of complying here. The first involves regular assessment of systems with recommendations as to how the system can be made more efficient. The second method relies on providing information to users on aspects of system efficiency with the aim that these recommendations will be adopted. There is a requirement that this second method produces the same savings as expected by the inspection method.

The aim of this directive is to initiate a 45million tonnes reduction in European CO_2 output. This is a 14% contribution to the overall EU Kyoto emissions reduction target of 330M tonnes required by 2010.

Technical

There are a number of new, re-discovered or improved technologies which can be used to reduce energy consumption and reduced CO_2 output whilst maintaining existing levels of thermal comfort, ventilation and lighting.

Carbon sequestration. One of the causes of rising CO_2 levels is the destruction of forests. The planting of new forests will help to absorb atmospheric CO_2 during their growth periods. Forests also help to promote bio-diversity by providing a habitat for wildlife. However, it is estimated that reforestation in the UK will only contribute a small proportion to the target CO_2 reductions set by the UK government.

Improve electrical generation efficiencies.

Higher efficiencies can be obtained from new coal fired generation and even higher efficiencies from gas generation. This is proven technology which is already contributing to reducing CO_2 output. However, there are commentators who believe gas should be reserved for distributed heating and CHP plant where efficiencies of 80-90% can be achieved and that more effort should be expended in producing cleaner coal fired electricity since coal reserves are more extensive than gas.

Renewable energy. Wind, solar, bio-mass and hydro electric power stations can be used to displace fossil fuel and nuclear generation. At the moment renewables are not cost competitive when compared to fossil fuel generated electricity. In many cases they also have their own environmental concerns. For example, windfarms are often rejected for their visual intrusion on hill tops and positioning within areas of natural beauty.

Building energy efficiency. It is generally accepted that cost effective energy savings as great as 40% can be made in existing buildings with poor fabric and services and that savings of 10-20% can be made on average across the whole buildings sector. These savings can be achieved often at little or no extra cost if energy efficiency methods are integrated during refurbishment or at the design stage.

From the above it is clear that low energy design in both refurbishment of old and construction of new buildings, is the method which is likely to have the largest impact on energy consumption and pollutant gas emissions within the UK. This also makes real sense since rather than provide new forms of supply, it is far more cost effective to reduce demand. This may also increase the viability of renewable energy schemes in the future which at current rates of generation can only supply a small fraction of UK electricity needs.

Low energy design

Virtually every aspect of a building's design, construction and services has an effect on its energy consumption. In order to reduce the energy consumption to a minimum, whilst maintaining comfort standards, we must first identify the role these design aspects play in energy performance. This knowledge will then inform us about the methods we can use to restrict energy use. This can be by careful design, adoption of new or improved technologies and materials or utilisation of traditional architectural techniques. The design elements can be broadly listed as the following.

Siting and climate can have a great affect on the amount of energy that is used to create a comfortable internal environment. It follows that the more severe the external climate the more energy is used. Landscaping can be used to create a less severe microclimate in which to place a building.

The form of the building dictates the size of the surface area and volume. These two factors in turn are directly proportional to the fabric and ventilation heat loss rates respectively. Form also dictates the ability with which natural energy can be collected and used, such as solar heat, light and natural ventilation.

Building fabric heat transfer characteristics of the external envelope determine fabric heat loss rates. Low density materials, insulators, can be used to slow the passage of heat. Dense, thermally massive materials can be used internally to help cool a building in summer.

Uncontrolled infiltration involves cold air entering a building and warm air being lost from it. The motors in mechanical ventilation systems consume electricity. Infiltration should be minimised and mechanical systems should operate efficiently and only as necessary.

Natural daylighting can be used to displace the use of artificial light created using electricity. The glazed openings of a building have the strongest influence on natural light utilisation.

Artificial lighting consumes electricity and so should be produced efficiently and only used as required.

Passive solar heating can be used to displace the use of mechanical heating created from burning fossil fuels. This requires well thought out solar collection strategies and heating controls that allow full advantage to be made of natural energy flows.

Mechanical heating systems consume fossil fuels to create heat and so should be operated efficiently and only as required.

Mechanical cooling systems consume electricity to create coolth. To avoid this means of cooling, passive methods such as prevention of heat gains and exposed mass with night time ventilation should be used as a first option. Where passive cooling is inadequate efficient mechanical systems should be chosen and operated only as required.

General services lifts, escalators, emergency lighting and other systems consume electricity and so efficient systems should be chosen and used only as required

Post occupancy energy management to monitor and adjust energy consuming equipment so that it operates efficiently. Building energy consumption can increase if it is not monitored and managed to remain on target.

The topics listed above have varying relevance depending on the building type and its services. For example, air-conditioning is rarely used in domestic buildings and some equipment intensive office buildings may only use space heating at the perimeter. The emphasis in any low energy strategy must be driven by a knowledge of predicted energy flows.

A general low energy strategy is indicated in Figure 1.3 The approach is to first reduce the demand for energy then make use of natural energy flows and finally supply the energy that is needed in an efficient and well controlled manner. The order to elements of the strategy is therefore:
1. Position and orientate the building in a "kind" microclimate by choosing an appropriate site or using landscaping techniques to

modify the climate.

2. Minimise fabric and ventilation heat loss rates.
3. Optimise any "free" sources of energy such as solar gains, daylight or natural ventilation.
4. Select the energy consuming plant to be as energy efficient as possible.
5. Control the energy consuming plant so that it operates only when required and to the level required.
6. Recover waste energy where viable.

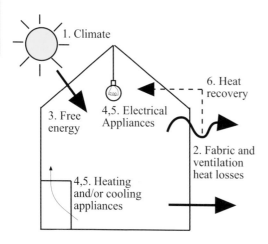

Figure 1.3. General low energy strategy.

Focus on carbon

If energy was free, limitless and non polluting its use would be of no concern to us. Unfortunately, as revealed earlier, this is not the case. In the past, the cost of heating and lighting a building was the only concern. Gas and electricity were both measured in units of energy but this was then converted to a cost. However, we are now very concerned about climate change and so we need to move our attention from the cost of using energy to the carbon released by it. So now when we measure the amounts of gas and electricity used, we often convert them to a carbon output which changes our perspective. This is illustrated in Figure 1.4 which shows two bar charts relating to a typical house. The left hand chart shows the contribution to the total energy consump-

tion of a building made by gas and electricity. The right hand chart shows the contribution to the total carbon output of the building made by gas and electricity. Figure 1.5 shows the same information for an air-conditioned office. In both figures the relative importance of electricity compared to gas increases when considering CO_2 output. It follows then that if we are interested in reducing the environmental impact of these two types of building then;

In domestic buildings space heating reductions remain a priority. In this case considerations should be made to reduce heat losses, optimise the use of passive solar space heating and provide efficent heating systems and adequate controls. Following this the electrical consumption of the lighting and domestic appliances should be reduced, as should energy used for water heating.

In office buildings electricity reductions through reduced artificial lighting, ventilation and cooling is the priority. In this case effort should be made to maximise the use of natural ventilation, passive cooling and natural light.

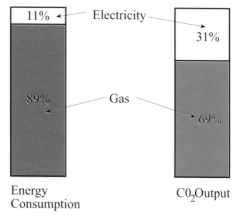

Figure 1.4. Percentage of total delivered energy use and CO_2 output attributed to gas and electricity consumption in housing.

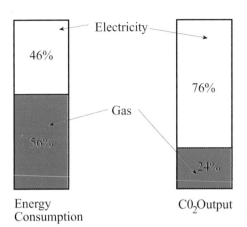

Energy
Consumption CO_2Output

*Figure 1.5. Percentage of total delivered energy use
and CO_2 output attributed to gas and electricity
consumption in an air-conditioned office.*

Conclusion

There are three factors that drive the increased
use of low energy principles in everyday design
decisions. These are;

Professional responsibility - given the value
of low energy design principles to producing
better buildings and reducing environmental
impact, it is the duty of professionals in the
construction industry to recommend low energy
solutions whenever alternative choices occur.

Increasing legislation - governments, in
recognition of the importance of energy issues

have introduced legislation that aims to reduce
building energy consumption. This legislation
must be complied with.

Client pressure - many businesses have green
policies covering the products sold or services
provided. In many cases this now extends to the
premises from which these businesses are run.
As a result, many clients are now demanding a
high level of energy efficiency from their new or
refurbished corporate headquarters.

The government's target is to reduce UK
greenhouse gas emissions to a level that is
12.5% less than 1990 levels by 2008 - 2012,
with a desire of extending this to a 20% reduction if possible. Architects, building services
engineers and other construction specialists
can assist in meeting these targets by making
energy conservation a consideration in all
design decisions. 🌐

References for Chapter 1

*1. DEFRA e-digest statistics about: the global
atmosphere. **www.defra.gov.uk/environment/statistics/
globatmos/index.htm***
*2. British Gas, Gas and the Environment. Publication
produced by British Gas Corporation Affairs, Grosvenor
Road, London, 1992.*

Further reading

*1. Chartered Institution of Building Services Engineers
(CIBSE). Guide F: CIBSE Energy Efficiency Guide. 1998*

2 Renewable energy

Introduction

There are two ways of reducing the carbon dioxide emitted from buildings. The first is to cut down on the amount of fossil fuels used, the second is to replace fossil fuel based energy with renewable forms of energy that do not emit carbon dioxide when used.

Renewable energy is energy that is obtained by tapping into the earth's natural processes. Both electricity and heat can be provided by renewable energy. The majority of renewable energy forms can be traced back to energy released by the sun. The exceptions are tidal energy which is due to the rotation of the moon around the earth and geothermal energy which is derived from the energy trapped in the core of the earth during its formation. There are two main advantages to renewable energy. The first is that the use of renewable energy does not result in the release of carbon dioxide or other pollutant gases to the atmosphere. The second advantage is that it is sustainable. Solar energy reappears every day and crops regrow to provide fuel.

Despite the advantages the amount of renewable energy utilised in the UK is small. This is because of a number of barriers to the uptake of renewable energy.

Energy content. Although the renewable energy potential is very large indeed, the energy content is low. The energy content is a measure of the amount of energy contained within the renewable source. For example, wind and a flowing river both contain kinetic energy. However if they were both flowing at the same speed the flowing water would have the greater amount of energy because there is more mass on the move than within the equivalent volume of air. With both air and water, increasing the speed of flow increases the amount of energy available for collection. This is why wind farms are situated on hilltops where windspeeds and

therefore energy potential are greatest.

Collection efficiency. The efficiency by which natural forms of energy can be collected and converted to forms useable in buildings (electricity and heat) is generally low. For example, crops used as biomass only collect 1% of the available solar energy. Man made devices, whilst better, are still inefficient. For example, the maximum collection efficiencies of photovoltaic panels and solar water heaters being 15% and 45% respectively. Typical values, though, are 10 and 30% respectively.

Environmental impact. We usually associate renewable energy as having a positive impact on the environment. However very few human activities leave the earth without change. Renewable energy is no exception and there are a number of negative environmental impacts associated with renewable energy some examples are listed in Table 2.1.

Form	Environmental Impact
Tidal barrages	Damage esturine life by changing the tidal pattern
Wind farms	Cause visual impact on hilltops
Waste burning	Releases pollutants such as dioxins

Table 2.1. Environmental impacts of some forms of renewable energy.

Some of the impacts listed in Table 2.1 have serious implications for human health, such as the potential for the release of cancer causing dioxins from the incineration of domestic waste. Others include the visual impact of wind turbines and possible bird strikes. Some observers appreciate them in the landscape, others strongly object to their presence.

Technical difficulties. As with many technologies difficulties are encountered in converting a planned method of harvesting renewable energy into reality. An example is in collecting geothermal energy from hot dry rocks. Here the slow speed at which the rocks recover their heat content after it has been extracted from them limits the viability of this form of energy.

Contribution of renewables

As a consequence of the above barriers, renewable energies only make up about 3.5% of the UK electrical supply (Figure 2.1)[1]. The total UK electricity availability per year in 2004 was 382.7 terrawatt hours TWh (T = terra = 10^{12}). However, It should be noted that the policy of the government is to increase the proportion of energy provided by renewables to 10% by 2010 and then 20% by 2025. A large modern coal fired power station has a peak electrical output of approximately 2000MW, the peak output of a nuclear power station is approximately 1300 MW. Renewable sources of electricity cannot currently match the levels of electrical output provided by these conventional power stations.

In order for renewables to make a rational contribution to UK energy consumption the following needs be implemented;

- the energy consumption of buildings, their services and appliances must be reduced by low energy methods. In this way the energy requirement of the building will more closely match the limited output of renewable

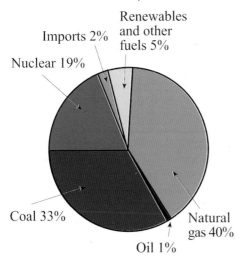

Renewables and other fuels 5%

Imports 2%

Nuclear 19%

Coal 33%

Natural gas 40%

Oil 1%

Figure 2.1. Breakdown of fuels used to provide the UK electricity supply.

sources
- the planning process can be used to encourage the uptake of renewable energy. For example, the Mayor of London has implemented a rule that new buildings must source 10% of their energy from renewable sources
- use of renewables must be further encouraged by government schemes such as the renewables obligation (RO). This requires electricity suppliers to work towards sourcing 10% of their electricity from renewables by 2010 and 15.4% by 2027. In this way the renewable energy industry will be encouraged to develop mass production techniques which will eventually reduce capital costs, raise efficiencies and help resolve technical difficulties. Suppliers can demonstrate compliance with this by obtaining renewable obligation certificates (ROCs). ROCs are issued by Ofgem, the UK energy regulator. They certify that one megawatt hour (MWh) has been generated from a qualifying renewable source. ROCs can be traded and so if a supplier does not have enough renewable generating capacity of their own a ROC can be purchased from a second party. This is useful to individuals who have renewable electricity systems at home because if their generating system qualifies, they can sell their ROCs for approximately £40/MWh. Since ROCs can be traded their value will vary depending on supply and demand
- one of the main barriers to the uptake of renewables is the poor economic viability of them. However, the capital cost can be reduced by obtaining a grant from the government's low carbon buildings programme (**www.lowcarbonbuildings. org.uk**). The level of support varies depending on the renewable technology involved. It is also worth contacting your local authority to enquire if there are any local schemes available. The low carbon buildings programme provides support for microgeneration technologies. The equivalent scheme in Scotland is the Scottish community and householder renewables initiative (SCHRI). ✎

Wind turbines

Wind turbines use propeller blades to catch the kinetic energy within a moving air stream and convert it into rotational movement. This rotation turns an electricity generator connected to the propeller and mounted at the top of a tower inside a housing. The tower gives ground clearance for the blades and also lifts them up into the faster moving airstreams. The larger turbines have a small electric motor that turns the blades into the direction of the wind, guided by data from a small wind vane. When a number of wind turbines are grouped together a wind farm is created. The turbines are usually separated from each other by 10 blade diameters. This is because the turbines remove energy from the wind and so if too close together would deprive their neighbours of energy further downwind.

A modern wind farm turbine (Figure 2.2) typically has two or three blades, with a swept area of 30 - 40m diameter, made out of glass fibre or wood-epoxy on a horizontal axis. The tower is 25 - 40m high and is made out of steel. The output of wind farm turbines ranges from 400kW to 1.5MW each. A typical wind farm will have a total output of approximately 10MW. This output is only 0.5% of that from a coal fired power station, but of course produces no pollutant gases.

An environmental benefit of 'wind farms' is that farming such as animal grazing can continue right up to the base of the tower. They create a fairly small environmental footprint on the ground but one of the main concerns of wind farms is their visual intrusion on the landscape. They are often sited on the top of hills within, or visible from, areas of natural beauty, as these are the places where windspeeds are greatest. As a consequence wind farm development must overcome strong opposition on visual impact grounds before planning permission is granted. To avoid this problem the next stage of development will be to construct offshore wind farms. One example is off the coast of Northumberland at Blyth where two

2MW turbines have been installed[2]. Remote and off-shore farms are, however, more costly to develop as a lengthy connection to the grid has to be created.

As well as providing electricity to the grid, turbines can be attached to buildings themselves or, if land and space permits, be sited within the grounds. Turbines attached to buildings tend to be small, since large units would create unacceptable stresses on the structure and would also contribute to airborne and structure born noise. One example of turbines attached to a building is the Green Building in Dublin[3]. The aim of this building is to demonstrate environmental technologies. It has three turbines attached to the roof. Each one is rated at 1.5kW. The total output of 4.5kW is said to contribute 80% of the building's lighting energy consumption.

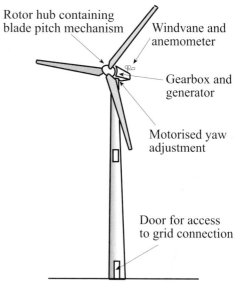

Rotor hub containing blade pitch mechanism

Windvane and anemometer

Gearbox and generator

Motorised yaw adjustment

Door for access to grid connection

Figure 2.2. Wind turbine.

An example of a larger turbine sited near to a building is the Sainsbury's East Kilbride distribution depot in Scotland. Here a 600kW turbine has been installed to generate about one third of the electricity required at the depot.[4]

Wind power demonstrates one of the general difficulties associated with renewable forms of energy, which is that it can be intermittent in delivery. The blades do not rotate when the windspeed is too low or so fast that damage would occur. As a consequence wind power could not form a complete electrical supply in itself. It would need to be supplemented by a more controllable and consistent method of power generation that can be used when wind generated electricity was insufficient or absent.

Building scale wind turbines

Smaller wind turbines are becoming available that are designed specifically for domestic scale installation or building mounting. The turbines can be either horizontal axis (Figure 2.3) or vertical axis (Figure 2.4) devices. A typical horizontal axis system has a blade diameter of approximately 1.75m and a (claimed) rated output of about 1kW at a constant windspeed of say 12m/s. Horizontal axis turbines are directed into the wind by a wind cock type tail fin. Vertical axis turbines do not need to be turned into the wind.

Figure 2.3. A typical horizontal axis domestic scale wind turbine.

The output is dependant on adequate wind in the range 3 to 16m/s and so siting is important. For example, the rated output of 1kW at 12m/s windspeed falls to approximately 125W (enough for two sixty watt bulbs!) at 6m/s windspeed, which is more typical in inland Britain. However, small turbines have a low inertia due to their

size and so can make use of gusts and rapidly fluctuating windspeeds. However, for urban applications it is unlikely that sufficient wind will be available at low level due to the obstruction of wind by the urban fabric, and so the turbines must be mounted at a height of approximately 15m i.e. on a pole in the garden or on the building itself.

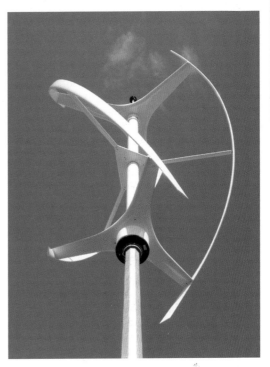

Figure 2.4. Prototype vertical axis wind turbine under development by quiet revolution. **www.quietrevolution. co.uk**

Small wind turbines produce DC electricity that must be passed through an inverter to produce useful AC electricity. The inverter is connected to the ring main in the house incorporating devices to bring the output into phase with the mains electricity and also to monitor that the mains electricity is present. If there is a power cut then safety systems that detect the absence of mains stop the turbine generating electricity. This prevents anyone working on the household wiring, having switched the power off at the consumer unit, becoming electrocuted by output from the turbine.

Practical considerations. A typical system could cost around £2000 installed, and to ensure that this generates savings, it is a good idea to monitor the windspeed at the site prior to purchasing. This is achieved using a portable windvane and anemometer connected to a data logger or PC. The windvane gives information on the wind direction, for example is it consistent or is it extremely variable due to turbulence arising from nearby buildings and trees. The anemometer, such as a rotating cup anemometer, gives information on wind speed which in turn dictates the electrical output of the device. Since it is unlikely that local conditions can be monitored for more than a couple of weeks, this local information can be compared with regional information such as that obtainable from local meteorological offices. If a correlation can be found between the two then the annual met office data can be used to give an indication of annual electrical output and hence savings. If there is no correlation then a risk must be taken when installing the device that there will be sufficient wind throughout the year to generate sufficient savings.

Wind turbines can be an icon of energy efficiency but they do create noise and their appearance is not to everyone's liking. For this reason the installation will need planning permission from the planning department of the local authority.

Export of electricity. It is possible to install export meters that measure the amount of electricity input to the grid from a renewable energy source. However, small scale turbines have a low output and it is likely that this will be taken by the base demand, such as refrigerators and freezers, and so little will be available for export, the cost of the export meters cannot usually be justified. Some companies are just starting to market some small wind turbines that are grid-linked but there are many that question the usefulness that these units will serve. ☙

Potential outputs from 1 - 2 metre diameter wind turbines

There has been a good deal of myth-making with regard to micro and small wind turbines, particularly regarding the pros and cons of small domestic scale wind turbines for attachment to buildings. Derek Taylor lays out a few facts.

Power versus wind speed curve

To assess the power output performance of a wind turbine one requires a power versus wind speed curve (sometimes called simply a power curve) ideally obtained under standard test procedures and preferably produced by an independent source. The power output of a wind turbine varies with the wind speed (V) experienced at any point in time, and this will generally be below the rated wind speed (Vr) for most of the time. Therefore to be able to estimate its likely variation of power output over time, and its likely annual electricity production in kilowatt-hours (kWh), one needs to have this information.

It is also worth pointing out that the rotor swept area of a turbine (and thus its diameter) with a given rated power output at a higher rated wind speed Vr will be smaller than one with a rated power (P) for a lower rated wind speed Vr. Historically, wind turbines designed for lower wind speed sites will usually have a lower rated wind speed, so the rotor diameter will be usually larger for low wind speed sites compared to high wind speed sites.

Wind speed frequency distribution

However in addition to power versus wind speed curve of the turbine, one has also to take account of the differences in wind speed characteristics at different sites. Every site has a different wind speed frequency distribution - in other words the number of hours that the wind blows at each wind speed; ie. the number of hours over the year that the wind blows at 1m/s, 2m/s, 3m/s, 4m/s and so on. Sites with the same annual mean wind speed (Vm) can have different wind speed frequency distributions.

This is important because the power contained in a wind stream is proportional to the cube of the instantaneous wind speed (V), so failing to take account of this can give an overestimate or an underestimate of the likely annual electricity production (E) in terms of kilowatt-hours per year (kWh/y).

To compare the annual electricity production outputs of different wind turbines under the same wind speed frequency distribution conditions and for producing budget estimates, we can assume a standard wind speed frequency distribution known as a 'Rayleigh distribution' which is a mathematical function based on annual mean wind speed (Vm). If one has a power versus wind speed curve for the wind turbine, one can therefore make a budget estimate of the likely annual electricity production from this wind turbine for a range of annual mean wind speeds (Vm).

Ball-park rule of thumb estimates of annual electricity production

A ball-park rule of thumb method has been derived from observations of annual electricity production of a range of wind turbines and based on the swept area of the turbine rotor. Though these have been generally medium scale wind turbines - rather than small wind turbines, which will inherently be less aerodynamically efficient because of the small geometrical size - so the estimates may err on the optimistic side and should be treated with some caution, but nonetheless they provide a useful guide if no other information, such as a power curve, is available.

A turbine's rotor swept area (A) is the area 'swept' by the turbine's blades as they rotate. It depends on the type of turbine, but in the case of conventional horizontal axis axial flow propeller type turbines, this is a circular disc with the same diameter as the turbine's rotor diameter.

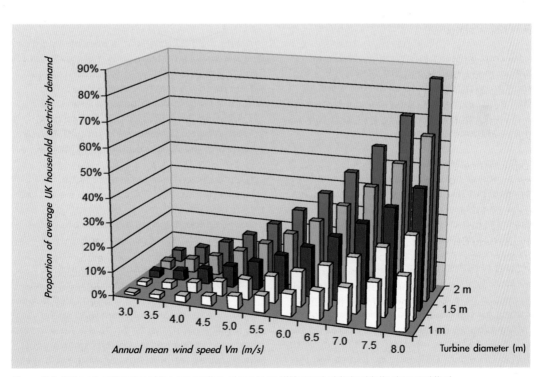

Figure 2.5. Ball park estimates of the proportion of average UK household electricity demand that could be contributed by small scale wind turbines of diameters ranging from 1 to 2 metres.

There is a need to check the current values, but the annual average household electricity demand in the UK - according to the Digest of UK Energy Statistics - is assumed to be about 4,700 kilowatt-hours per year per household - though it is suspected that it may now be greater than this.

On this basis we can estimate the proportion of UK annual average household electricity demand that can be reasonably assumed to be able to be generated by wind turbines with this range of diameters (e.g. 1, 1.25, 1.5, 1.75 and 2 metres) as indicated by Figure 2.5. On this basis a 1.5m diameter wind turbine would need to be sited with an annual mean wind speed Vm of over 7m/s to generate a third of the average UK household electricity demand.

Similarly a 1.75m diameter wind turbine would require an annual mean wind speed Vm of between 6 and 6.5m/s to generate a third of the average UK household electricity demand and between 7 and 7.5m/s to generate half of average UK household electricity demand.

A 2m diameter turbine would require an annual mean wind speed Vm between 5.5 and 6m/s to generate a third of the average UK household electricity demand and between 6.5 and 7m/s to generate half of average UK household electricity demand.

On open sites in certain rural areas some of these annual mean wind speeds might be experienced, but these are much higher annual mean wind speeds than are likely to be experienced at buildings in most urban areas - which could lie between 3 and 5m/s.

Power coefficient estimates

Another way we can assess a turbine's performance is to base it on the claimed rated power output for the cited rated wind speed. With this information we can estimate the overall power coefficient CPoa (a measure of efficiency of the turbine in which 100% is 1), by comparing the claimed output against the estimated power contained in the wind stream.

The maximum theoretical aerodynamic

power coefficient CP that is possible for a non-augmented wind turbine is 0.59 and this is known as the Betz Limit after Albert Betz who first calculated it.

Each wind turbine rotor will have an aero-dynamic power coefficient CP which varies according to the relationship between rotor speed and wind speed, known as the tip speed ratio, and it will have a peak aerodynamic power coefficient for a narrow range of tip speed ratios - which usually means a drop in performance if the turbine deviates from this optimum tip speed ratio.

A small wind turbine is unlikely to achieve an aerodynamic power coefficient CP greater than 0.35 and is likely to be much less. The overall power coefficient CPoa takes account of the generator efficiency. The overall power coefficient CPoa for a wind turbine of a given rotor swept area A, given electrical rated power output Pelec and rated wind speed Vr, can be calculated as shown in Figure 2.5.

Using this relationship it is possible to check whether the claimed output is realistic or not. Table 2.2 shows a range of feasible electrical rated power outputs for rated wind speeds and for a range of wind turbines with 1, 1.25, 1.5, 1.75 and 2m diameters. These assume an aerodynamic power coefficient of 0.35 and a generator efficiency of 90%. This should only be used as guide, however, as even if this power coefficient was achievable at the rated wind speed indicated, that does not mean that the turbine will necessarily be operating at this power coefficient across the range of operational wind speeds.

From Table 2.2, it can be seen that the choice of rated wind speed influences the size of the rotor swept area for a given rated power output. For a low annual mean wind speed site it will generally be better to opt for a lower rated wind speed so for a given power output, wind turbines for this situation will have larger swept areas and hence larger rotor diameters.

On this basis a non-augmented wind turbine of 1.25m diameter would need a rated wind speed Vr of 13m/s to achieve a rated power output of 500 watts. A 1.5m diameter would need to have a rated wind speed Vr of 15m/s to achieve 1kW rated power. Similarly a 1.75m diameter turbine would need to have rated wind speed Vr of 13m/s to achieve 1kW and just under 15m/s to achieve a rated power output of 1.5kW. A 2m diameter turbine would need to have a rated wind speed Vr of just under 12m/s to achieve 1kW and between 13 and 14m/s to achieve 1.5kW and between 14m/s and 15m/s to achieve 2kW.

Factors affecting turbines attached to building

A big advantage of attaching a wind turbine to a building is the saving of the cost of the tower and foundations and cabling - items which form a high proportion of the cost of conventional micro and small wind turbines.

However against that has to be taken into account any structural modifications required and additional weights, side loads, point loads and bending moments imparted to the structure. The magnitude of these loads will usually require that the turbines used are geometrically small so it will be a question as to whether

the relatively low power outputs and energy production justify the installation. Vibration and noise levels can be minimised or avoided, but are likely to be influenced by the particular characteristics of the host building and do need to be given consideration.

Because of the 'roughness' of the terrain in urban locations, wind velocities are usually retarded by the effect of groups of buildings and/or trees. Therefore the wind energy potential tends to be low in urban areas and to date these areas have not been considered sufficiently windy to be economically viable because of the probable low outputs for the relatively large capital investment per kilowatt required for small wind turbines.

There may be some level of wind speed acceleration achievable simply by locating the turbine on a pitched roof - though this would need to be confirmed and even if it were achievable it is likely to be some distance above the roof and it would be unlikely to apply to winds from all directions. Additionally it would also be dependent on the orientation of the building, the shape and treatment of the roof, eaves, roof edge and ridge edge characteristics.

In addition there are potential factors that may degrade the performance of building attached turbines, such as locating the turbine on the wall of a building such that the wind flows may well be very turbulent. This could mean that the wind turbine keeps 'hunting' the wind direction and is potentially similar to attaching a turbine next to a 'cliff' edge and historically this has usually not been recommended by wind turbine engineers.

For these reasons many long established manufacturers of micro and small wind turbines may advise against installing their (non-augmented) wind turbines on buildings - so if it is to be undertaken it has to be considered very carefully.

Rotor Diameter (m) Swept Area (m²)						
Rated	1.128 m	1 m	1.25 m	1.5 m	1.75 m	2 m
Wind Speed	1 m²	0.79 m²	1.23 m²	1.77 m²	2.41 m²	3.14 m²
Vr	Output in watts					
m/s	W	W	W	W	W	W
10	190	150	230	340	460	650
11	250	200	310	450	610	870
12	330	260	410	590	800	1130
13	420	330	520	750	1020	1440
14	530	410	650	930	1270	1800
15	650	510	800	1150	1570	2220

Based on CP of 0.35, generator efficiency of 90% & air density of 1.2256 kg/m³

Table 2.2. Feasible electrical rated power outputs for 1.128, 1, 1.25, 1.5, 1.75 & 2m dia. wind turbines for rated wind speeds between 10 & 15 m/s.

Conclusion

The ball-park rule of thumb method may or may not be fair to the estimated outputs from turbines, but it does indicate that sufficient information should be provided to accurately judge the probable performance of such devices.

The power outputs for wind turbines should be based on accurate wind speed v power curves, and the annual electricity output and CO_2 saving claims made for them should be clear and be based on established techniques for a range of annual mean wind speeds.

Many potential customers of micro and small wind turbines are very probably located at sites with relatively low annual mean wind speeds, and as such it would seem very unlikely that non-augmented turbines of 1 to 2m diameters located at such sites will achieve a high proportion of average annual household electricity demand. ☙

The above is from an article by Dr Derek Taylor, first published in Building for a Future magazine Volume 15, No. 3.

Figure 2.6. Roof mounted wind turbines shown here with a PV generating system.

Water power (hydro)

The movement of water has traditionally been used as a mechanical energy source in mill buildings, collected using water wheels. However the movement of water can also rotate a turbine in order to generate electricity. The most impressive examples are hydro-electric power stations where water, held in a reservoir behind a dam is allowed to flow down to a lower level through ducts containing a turbine. Countries such as Canada and Norway have hydroelectric power stations with outputs of several thousand megawatts which is comparable to fossil fuel power stations. In the UK hydroelectric power contributes 2% of the UK electricity supply. The biggest hydroelectric power stations are found in hilly regions such as Scotland where there are the necessary height differences through which the water can fall and plenty of rainfall. The potential for new large scale generation is very limited due to the lack of suitable sites. Future developments will be in small scale hydro power. This is defined as generation up to 5MW output. Small scale hydro turbines utilise the kinetic energy of fast flowing rivers or the potential energy built up in the head of water created by a small weir or reservoir. For example, a unit at Roadford Reservoir, Okehampton, Devon generates just under 1MW of electricity[5]. So long as there is sufficient and continuous rainfall the electrical output of hydro - electric schemes is continuous and therefore available when required.

Tidal barrages

A tidal barrage is a low dam constructed across the mouth of a tidal estuary. When the tide rises sea water is allowed to pass through a gate in the barrage and collects in the area behind it. At high tide the gates are shut and as the tide falls the sea water can only escape by passing through an opening in the barrage in which a turbine is placed. There are no tidal barrages in the UK although estuaries on the rivers Severn, Mersey, Wyre and Conwy have been considered[6]. There is a barrage at La Rance in France which generates electricity. The electrical output occurs twice a day during the ebb of the tide. The opportunities for future barrages is small in the UK. One of the reasons are the ecological concerns arising from altering the ebb and flow of tides in the estuary which would disturb estaurine life. Estuaries are the home to a great diversity of shellfish, sea weeds, marine and brackish water organisms and bird life that could be affected by this technology.

Pumped storage

Pumped storage is not a form of renewable energy but does allow the rest of the electrical generation network to operate more efficiently. At night surplus electricity is used to pump water from a low reservoir up to a high reservoir where it is stored. If there is a sudden demand for electricity, such as can occur during commercial breaks in major televised sporting events when many kettles are switched on at once, water is allowed to fall back down to the lower reservoir through a turbine. This generates the electricity needed for the surge in demand. This short term rapid generation of electricity is very useful since it avoids the need to fire up a conventional power station which is inefficient for short duration peaks in demand. There is an example of a pumped storage power station at Dinorwig in Wales.

Wave power

Waves contain a large amount of energy. Many systems have been devised over the years to try and harness the energy in waves. Floating systems, such as cam shaped buoys that rotate when a wave advances on them turning a generator, had major maintenance problems and so have fallen out of favour. The current interest lies in coast based systems where access can be more easily obtained for maintenance and sea conditions are slightly less severe. Figure 2.7 shows a section through a system which is based on the compression of air when a wave enters a cave.

The generator is constructed to resemble a sea cave. As a wave enters the mouth of the generator the air within it rushes out of the only escape route which is a duct in the roof of the generator. A turbine in the duct, called a Wells turbine (named after professor Alan Wells),

rotates when the air passes through it, thereby generating electricity. As the wave subsides a negative pressure is created in the cavity and air is drawn in the reverse direction through the turbine. Gearing in the system ensures that regardless of the direction of air flow the electrical generator turns in the same direction. An example of this type of system is installed and operating on the Isle of Islay in the Inner Hebrides and is rated at 0.5MW (**www.wavegen.com**).

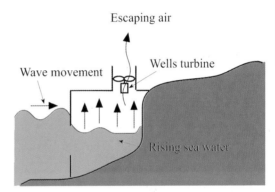

Figure 2.7. Wave power generator.

'Small' and 'micro' hydro power

Small and micro hydro systems have perhaps the lowest environmental impact of all energy sources, including other renewable energies.

A study carried out in Spain in 2001 concluded that micro hydro has the least environmental impact of a range of renewable technologies;
- renewable energies have 31 times less impact than conventional energy sources, and 1kWh produced by small hydro is 300 times 'cleaner' than the equivalent produced by lignite
- small hydro does not have a significant impact on the environment: there are no emissions of gases such as SO_2 CO_2 or NOx, nor is there anything that causes ground or water acidification, acid rain, climate change, ozone layer depletion, etc.

The unit used in the study for measuring

the environmental impacts of the eight, tested generation systems is the 'ecopoint' - a unit of environmental penalty. These were calculated by considering the following environmental factors: global warming, ozone layer depletion, acidification, eutrophication (oxygen depletion of water), heavy metal pollution, emission of carcinogenic substances, winter smog, summer smog, generation of industrial wastes, radioactivity, radioactive waste and depletion of energy sources. The more ecopoints obtained by a generation system, the greater environmental impact it will have. The full listing is given in Table 2.3. ✆

Fuel	Ecopoints
Lignite	1735
Fuel oil	1398
Coal	1356
Nuclear	672
Solar PV	461
Natural gas	267
Wind	65
Small hydro	5

Table 2.3. Fuels ecopoint rating for a range of fuels.

CONSULTING WITH A PURPOSE
work with people towards making a safer, more energy effective environment.

CWAP
advise organisations and individuals on their environmental obligations and how to capitalise on the latest environmental developments.

CONTACT:
Gideon Richards
45 New Laithe Hill, Newsome, Huddersfield
HD4 6RF
T: 01924 261341
E: gideon@cwap.co.uk

Biomass

Biomass is material derived from plants and animals. This material contains energy which can be released in a number of ways, such as burning the raw material, burning waste from the material, or processing it to produce new fuels. The use of crops to produce energy is considered to be carbon neutral as carbon dioxide released during combustion is re-absorbed when new plants grow.

The use of animal litter as fuel is not carbon neutral as the animals emit metabolic carbon dioxide in life and burning of the litter also releases CO_2. However, burning organic waste is preferable to allowing it to decompose in an oxygen depleted environment. This is because the anaerobic digestion produces methane instead of carbon dioxide and methane is 30 times more potent than CO_2 as a greenhouse gas (see processed biomass below).

Wood burning has traditionally been used to provide energy and still represents the majority of energy released in the world. However it has been replaced as fuel for space heating and cooking in the UK by gas and electricity. There has however been a recent resurgence in interest in efficient wood burning stoves as a means of heating sustainable low energy housing and small commercial buildings.

Coppice
Coppicing is the cultivation of crops to be burned as fuel. The most common example is the growing of willow trees. Willow is fast growing and after a few years the branches are cut off to be chipped or pelletised, then burned in solid fuel burning heaters. New shoots appear at the base of the cut branches and so new growth is regenerated. Rotation is needed so that the coppice is at various stages of growth. Areas are required to reach maturity each year to maintain the fuel supply.

Large areas of land are needed to produce biofuels since only 1% of the solar energy is captured and converted to useable energy.

However, in Finland in 1995 wood fuels accounted for 15% of the total energy requirement (heat and power) and 10% of the total primary fuel used to generate electricity [7].

The number of wood burning boilers to provide central heating for domestic and commercial buildings is rapidly growing in the UK. They require a store of woodchips, pellets or logs. The pellet and woodchip boilers can be highly mechanised with screw-feeds or injectors to deliver carefully calculated fuel quantities to the burners.

Waste as fuel

Waste can arise in a number of forms, including thinnings and chippings from the timber industry, farming waste and also paper packaging which is found in domestic refuse.

There are a number of large scale examples of energy from waste in the UK. For example Sheffield has a municipal refuse incinerator which burns 120,000 tonnes of waste each year and produces 28MW of heat which is used within a city wide district heating scheme[8]. Amongst the wide variety of materials contained in domestic waste are processed biomass products such as paper and plastics. As well as heat from waste there are also waste burning power stations.

One example is in Humberside that burns straw waste from farming. Another at Eye in Suffolk burns chicken droppings mixed with straw and woodshavings or woodchips. This latter example produces 12.5 MW of electricity. The plant burns 125,000 tonnes of poultry litter per year, approximately half of Suffolk's chicken farm output. The station produces power and avoids the problem of nitrates leaching out of the litter into river and groundwater systems.

Processed biomass

Biomass can be processed in a number of ways to make it into a more versatile fuel. One simple example is the chipping of timber to make it easier to feed in to a wood burning appliance. Natural processes can also be utilised. One example is the creation of methane gas from

the anaerobic digestion of organic waste by bacteria.

The most common examples are the collection of methane from the digestion of human sewage at sewage treatment plants, the digestion of animal sewage on farms and the collection of methane from landfill sites, produced from the breakdown of organic material in the refuse. In each case the methane can be collected, cleaned to remove impurities, compressed and then used as a fuel in a combined heat and power plant. A typical medium sized anaerobic digestion chp scheme would generate 100kW of electricity. The combustion of methane means that this extremely potent global warming gas is not released to the atmosphere.

Crops can be grown specifically to be processed into a more versatile fuel source. An important example of this is the growing of sunflowers so that the oily seeds can be utilised in the production of biodiesel. This is a fuel which is used extensively as a motor fuel but can also be used in building heating systems and power generation. Another example is the production of alcohol from the fermentation of biomass. This is already used extensively in Brazil as a fuel for cars. ◔

Figure 2.8. Woodchips being used to power a CHP biomass power station. Fuels can often be varied to suit crop availability or localised waste streams.

Geothermal energy

The core of the earth is composed of molten iron and so is extremely hot. Some of this heat makes its way towards the earth's surface by conduction. This heat manifests itself in three forms; hot aquifers, steam and hot dry rock. This section will also consider a method of extracting low grade geothermal energy using ground loop heat pumps.

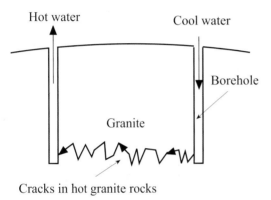

Figure 2.9. Boreholes used to extract heat from hot dry rock.

Hot aquifers. At certain locations in the world ground water passes through hot, porous rock and becomes heated. If a borehole is drilled to this porous rock the hot water can be extracted and used in a building's heating system. This is common in places such as Iceland, where water up to 100°C may be obtained. In the UK hot aquifers do not represent a significant heat source as the geological conditions which are favourable for hot water collection are not near major urban areas and it is impractical to pump hot water over large distances.

Steam. If the temperature of a hot aquifer increases above 100°C steam is produced. This can be collected and used in space heating or if passed through turbines can produce electricity. Unfortunately, whilst geothermal steam is used to produce electricity in Iceland, Italy and New Zealand there are no geothermal steam resources in the UK.

Hot dry rocks. Hot dry rock is present everywhere in the world at depth. It is referred to as dry as it is solid and therefore has no water held within it which could be extracted. Instead two boreholes are drilled some distance apart from each other. Water is injected into the first borehole at pressure which creates a crack pathway between it and the second borehole (Figure 2.9.). Water can then pass from the source borehole to the collection borehole and is heated en route. Tests on hot dry rock have been carried out in the granite beneath Cornwall. So far technical difficulties involved with drilling to a depth of 2000m and creating fractured rock have meant that this source of energy has not been realised.

Ground source heat pumps (GSHP)

One method of extracting low grade energy from the ground is to utilise a ground loop heat pump system. In this method the geothermal energy compliments an electrically driven form of space heating.

Heat pumps are like a refrigerator working in reverse. A refrigerator removes heat from the ice box making it colder and discards the heat which has been removed as waste into the kitchen. The device is called a heat pump as it takes heat from a low grade source, a cold place, and converts it into a higher grade form by releasing it in a warmer place.

The basic components of a heat pump system are shown in Figure 2.10. The main components are an evaporator coil, a compressor, a condenser coil, and an expansion device. These components are connected together using copper pipe through which refrigerant circulates in a closed loop. Heating is achieved in the following way:

Liquid refrigerant is forced through the expansion valve. As the refrigerant leaves the expansion valve its pressure is reduced. This allows it to evaporate which removes heat from the air flowing over the evaporator coil. The refrigerant, now in a vapour state, leaves the evaporator and passes through the compressor. The pressure is increased causing the refrigerant vapour to condense. This occurs at a relatively high temperature. As the refrigerant condenses it releases the heat it absorbed during evaporation. This heats up the condenser coil. Air passing over the condenser coil is heated and is used to warm the living space. The cycle then repeats.

In terms of a domestic refrigerator the evaporator is situated in the ice compartment and the condenser is the grid of piping at the rear of the refrigerator. The evaporator and condenser coils are simply arrays of copper pipe with aluminium fins mechanically bonded to their surface to increase the area for heat transfer.

The efficiency of a heat pump is at its greatest when the evaporator and condenser coils are at similar temperatures. However, when space heating is required, the condenser coil is in a warm room at 21°C and the evaporator coil is outside at temperatures around 0°C. This has two effects. The first is that the efficiency with which electricity is converted to space heating is reduced and secondly the evaporator coil

can ice up, reducing its ability to transfer heat. As a consequence air to air heat pumps may incorporate an electrical heater to periodically defrost the evaporator coil. The use of electricity for defrosting also reduces the efficiency of the device.

The problems of icing up and low efficiency can be eliminated if the evaporator coil is placed in a warm environment. Examples of such environments are lofts and conservatories heated by solar collection and ground waters heated by geothermal energy. One way of taking heat out of the ground is to bury a network of pipes which are filled with water, known as a ground loop (Figure 2.10). During winter, the ground loop will always be at a higher temperature than air temperature as it is picking up geothermal heat from the ground. The water in the loop is pumped to a shell surrounding the evaporator coil thereby raising its temperature. Water leaving the evaporator shell will have been cooled, and so it is returned to the ground loop to pick up more geothermal energy. A large network of piping is required to absorb heat from the ground. ☙

Figure 2.10. Simplified schematic diagram of a loop heat pump system.
(Diagram Courtesy of Ice Energy).

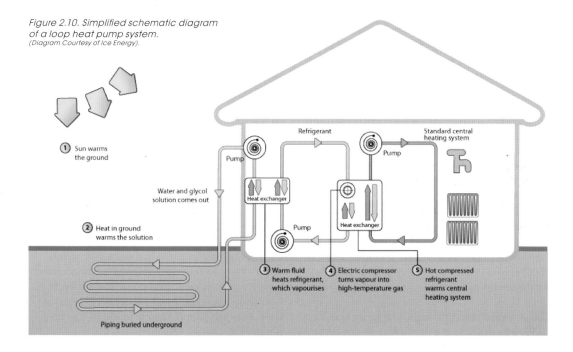

Solar energy

Passive solar heating

Passive solar space heating is simply the collection of solar energy by a building without utilising special devices, such as solar panels. However, elements of the building may be modified to optimise solar collection such as increasing the area of south facing glazing.

The usefulness of passive solar space heating varies depending on the type of building. In housing the entry of sunlight is considered psychologically pleasing and the heat it carries can offset the need for mechanical space heating. It is estimated that passive solar heating can reduce space heating energy consumption in a typical house by up to 10%. Small non-domestic buildings, such as schools and health centres where space heating energy consumption is the predominant energy usage, can also benefit from passive solar design. However, in commercial buildings, where heat gains from occupants, lighting and equipment are already large, the entry of solar energy can cause overheating leading to discomfort and, in extreme cases, to the use of air conditioning. In offices there is also a need for a good visual environment. Entry of sunlight can create glare either directly through windows or as reflections from computer screens. A common occurrence associated with this is that blinds will be drawn and artificial lighting switched on leading to increased electrical energy consumption.

For a passive solar design to be successful the following must be considered:

Availability of solar energy. The availability of solar energy varies depending on time of year and atmospheric conditions. These factors are beyond our control, however, the solar collector can be orientated to optimise solar collection when it is available.

Solar collection methods. The most common collection systems are windows and conservato-

ries. There are also less common systems such as trombe walls. Each system has different solar collection abilities, heat loss characteristics and means of transferring the energy into the building. Problems of high heat losses, over-heating and glare can arise and would reduce the effectiveness of the solar collection system unless eliminated at the design stage.

Thermal storage. Solar energy is unpredictable both in timing and quantity. Thermal storage is needed to improve the utilisation efficiency of solar energy.

Heat distribution. Solar energy is a south side phenomenon in the northern hemisphere. Methods are required to re distribute some of the heat to the north side of the building.

Mechanical heating system. Passive solar heating only saves energy if the mechanical heating system can reduce its output quickly in response to the incoming solar gains.

Availability of solar energy

A large amount of solar radiation is received by the earth. The solar constant, the amount of energy outside the earth's atmosphere, is equivalent to 1.2kW/m². Some of this energy is removed by absorption and scattering in the atmosphere so that the maximum direct solar intensity falling on a horizontal surface in the UK is 0.8kW/m². This will occur at noon on a clear day in mid summer. When averaged over a full day, to take the daily variation into account, the average solar intensity in the summer is 0.35kW/m².

The total amount of energy falling on a surface depends on the number of hours of sunlight, the solar intensity and the orientation of the surface. As the sun's position and number of sunlight hours changes with month of the year, the average daily solar intensity also varies. This is illustrated in Figure 2.11 which shows the average daily solar intensity on north, south and east/west facing vertical surfaces. The solar intensity on a horizontal surface is also shown. The following features can be observed:

© Green Building Press

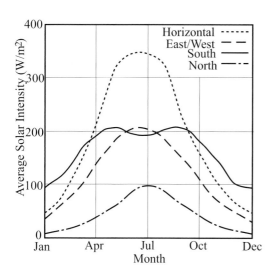

Figure 2.11. Solar intensities on various surfaces through-out the year.

The highest value of solar intensity occurs on the horizontal surface in summer. This is because the solar intensity on a surface is greatest when the solar radiation falls perpendicularly onto the surface. In summer the sun is high in the sky and so is closer to this situation than in winter when the sun is lower in the sky. The low altitude of the sun causes a reduced solar intensity on the surface as illustrated in Figure 2.12. This figure represents the solar radiation as a series of equally spaced parallel lines. It can be seen that more of these lines hit the given area (i.e. providing a high solar intensity) when the sun is high in the sky in June than when it is low in the sky in December.

The curve for solar intensity on a north facing vertical surface is lower than the other curves at all times of the year. This is because it only receives direct radiation from the sun in the early morning and late evening in summer. The rest of the time north facing surfaces are in shade as the predominant direction of the sun is from south east to south west. When in shade north facing surfaces only receive solar radiation that has been scattered back on to it from moisture and pollution in the atmosphere.

The solar intensity on east and west facing

vertical surfaces have the same curve. However, the curve does not show that the east facing surface receives its sunlight in the morning and is shaded in the afternoon and the west facing receives sunlight in the afternoon and is shaded in the morning. West facing glazing in office buildings exposed to the sun is of particular concern. This is because the sun will enter it at the end of the day. At this time the fabric of the building will have been heated up by other casual gains during the day. The additional solar gains cannot be absorbed by the fabric and afternoon overheating will occur.

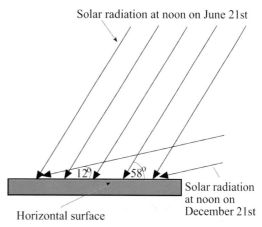

Figure 2.12. Diagram showing how solar intensity on a surface is reduced at acute angles of incidence.

The solar intensity on the south facing surface follows a curve with two peaks. This pattern of solar intensity across the year is very beneficial to passive solar heating. The trough between the peaks occurs when overheating is of most concern and the peaks are moved out towards the start and end of the heating season when the heat is more useful.

It follows from the above that the optimum orientation for a solar collection system is facing south. However, it is usually assumed that a collector orientated within +/- 30° of south will still receive the majority of available solar energy. Useful morning heating can be achieved using an east facing collector and evening warming using a west facing collec-

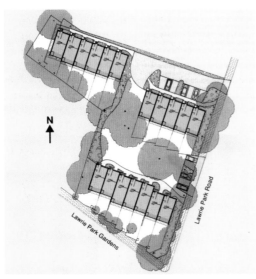

Figure 2.13. Estate layout for solar collection. diag. from GPCS 90 Lowri Park Road - passive solar design. Crown copyright (1992).

tor. This then dictates the orientation of the buildings themselves as shown in Figure 2.13. which shows an estate of houses arranged to orientate their solar collectors towards the sun. Horizontal space heating solar collectors should be avoided as there is a peak during the summer when space heating is not required. However they may be useful for systems such as outdoor swimming pool heating which tend to be used during the summer months.

Passive solar collection

The two requirements of a successful passive solar collection system are that it must transmit solar energy into the building when required whilst at the same time maintain the insulating properties of the fabric. The two most common collection systems are windows and conservatories. There are also a number of less common solar collectors such as trombe walls.

Windows

The simplest solar collectors are the windows already present in buildings to provide daylight, views and ventilation. However since windows are the main route for fabric heat losses from the building, care should be taken to ensure there is a net gain of energy through them

during the heating season i.e.

Heat gains	< must	Heat losses
through glazing	outweigh >	through glazing

This balance is very difficult to achieve. As is shown in Figure 2.14. which shows the net heat gain over the heating season for south facing single glazing, double glazing and low emissivity double glazing with night time insulated shutters[9].

It can be seen that single glazing experiences a net loss of heat for about one half of the heating season. Net gains are confined to the early and late parts of the heating season. For double glazing the situation is improved but there are small net losses from November to February. The system which gives net gains throughout the entire heating season is low emissivity double glazing combined with night-time shutters.

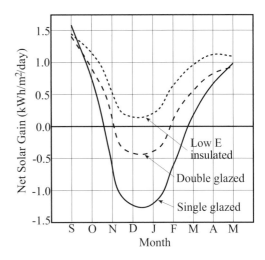

Figure 2.14. Net solar gains through various types of glazing[9].

It follows from the above that to be effective as a solar collector windows should;
- have as low a U-value as possible i.e. double glazed with low emissivity coating and possibly argon gas filling
- be covered with insulation at night such as thick curtains or insulated shutters to reduce heat losses when no gains are

available
- face within + or - 30° of south
- the overall area of glazing on the building should not be increased. Instead glazing on the east, west and especially north facades should be reduced and an equivalent area transferred to the south facade. Note windows on east west and north faces should not be reduced to the extent that adequate daylighting is lost.

Conservatories

A more complex type of solar collector which has marginal energy saving benefits is a south facing conservatory (Figure 2.15). Sunlight entering the conservatory raises the internal air temperature. Some of the solar energy is stored in the mass of the masonry outer wall and ceramic floor tiles on a concrete base. The elevated temperatures in the conservatory reduce fabric heat losses through that part of the outer skin of the building that is buffered by the conservatory. However, as U values in the outer walls are reduced by Building Regulation requirements, the buffering effect becomes less valuable. The air within the conservatory can be used to ventilate the building. This air can move into the building via open patio doors, windows or trickle ventilators. More complex arrangements involving ducting and fans to move the heated air can also be used. The duct could be formed from a hollow core within an intermediate concrete floor slab, providing additional thermal mass to the system. The benefits of a conservatory collection system are:
- it acts as a buffer between the solar collection and the occupied space. Gains can be accepted, or if not required, rejected
- it avoids the need for large windows in the external shell of the building and so the thermal integrity of the building is maintained
- it creates an extended living space. Shelter and solar gains make the conservatory habitable from early spring to late autumn

This latter feature is also the main cause for concern with conservatories. If they become important living spaces there may be a desire to fit them with space heating to be used in winter.

This should not take place as the heat losses through the highly glazed structure would outweigh any gains made. In summer owners may wish to cool the conservatory using a portable air conditioner. This should be avoided and instead the temperature should be controlled using shading, thermal mass and ventilation.

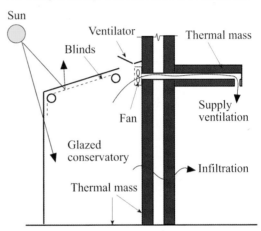

Figure 2.15. Conservatory as a solar collector.

Other passive solar collectors

A variety of other passive solar collection systems have been proposed. One such example is the trombe wall. Trombe walls form part of the south facing wall of the building (Figure 2.16). Sunlight passes through a transparent outer panel, such as glazing or transparent insulation, and is absorbed by the structural wall at the back. The air in the cavity is heated by this action. If the house does not require space heating, the warm air can be vented outside. This in turn draws ventilation air through the adjacent room, entering the trombe wall cavity from a low level vent. If space heating is required the external high level vent is closed and warm air will move out of the trombe wall into the living space by its own natural buoyancy. Convective cycling of air is created through the trombe wall via the high and low level room vents. The trombe wall has thermal storage mass built into it as part of its construction. One of the disadvantages of trombe walls is that they do not provide daylight or views out of the house. This can be overcome by forming the lower part of the

wall as a solar collector and having standard windows within the remaining wall. Note, if the trombe wall is created below sill height it must be at least 1m in height to set up a sufficiently strong convection current for heated air to escape from it.

Few examples of effective trombe wall heating systems exist due to the difficulty in designing the system for effective convective heat transfers integrated with opening/closing of vents as required.

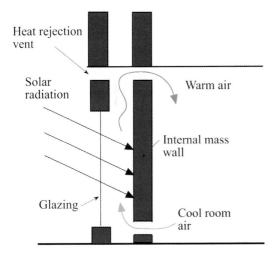

Figure 2.16. Trombe wall passive solar heating system.

Control of heat gains

A drawback of passive solar collection devices is that the energy is deposited directly in to the living spaces behind the glazing. Solar gains are very different to the heat input to a building by a mechanical heating system. A mechanical heating system releases heat into the room in a controlled manner. When the room is warm enough the heat input is stopped or reduced. With solar heating the quantity and timing of the heat gains are unknown. This can cause overheating in the living space and thermal discomfort. To avoid this some control of the solar gains is necessary. This is usually achieved using three mechanisms; solar blinds, ventilation and exposed thermal mass.

Blinds. Raising and lowering of blinds can vary

the solar heat input to a space. When fully retracted full solar gains are achieved. If the temperature rises above comfortable limits then the blinds can be lowered to reduce the solar gain input. Varying the position and pitch of venetian blinds can give good control over solar gains. However adjustment is a manually intensive process which may not be appropriate in commercial buildings. Here motorised systems can be used which adjust the position of the blinds in response to data from indoor air temperature and external solar energy sensors.

Ventilation. Ventilation of a space can be used to carry unwanted solar heat out of the building in the form of hot exhaust air. This can be achieved by opening windows or by operating a mechanical extract fan. The fan should be controlled by an air temperature sensor so that it switches off when temperatures have returned to acceptable levels.

Thermal mass. The thermal mass of a building is a description of its internal fabric in terms of its ability to absorb heat.

When a material absorbs heat its temperature increases. Some materials can absorb more heat than others for each degree of temperature rise. Their ability to do this is described by the specific heat capacity (SHC). The SHC is a measure of the quantity of heat absorbed by 1kg of material in order to raise its temperature by 1°C. A material with a high thermal capacity can absorb a lot of heat for each degree of temperature rise. High thermal capacity materials are usually dense such as blockwork and concrete. Low thermal capacity materials have a low density such as timber, insulation and plasterboard.

A high thermal mass room would be one that had tiled solid concrete floors, unplastered, dense blockwork or stone internal walls and an exposed concrete ceiling. A low thermal mass room would have timber framed external walls, suspended timber floors and timber stud and plasterboard internal walls.

Thermal mass provided by exposed blockwork walls acts as a heat store. When the air temperature is higher than that of the wall heat moves from the room air into the walls. This reduces the air temperature. When the air temperature is lower than the wall temperature heat will move back out of the walls into the room air. This raises the room air temperature. The effect of this movement of heat into and out of the walls is to improve the utilisation of solar gains. In a low thermal mass room sunlight entry would cause the air temperature to rise rapidly. Thermal discomfort would occur and windows would be opened to reject the solar heat gains. If thermal mass were present the peak temperature would be reduced, the windows would remain closed and the solar gains would be retained within the room air and fabric. Some of the heat absorbed by the fabric would reappear at a later time. By this process, thermal mass reduces peak air temperatures and raises troughs in temperature to give a more stable internal temperature profile.

Orientation	Solar gain (kWh/m²/day)		
	Light	Medium	Heavy
South	0.75	0.90	1.04
North	0.23	0.27	0.31
East/West	0.45	0.54	0.62

Table 2.4. Average useful solar gains through one square metre of glass for various orientations.

The improved utilisation of solar energy by the provision of a thermally heavy building is illustrated in Table 2.4[10]. The table illustrates two things. Firstly, that south facing glazing achieves the highest solar gains followed by east/west then north facing glazing. Secondly, that for all orientations of glazing the solar gains are improved as the thermal mass increases. The values given are for single glazing and should be reduced by 10% for double glazing. They are averaged over the heating season assuming space heating is operating between 0600 and 2300 hours.

Heat distribution

One of the limitations of passive solar heating is that it occurs predominantly on the south side of the building. For most domestic buildings this

is acceptable as heat can travel short horizontal distances towards the north side of the building and rising warm air will heat the upper floors. However, as the building becomes large, such as a health centre or school then clear north/south zoning occurs. The south side may not require any mechanical heating due to the solar gains but the north side may require heating due to the absence of solar gains.

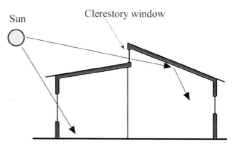

Figure 2.17. North side heating using multiple solar collectors.

There are two methods for creating a more even horizontal distribution of heat through large floor plan buildings. The first is to provide solar collectors, such as windows, at more than one location, as shown in Figure 2.17. The second is to use ducting and fans to take warm air from the south side of the building and convey it to the north side (Figure 2.18).

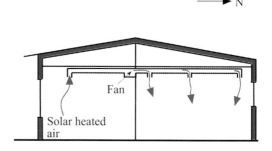

Figure 2.18. Solar heat distribution using fans and ducting.

Long term heat storage

One of the problems with passive solar heating is that the majority of solar energy appears in the summer when it is least needed for space heating. It has generally been considered impractical to collect and store heat in the summer for use in the winter. This is because a thermal store of similar size to the building would be required. However, a number of contemporary sustainable buildings have made an attempt at achieve this goal. One example is the conference building at the 'Earth Centre' near Doncaster. This has a large water tank in its basement which is heated during the summer using evacuated tube solar water heating panels. In autumn the stored hot water is used in the heating system to provide space heating.

In the above example water was used to store heat by virtue of its thermal capacity. Another storage medium is rocks, solar heated air is blown through spaces between the rocks heating them up. In the heating season air entering the building is pre-heated by passing it through the rock store. Research is continuing into phase change material as thermal storage media. These materials do not store heat by heating up but by changing state. For example they are a solid material and when they absorb heat they become liquid. This does not increase the temperature of the material and so sensible heat losses are small. When the phase change material changes back to a solid heat is released which can be used for space heating. Examples of materials that change phase around room temperature are inorganic hydrated salts such as calcium chloride hexahydrate, another is paraffin waxes. The heat, known as the latent heat of fusion, that is absorbed by a phase change material to melt it, is much greater than that absorbed during temperature rise of a conventional sensible heat store. This means that the size of the thermal store can be greatly reduced.

Integration with mechanical heating

It was stated at the outset that passive solar space heating is only useful in reducing energy consumption if the output of the space heating system can be reduced or turned off in response to the entry of solar energy. This can only occur if the heating system has been designed to take advantage of solar gains and there are adequate control systems in place.

Control The heating system must be zoned so that areas not receiving solar gains, such as the north side of the building, can be heated independently from the south side. Sensors, placed out of direct sunlight, must be employed to detect solar gains. In response, as room temperatures increase, actuators are used to modify the heat output from heat emitters.

Thermal response. The heating system and in particular the heat emitters must have a quick thermal response time. This means that the time between receiving a command to reduce heat output and the commencement of reductions in heat output must be short. High thermal capacity systems such as under-floor heating, electric storage radiators or high water content radiators are unsuitable as they have a slow thermal response time. Even if the flow of hot water to them were to be stopped instantly the stored thermal energy within them would still be released for some hours before reducing significantly. Instead, low water content radiators or fan convectors should be used. Switching off the fan of a fan convector rapidly reduces its heat output. This means that if solar gains change as a result of movement of cloud cover, the heating system can respond to these changes quickly by turning the fan on as temperatures fall and off as temperatures rise above set point.

A passive solar strategy

An example of a strategy to supplement space heating in housing using a passive solar heating is described below.

For passive solar design to work effectively a number of elements need to be considered simultaneously (Figure 2.19). This will ensure that optimising one element does not cause detrimental effects elsewhere. Many of the methods used to optimise solar energy collection can lead to an increase in energy consumption or discomfort if not applied carefully.   >>>

The first stage in the strategy is to consider the usefulness of the solar gains. In a commercial building solar gains may be rejected as they would simply add to other gains and cause over heating. This also applies to domestic buildings in hot climates. If solar gains are considered to be of benefit then the following issues should be addressed.

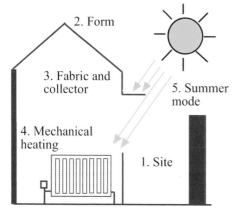

Figure 2,19. Elements of a passive solar space heating strategy.

Siting - allow good solar access to the site but make sure buildings that are collecting solar energy for themselves do not overshadow nearby buildings to the north. The spacing out of buildings to avoid overshadowing of neighbouring buildings can allow local wind speeds to increase which would increase ventilation heat losses.

Form - extend south facing facade to increase the area for solar collection. Plan rooms so that habitable spaces are to the south and service rooms to the north. Increasing the surface area of a building increases the area through which fabric heat losses occur.

Fabric - increase the glazed area on the south side and reduce it on the north side. At night and on overcast days solar gains will be non existent or minimal but heat losses will continue through the thermally weak glazing. During the day glare will occur if a bright window appears in the field of view. The building should be highly insulated but this, combined with solar heat gains, can result in overheating in summer.

Reductions in the size of north facing glazing can lead to inadequate daylight levels.

Services - the heating system should be responsive, modulating its output in response to solar gains. Savings in energy will not be made and discomfort will be caused if the output of the mechanical heating system is not reduced in response to solar heat gain.

Cooling - provide shading devices on windows and thermal mass in the interior to avoid summertime overheating. Shading devices should be selective, allowing gains in winter but rejecting them in summer. Blinds and shades should not significantly reduce daylight levels.

Low energy design principles must be applied with care. There are numerous interactions that take place between form, fabric and services. A successful low energy design considers the building holistically, carefully assessing the impact any decisions have on the buildings overall performance.

Planning orientation using sun path diagrams

Sun path diagrams highlight the path which the sun appears to take across the sky and explains how the position of the sun in the sky at any time is specified using two angles.

The sun is stationary relative to our solar system but the spin of the earth and its orbit around the sun gives observers on the earth's surface the impression that the sun moves across the sky. The path that the sun takes varies with each hour of the day, and day of the year. but the general pattern is well known. To an observer in the Northern hemisphere, such as someone in the UK, the sun rises in the east, reaches a maximum altitude at noon in the south and sets in the west (Figure 2.20). In summer the UK is tilted towards the sun and so the sun rises early towards the north east, has a high sun path and then sets north of west. The long sun path is experienced as a long day. In winter the UK is tilted away from the sun so the sun rises towards the south east, reaches a relatively low maximum altitude at noon then sets in the south west. This low, short sun path gives a short day. The position of the sun in the sky at any time of the year can be specified using two angles.

The first is the angle of azimuth. This is the angle between the north point and a vertical plane passing through the centre of the sun from the point of observation. The second angle, the angle of altitude, is the angle between the horizontal and a line passing through the centre of the sun and the point of observation. Tables of solar altitude and azimuth for any given time of day and for 5° increments in latitude on the earth are published in 'CIBSE Guide A'.

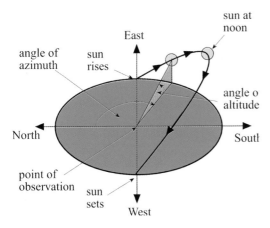

Figure 2.20. General sun path showing angles of azimuth and altitude.

Sun path diagrams explained

The sun path is three-dimensional. However, it can be depicted on a two-dimensional chart called a sun path diagram. There are two types of sun path diagram; one that projects the sun path information horizontally and one that projects the sun path information vertically.

Horizontal projection

An example of a horizontally projected chart is given in Figure 2.21. The y-axis represents solar altitude so the further up the chart a point is the higher the sun is in the sky. The x-axis represents the solar azimuth. Due south is in the centre of the chart. Three sun paths are

shown for latitude 51° north. Other latitudes have a slightly different set of sun paths. The further north in the UK, the lower the angles of altitude for any particular time of year.

The three traces shown represent the extremes and mid point of the sun path. The uppermost trace is the sun path for the summer solstice. This is the longest day of the year (indicated by the length of the sun path when over the horizon) and when the sun reaches its maximum altitude at noon. The lowest trace is the sun path for the winter solstice. This is the shortest day of the year when the sun reaches its lowest altitude at noon. Finally, the central trace is the autumn and spring equinox. On this day the sun rises due east and sets due west. With each day passing from the summer solstice the sun becomes lower in the sky and the day begins to shorten. The autumn equinox position marks the mid point between the summer and winter solstice. Following the winter solstice the sun's altitude increases again daily at any given time until it passes through a second mid position, the spring equinox.

Vertical projection

The vertically projected chart is shown in Figure 2.22. It can be seen that the graph paper used is different to the usual rectangular x - y arrangement. Here the outermost concentric circle represents the horizon or 0° altitude. Successive concentric circles represent increasing altitude in 10° intervals until the centre point represents 90° altitude, directly upwards. The building is considered to be under this centre point. The nearer a point on the graph is to the centre of the circle the higher it is in the sky. The radial lines represent angle of azimuth. These begin with the vertical radial line which represents north. Successive radial lines moving in a clockwise direction are 10° increments of solar azimuth. 90° azimuth represents east, 180° represents south and 270° represents west. The same three sun paths as depicted on Figure 2.21 are also shown on Figure 2.22.

Both types of sun path diagram show the same information - angles of altitude and

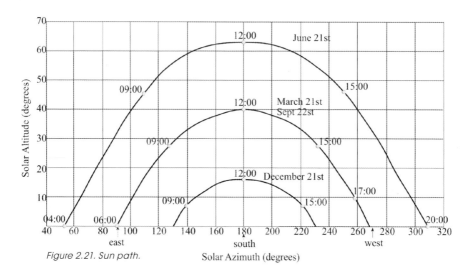

Figure 2.21. Sun path.

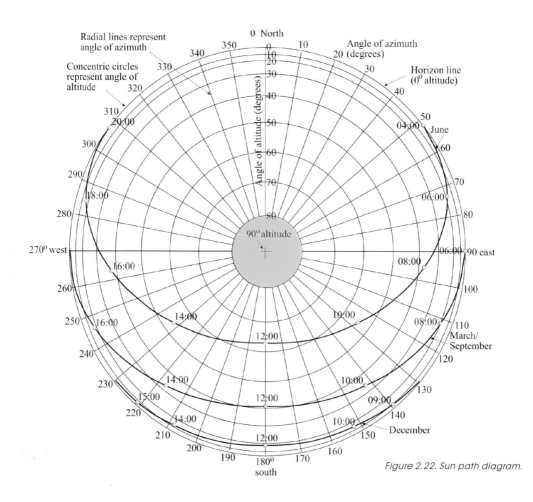

Figure 2.22. Sun path diagram.

azimuth. However the horizontal projection of Figure 2.21 is better for visualising solar altitude whereas the vertical projection in Figure 2.22 is better for visualising solar azimuth.

Using the charts

The sun path diagrams are useful in studies of passive solar heating and passive cooling. The former by attempting to encourage the entry of sunlight into the building, the latter by preventing the entry of sunlight into the building. A simple example, using the circular sun chart shown in Figure 2.22, is the determination of which face of a building the sun falls on at a particular time and date of the year. A small outline of the building under investigation is placed at the centre of the sun path and is rotated to the correct orientation. The chart requires a sun path that relates to the latitude of the site and the day of interest. By connecting a point on the sun path at the time of interest to the centre point, the surface that this line crosses will be that which is affected by the sun.

The information carried on the sun path diagram is also used in environmental design software. The size, position and orientation of windows are defined either in terms of data or as a CAD image file. The software will then call upon inbuilt sun path information to determine external overshadowing of the site by adjacent structures, shadows cast by the building itself and finally, if data is also available on solar intensity as well as position, heat gains to the building through the glazing. Most software systems also have the benefit of being able to repeat these calculations at different times of the day, such as at hourly intervals. The daily heat gain can be calculated and animations created showing the movement of shadows and pools of sunlight within and surrounding the building. ☙

Various solar strategies in a south facing courtyard.
Floor mounted solar panel.
Triple glazed solar roof for passive solar heating.
Glazed, passive solar 'bottle' wall.

Solar water heating

Unlike space heating which is only required during the winter months, hot water is required all year round. This is useful as the sun's greatest availability is in summer when space heating is not required. A solar water heating system can provide all of the hot water requirement of a typical 2 adult, 2 children family during the summer months but only part of the hot water requirement in winter, when the solar availability is reduced.

The system could be sized to provide full hot water delivery in winter but would then be greatly oversized in summer. As a consequence a typical solar water heating system, based on 1m² per person, provides approximately 50% of the annual hot water requirement of a typical family. The capital cost of a solar water heating system is between £1750 and £4000. If we assume the cost is £2000 to provide 4m² of solar collector and this provides 33,000 litres of hot water per year, normally heated by electricity, then the result is a simple payback period of approximately 10 years. The payback is considerably longer if the solar water heating system is displacing gas.

There are two main parts to the most common type of solar water heating system. The first is the solar collector that traps solar energy and transfers it into the water flowing through it. The second is the system that transfers the heat within the collector to the water stored in the domestic hot water storage tank.

Solar collectors

Modern solar collectors take generally one of two forms. These are flat plate collectors and evacuated tube collectors. Both types of collector have to carry out the twin functions of maximising the collection of solar energy whilst minimising heat losses. Both types must also be extremely robust since they are mounted outdoors and have to withstand thermal cycling between low temperatures caused by radiant cooling to the night sky and high temperatures caused by the absorption of solar energy.

Flat plate collectors are rectangular and are typically 0.6m by 1.5m in size. Multiple collectors can be plumbed together in series to form a collector array which will increase the amount of hot water that is created. A typical flat plate collector is shown in Figure 2.23. It is composed of a steel or aluminium frame which holds all of the components in place and allows the collector to be fixed to a suitable south facing mounting location such as the rooftop.

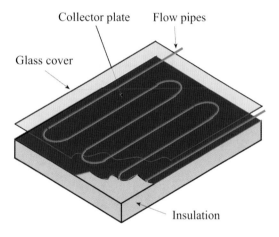

Figure 2.23. Flat plate solar collector.

The uppermost layer in the flat plate collector is a sheet of glass. This allows the solar radiation to pass through to the collector plate below where it is absorbed. The glass sheet has two functions. The first is to create a greenhouse effect, trapping heat within the air gap above the collector plate. The second is to reduce convective heat losses from the collector plate. This last function is necessary to increase collector efficiency since, in winter, the collector will lose heat to the cold surrounding air. Heat losses are reduced further if low emissivity double glazing is used. Standard thermal insulation forms a layer behind the collector plate to reduce backward heat losses. The collector plate is composed of a steel or aluminium panel onto which tubing is fixed. The tubing is placed in close contact with the plate to ensure that solar heat absorbed by the plate is transferred into the water that circulates through the pipes. Low cost collector plates are simply finished in matt black paint. This finish is the most efficient at absorbing solar heat. More expensive units have collector plates coated in a metal oxide layer. This has a high heat absorptivity and a low heat emissivity. The coating therefore reduces radiant heat losses from the collector plate without affecting the absorption of solar energy.

Evacuated tube collectors have a collector plate similar to a flat plate collector but it is in the form of a strip that has the water circulation tubing running down its centre (Figure 2.24). The tubing terminates in a connector which allows it to be fed into a header pipe. Other collector tubes are added to this header to form a collector array. Arrays can then be added together in series to increase the collector area. There is no thermal insulation at the back of the collector plate. Instead the glass envelope surrounding the plate has had some of the air removed from it. This reduces the convective heat losses from the collector plate. This, combined with a selective high absorbance/low emissivity coating, makes the evacuated tube collector the most efficient unit available for collecting solar energy.

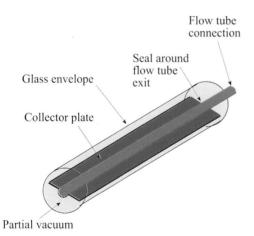

Figure 2.24. Evacuated tube collector.

Mounting angle. So that the sunlight strikes the collector plate at an angle that is close to right angles to the surface, both types of collector must be tilted towards the sun. The rule of thumb for the mounting angle is at

latitude + 10° to the horizontal. At a latitude of 54° in the UK this would result in a mounting angle of 64° as shown in Figure 2.25.

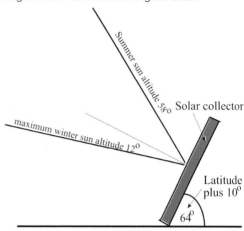

Figure 2.25. Tilt of solar collector to optimise collection in winter.

It can be seen that this aligns the normal to the collector plate towards the noon winter solstice solar altitude rather than the noon summer solstice solar altitude. This is because there is less solar radiation in winter and therefore its collection must be optimised at this time.

One of the advantages of evacuated tube collectors is that the array can be mounted on a vertical surface such as a wall. Individual tubes are then rotated to the appropriate optimum collector angle (Figure 2.26). >>>

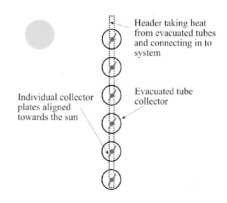

Figure 2.26. Vertical array of evacuated tube collectors.

System types

There are three basic solar water heating systems into which the solar collectors described previously can be integrated.

Low cost systems which use the buoyancy of warm water to circulate the heat to the hot water storage tank (Figure 2.27). These are most often used as water heaters in developing countries as they do not require an electrical pump and have a low capital cost.

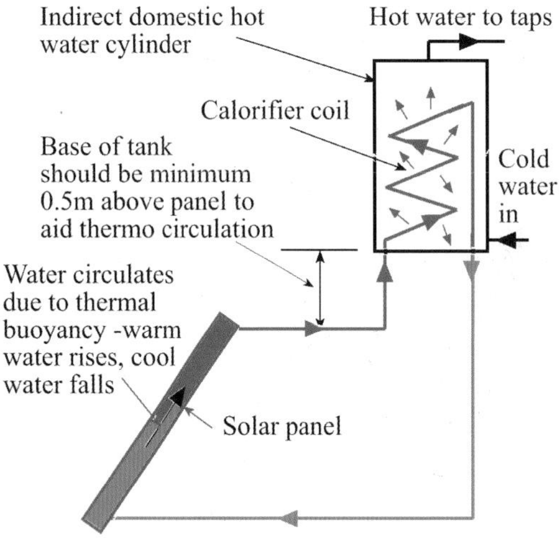

Indirect domestic hot water cylinder

Hot water to taps

Calorifier coil

Base of tank should be minimum 0.5m above panel to aid thermo circulation

Cold water in

Water circulates due to thermal buoyancy -warm water rises, cool water falls

Solar panel

Figure 2.27. Low cost thermo-siphoning solar water heating system.

Intermediate systems which use pumped circulation, minimal electronic controls and a single hot water storage tank (Figure 2.28). The pumped circulation means that the storage cylinder can be situated below the solar panel. These systems suffer from the fact that low grade heat from the panel cannot be used. For example if an immersion heater is used to raise the stored water temperature to 65°C, water coming off the collector at 35°C and circulating through the calorifer (indirect) coil would actually cool the stored water down.

High efficiency systems with a pre-heat storage tank (Figure 2.29). This system has the most components and is therefore the most costly. It does, however, use low grade heat coming off the collector to pre-heat incoming mains water as it passes through the primary tank. ☻

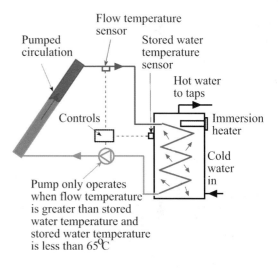

Flow temperature sensor

Pumped circulation

Stored water temperature sensor

Hot water to taps

Controls

Immersion heater

Cold water in

Pump only operates when flow temperature is greater than stored water temperature and stored water temperature is less than 65°C

Figure 2.28. Single tank solar water heating system.

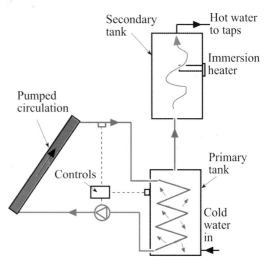

Secondary tank

Hot water to taps

Immersion heater

Pumped circulation

Controls

Primary tank

Cold water in

Figure 2.29. Dual tank solar water heating system.

Photovoltaics (PV's)

The construction of a photovoltaic cell is shown in Figure 2.30. The central component is a single crystal of silicon. Because of its atomic structure, an electric charge moves around naturally inside the crystal but in a random manner. The current can, however, be encouraged to flow in one direction by joining two types of silicon together; one acting as a positive terminal (*p*- type) and the other acting as a negative terminal (*n* - type). The two forms are made by adding impurities to the silicon, called doping. *n* - type is formed by adding arsenic and *p* - type by adding boron. When sunlight falls on the *p* - *n* junction the energy contained in it causes more electrons to be released increasing the electric current available for collection.

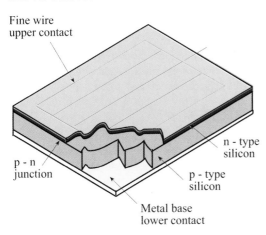

Fine wire
upper contact

p - n
junction

n - type
silicon

p - type
silicon

Metal base
lower contact

Figure 2.30. Silicon crystal PV cell.

As with all electrical devices connections are required to pick up and channel the available electricity. The back of the crystal has a copper layer deposited on to it to make up the lower terminal. The upper terminal sits on the side of the semiconductor facing the sun. If the entire face were to be covered in copper, the crystal would be shaded from the sun. To avoid this the upper terminal is made out of a network of extremely fine wires deposited onto the surface. Sunlight can pass between the gaps in the wire grid and hit the crystal. The amount of

semiconductor obscured from the sun by the upper terminal is one of the factors that reduce photovoltaic efficiency. Finally, the whole cell is protected by being encased in a glass sandwich. Small cells are used widely to power pocket calculators and watches. Larger arrays are now being manufactured to produce electricity for use in buildings.

The photovoltaic panels form part of a system, comprising PV panels, batteries (if used), an inverter and an export electricity meter. The electricity produced by the panels is in the form of direct current (d.c.), like that obtained from batteries. Buildings use alternating current (a.c.) and so an inverter is used to convert the direct current to alternating current. If the electricity is not required at the time of generation it can be stored in batteries, or converted to a.c. and exported to the grid. The export meter allows the building operator to charge the utilities for the electricity that has been supplied to the grid.

Financial and practical constraints of PV's

Photovoltaics are an interesting concept for powering buildings. Unfortunately, the cost of photovoltaic arrays are still too great for them to be economically viable. For example 10m² of PV cells would give a peak output of 1 kilowatt. This array would produce approximately 700kWh of electricity each year. If electricity for a house can be purchased from the grid at 11.0 pence per kilowatt hour then the value of this electricity is £77.00 per year. The capital cost of the PV array is approximately £400 for commercial and £600 for domestic buildings per square metre. The lower cost of commercial systems arises due to economies of scale. If we assume £6000 for our 10m² array, this results in a simple payback period of 78 years! This is too long a period considering the estimated 30 year lifespan of PV cells. The sections below consider the factors involved in improving the economics of PV cells, but possibly a better way of justifying them is in terms of a carbon payback period, as they produce CO_2 free electricity. The only CO_2 associated with them is that produced during manufacture and transport.

Economic viability can be improved. This might come about if the current large rises in the unit cost of electricity from the grid were to continue. Other aspects that would make them more competitive would be:

The efficiency is increased. The efficiency of a PV panel is a comparison between the amount of solar energy hitting its surface and the electrical energy it produces. The maximum theoretical efficiency of a PV panel is approximately 28%. The actual peak effciencies of a single crystal silicon array is 15% and that for an amorphous silicon array is 5%. Improvements in efficiency can be brought about by reducing the area covered by the upper electrical contact, keeping the PV panel cool and using multiple semiconductor materials which can absorb more of the solar spectrum. It is important that the PV panels are kept cool as their efficiency falls by 0.4% for every 1°C rise in temperature above 25°C. This usually means that the panels must be mounted with an air gap behind them so good air circulation is encouraged to remove heat from the panels.

The capital cost of the panels is reduced. Single crystals of silicon, each up to 0.1m square, are very expensive to produce. Since they form the basis of PV panels, the panels themselves are also very expensive. Mass manufacturing techniques arising from increased uptake of the technology may help to reduce this high capital cost. It has been suggested that part of the capital cost of a PV array could be offset by replacing expensive cladding materials on commercial buildings with PV cells. So, for example, if the PV array costs £400 per square metre and prestige cladding panels cost £300 per square metre it could be argued that by replacing the cladding with PV the additional costs are only £100 per square metre. This creates a low 'apparent' capital cost but only for commercial buildings. An alternative is to create PV arrays from amorphous silicon. This is silicon which is not a single large crystal but is made up of numerous tiny crystals. These PV panels are much cheaper but unfortunately, as explained above, their efficiency is only 5%. It is possible that mass production techniques

used by the glass industry to create float glass with specialised coatings, could be used to make these panels extremely cheaply in the future. Their low efficiency would be offset by the ability to cover large areas of the building cheaply.

There are a variety of options for the integration of PV panels into buildings. They can simply be stand alone panels attached to south facing vertical surfaces of the building or mounted at an angle on the rooftop (Figure 2.31). An interesting alternative in domestic buildings is the availability of PV roof tiles that have a similar appearance to traditional roofing tiles and when used to form a domestic roof avoid some of the visual intrusion created by the appearance of a stand alone panel. In commercial buildings it is common for the glass substrate, onto which the silicon cells are placed, to be coloured the same as the silicon cell. One alternative option that has been used is to leave the glass clear so that light can pass through it. When these panels are used as part of a glazing system, the dual benefit of daylight, passive solar heating and electricity production is achieved. ☙

Figure 2.31. Photovoltaic and solar water heating panels in a bespoke framing system on the roof of a contemporary building.

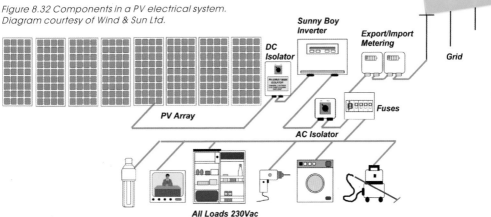

Figure 8.32 Components in a PV electrical system.
Diagram courtesy of Wind & Sun Ltd.

Sunny Boy
Inverter

Export/Import
Metering

DC
Isolator

Grid

PV Array

Fuses

AC Isolator

All Loads 230Vac

Case study
PVs at Lockton Youth Hostel

The client brief asked the architects (EcoArc) to breathe new life into the dilapidated building and provide high comfort standards for visitors. The architects were asked to exceed current building standards wherever possible, with a strong environmental agenda to reduce running costs, using renewable energy. The challenge was to do this within the permitted guidelines of the National Park Authority in a North York Moors village of high conservation value.

An early proposal of a 2.5kW wind turbine on an 11m high tower was ruled out by the planning authority as it was seen as inconceivable to permit it within the traditional vernacular village setting that the hostel was in. To the architects pleasant surprise the local planning authority warmly embraced all other ecological innovations and in fact provided £80,000 seed funding from their North York Moors National Park Authority Sustainable Development Fund to support the project.

The completed renovated building demonstrates a simple sustainable model within an existing rural context. It has been conceived as an integrated eco system within the boundaries of the site and aims to be as self-reliant as possible in terms of its service energy supply systems and the treatment of its waste streams. The building has been adapted to make more efficient use of the available space and consume less energy in

use. Electricity is provided via photovoltaic panels mounted on the south roof.

The architects worked with Steve Wade, from Wind & Sun, to design and install a solar PV system. The Youth Hostel uses a grid-connected 1.28kWp photovoltaic (PV) system consisting of 8 BP Solar 160Wp monocrystaline PV panels, which were installed above the existing slate roof. PV generated electric power is first used by the hostel internal loads; any surplus being exported to the national grid. At night or when power consumption exceeds power generated, electricity is imported from the grid as normal. All power flows are 'seamless' from the point of view of the user.

The system should produce approx. 1000kWh of electricity per annum. A display is incorporated in a 'Sunny Boy' PV inverter to show people staying at the hostel how much is being generated. Inclusion of the originaly proposed 2.5kW wind turbine would have meant the Hostel could have been a net exporter to the grid. However, due to financial constraints the PV array is not large enough to produce 100% of energy demand. Regardless of this, the PV array at Lockton makes a significant contribution and has been important in terms of raising awareness of PVs, which are rare in the North York Moors National Park. ◑

References for Chapter 2

1. Department of Trade and Industry. Energy Statistics 2005

2. Website of the British Wind Energy Association. www.bwea.com

3. Brister, A. Dublins Green City. Building Services Journal pp 32-33. August 1996.

4. Wind Power for Sainsbury's. Energy and Environmental Manager, p11. McMillan Scott 2001.

5. Department of Trade and Industry, Technology Status report 002. Small Scale Hydro Power, October 1993

6. Energy Technology Support Unit. Technology Status Report 003, Tidal Power. June 1993.

7. Anon. Renewable Energy is a Burning Issue. Energy in Buildings and Industry. p18. March 2001

8. Building Research Energy Conservation Unit. Case Study 81: Community Heating in Sheffield. HMSO. November 1994.

9. King, C. Passive Solar Heating. p10. Report written by the Energy Research Group Dublin for the European Commission Directorate General XII for Science Research and Development. 1995.

10. Uglow, C. E. The Calculation of Energy Use in Dwellings. BSER&T, Vol 2, No.4, pp1-14. 1981.

Further reading

BRE CP75/75 Availability of Sunshine. 1975

GIR27: Passive Solar Estate Layout. 1995

GPG73: Energy Efficient Housing Design - Exploiting Solar Energy.

GIL22: Passive Solar House Design

Financial aspects

Financial assistance may be available to assist in purchasing a wind turbine, or other renewable energy device, under the Energy Saving Trust (EST) low carbon buildings programme (www.lowcarbonbuildings.org. uk). Local authorities may also have locally available grants.

© Green Building Press

Proven energy generation
The **C21**e solar roof tile.

C21e solar electric roof tiles are easy to install, use the most efficient solar cells available and integrate seamlessly with conventional tiles.

Don't just take our word for it:

Best Exterior Product	Interbuild 2004	
Award for Innovation	Building 2005	
Best Sustainable Product	Construct 2006	
Best Overall Product **Best Product for the Building Envelope**	Interbuild 2006	
Innovator of the Year award for C21e	REA Awards 2006	

solarcentury

Call **020 7803 0100**
email **C21@solarcentury.com**
or visit **solarcentury.com**
to find out more about C21e solar roof tiles

3 Site and climate

Introduction

Buildings are constructed so that humans can carry out their various activities in an appropriate environment, efficiently, safely and in thermal comfort. The shell of a building is a barrier between the varying external environment, which can be uncomfortably cold or hot, and the stable, comfortable internal environment. The building fabric acts as a moderator of climate but it is usual, during seasonal extremes, to use energy to maintain internal conditions. It follows therefore that the greater the deviation of the external environment away from the required internal conditions the greater is the need for energy consumption.

In this chapter we will consider how the climate at a particular site is determined by geographic and topographic factors and how this climate affects the energy consumption of a building. We will consider how excess energy consumption can be limited by firstly modifying the site using landscaping and then enhancing the building itself.

Climate and energy

The energy used to heat a building does not remain in the building but is lost from it via two routes known as fabric and ventilation heat losses. This section will consider these two forms of heat loss and introduce the effect of the climate on them.

Fabric heat losses arise when heat is transferred from the warm interior to the cold exterior through the external surfaces of the building. This occurs by a combination of heat transfer mechanisms; conduction through the solid materials such as masonry, convection across air spaces such as cavities, and radiation across cavities and from the external masonry surface. Thermal properties of the fabric and various construction materials are discussed more fully in Chapter 4.

Ventilation heat losses occur when the warm air inside the building leaves and is replaced by cool air from outside.

The speed with which heat is lost by these processes is known as the heat loss rate, measured in joules per second (J/s) otherwise known as watts (W). The equations that are used to calculate the steady state heat loss rate from buildings for both fabric (Q_f) and ventilation (Q_v) heat loss rate are shown in Figure 3.1 and explained more fully in *'Thermal properties of construction materials'* in Chapter 5.

The effect of climate on buildings

Figure 3.1 shows the variables involved in determining the fabric and ventilation heat loss rates. Some of these are constants, determined by the building form and fabric others are variable depending on the external climate.

$$Q_v = \tfrac{1}{3}.n.V.\Delta T$$

$$Q_f = \Sigma(U_x.A_x.)\Delta T$$

Figure 3.1. Equations for ventilation (Q_v) and fabric (Q_f) heat loss rate

Constants. The area, volume and internal temperature are all constant. The first two determined by the building form, the latter by the building services that function to maintain a constant internal temperature.

Variables affected by the climate. In the following sections we will find that; the ventilation rate increases as the wind speed increases. The temperature difference between inside and outside increases as the external temperature falls, and the U-value of masonry walls increases when wind and rain exposure increases. Each of these increases will result in larger heat loss rates.

MSc Architecture: Advanced Environmental and Energy Studies

AN INNOVATIVE POSTGRADUATE PROGRAMME OFFERED JOINTLY BETWEEN THE UNIVERSITY OF EAST LONDON AND THE CENTRE FOR ALTERNATIVE TECHNOLOGY, EUOPE'S LEADING ECO CENTRE

The programme examines the relationship between human beings and the environment and in particular offers an ecological perspective on building. The programme runs as ten five-day residential sessions every month except August and December. Students choose to complete eight of the ten sessions either by attending at CAT or by Web based study. The programme is suitable for all those with an interest in developing expertise in an area of rapidly increasing importance where skills shortages are being reported. The programme offers an opportunity for those seeking a career change and/or needing to upgrade their existing skills and welcomes those who have experienced significant breaks in their education. The programme is open to students with a wide range of experiential and educational backgrounds who are expected to have a first degree. Mature students who do not possess formal qualifications but have been engaged in activities that are relevant and/or considered likely to benefit from the programme may be accepted. The programme is accredited by the Energy Institute and selected Units are offered via the RIBA CPD providers network. An extended version of the programme to give exemption from the requirement of the RIBA part II examination is being developed.

Course materials, food and accommodation (while at CAT) are included in the programme fee

for more information visit **www.cat.org.uk/msc**
or email **m.w.thompson@uel.ac.uk** or **a.pooley@uel.ac.uk**

University
East London

Centre for Alternative Technology   . energy
INSTITUTE

Macroclimate and microclimate

Climatological processes arising from variations in energy deposition on the earth by the sun dictate the patterns of weather we encounter. The variation in solar energy deposition repeats annually. As a consequence the climatic variables, including temperature, wind-speed and direction, solar intensity and humidity can be anticipated each year, on a national scale, with a reasonable degree of accuracy.

At this stage the distinction between weather and climate must be made clear. The weather is the climatic conditions prevailing at a particular time; wind speed, wind direction, insolation, air temperature, relative humidity and precipitation. Climate on the other hand is a statistical set of data based on weather records taken over a number of years. For example, a standard set of data used by building scientists is based on the period 1961 to 1990. From these records patterns can be determined. For example, the most common wind direction in December in the UK is from the south west. This gives us information with which to make a good prediction of what the wind direction is likely to be in December, but in reality, on any given day in December, the wind can come from any direction. Weather data is gathered by meteorological offices in the major cities in the UK. From this, tables of data are prepared giving us a good indication of what the climate is most likely to be for each month of the year. This is known as macroclimatic data since it is relevant for a large area within the UK.

The physical processes that dictate macroclimates can be modified on a local scale by variations in topography. For example the presence of coasts, valleys, dense woodland or hills all interact with the general climate of the region and cause local variations. Buildings and other discrete features can further modify the local climate by wind channelling, solar trapping and overshadowing. These variations create a small region of distinctly different climatic conditions known as the microclimate.

Choice of site

It is impractical to suggest choosing a site for a new development on the basis of low energy consumption. This is because in practice little choice is available. Planning restrictions, the need to build at a particular location, say for transport or closeness to commerce, land availability, cost of land or use of an existing site all limit the choices available. However, much can be achieved by considering the building and its relationship with the site to minimise the effect of climate on energy consumption.

Four areas of knowledge would allow us to minimise the effect of climate on buildings;

- how climate varies with location. The location of a site has a profound effect on the climate it experiences. Site knowledge through local monitoring or meteorological office data will enable the more extreme climatic variables affecting the site to be identified
- how climate affects heat loss. Wind, rain, solar intensity and external temperature all have a direct affect on a building's heat loss or gain rate. An understanding of climate related heat loss processes is a necessary precursor for suggesting methods for preventing such heat loss
- how the landscape can be designed to minimise the effects of climate. A range of techniques are available that modify the general climate to create a 'kind' microclimate
- how the building fabric and its form can be reinforced so that it acts as a climatic moderator.

The above will be addressed in each of the environmental variables affecting heat loss later in this section.

External temperature

The space heating energy consumption of a building is directly proportional to the difference between inside and outside environmental temperatures. Assuming we input heat to the building to maintain a constant internal temperature, then the factor which determines the magnitude of the temperature difference is the level of the external temperature. The lower the outside temperature the greater the rate of heat loss for both fabric and ventilation routes.

UK temperature profile

There are two factors which strongly influence the temperature at a particular location in the UK. These are the altitude and latitude of the site.

At a fixed latitude (fixed angular distance from the equator) temperatures decrease with increasing latitude. Figure 3.2 shows the average external temperature at sea level for the UK in winter. It can be seen that the further north the lower the average outside temperatures. This is further illustrated in Table 3.1 which shows the average winter temperatures for Southampton, Manchester and Aberdeen. On average the temperature in Aberdeen is 1.5°C cooler than Manchester and 2.3°C cooler than Southampton.

At a fixed altitude, (fixed height above sea level) temperatures decrease with increasing altitude. Typically the reduction in temperature is 0.6°C per 100m increase in altitude[1].

There are local variations in addition to these general rules. For example, the west coast experiences higher temperatures than average due to the effect of warm sea currents. Absorption of solar energy can create warm islands, and depressions in the land experience lower than average outside temperatures due to cold air sinking into and collecting in them.

Degree days

The effect of lower outside temperatures on heating energy consumption is usefully illustrated by using a system known as degree days[2]. This is a method of expressing the depth and length of time the outside air temperature fell below a certain threshold. The threshold is known as the base temperature. The base temperature is 15.5°C and it is assumed that if the outside temperature is at or above this figure then no heating is required in the building. If the outside air temperature falls below this threshold then space heating will be required.

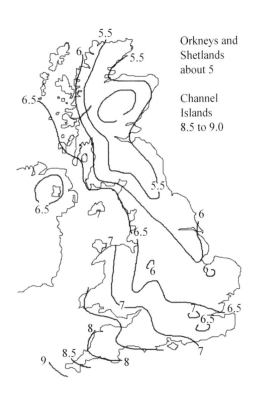

Orkneys and
Shetlands
about 5

Channel
Islands
8.5 to 9.0

Figure 3.2. Sea level dry bulb temperatures averaged over the heating season (October - April inclusive (taken from CIBSE Guide A).

Location	Average External Temperature (°C)
Aberdeen	5.9
Manchester	7.4
Southampton	8.2

Table 3.1. Average external temperature at three locations measured over the heating season September-May.

Degree days are calculated by summing the number of 24 hour periods over which the external temperature falls 1°C below the base temperature. For example, if the external temperature is 13.5°C for 12 hours, this is equivalent to 12 hours x 2°C below base line = 24 degree hours or one degree day. It follows therefore that the larger the number of degree days, the more cold the climate and the greater the demand for space heating. Table 3.2 shows the total degree days for four regions measured over the heating season (September - April) for the period 1984 - 1985. It can be seen that the south west of England has the lowest degree day total and the figures for the other locations increase the further north the location. Figure 3.3 shows isopleths of the 20 year average degree days for the UK. The darker the shading the higher the degree day total and greater the demand for space heating.

Location	Number of degree days
Cornwall	1800
London	2100
Manchester	2300
Central Scotland	2600

Table 3.2. Average degree day totals for four regions (Sept-April).

This figure confirms the two principles governing outside temperatures described above. The further north in the country, the higher the degree day totals. Also the high lying parts of Devon and Cornwall show higher degree day totals, as do the Pennines and the highlands of Scotland.

As well as describing the severity of the climate, degree days can be used in energy management (see Chapter 11). One example is in the normalisation of energy consumptions in similar buildings in different parts of the UK. For example, a business may have identical offices in Aberdeen and Southampton. The energy manager cannot compare the relative perform-ance of these buildings directly as it is colder in Scotland, therefore the building located there will naturally consume more energy. However, this extra energy consumption could be masking additional energy consumption arising from a heating system fault. By dividing the energy consumptions of both buildings by the degree day totals in their respective loca-tions, the energy consumption per degree day is determined. This eliminates the difference caused by the lower external temperatures and reveals any differences in energy consumption due to other factors.

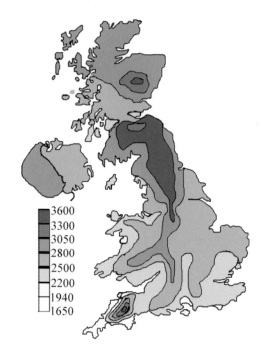

3600
3300
3050
2800
2500
2200
1940
1650

Figure 3.3. Degree day isopleths. Diagram from Fuel Efficiency Booklet 7: Degree Days. (1993). © Crown Copyright.

Landscape and site

The essential requirement for raising external temperatures is to allow good solar access to the site. For this to be achieved overshadowing by tall objects such as hills, trees or buildings to the south of the site must be avoided. On an existing site with obstructions to the south, the degree of overshadowing can be estimated using geometry from a knowledge of the sun's angles of azimuth and altitude (see the sun path diagrams in Chapter 2), the height spacing and arrangement of buildings and any obstructions.

Figure 3.4 shows the minimum shadow lengths created by a house with a roof ridge 8m above the ground at latitude 55° north. Two shadows are shown, the first is for the worst case situation i.e. noon on the winter solstice, December 21st, when the sun reaches its lowest mid day position in the year. This gives the maximum noon shadow length. The second line shows the position at noon on March 21st and September 21st i.e. around the beginning and end of the heating season. It can be seen that the second dwelling, shown 24 meters to the south of the first, will be overshadowed during the depths of winter but will receive sunlight at the beginning and end of the heating season.

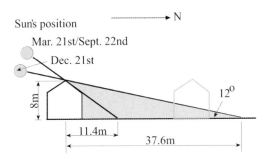

Figure 3.4 . Shadow length at noon winter solstice and spring/autumn equinox.

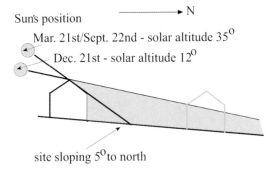

Figure 3.5. Effect of a sloping site on solar access.

Sites on north facing slopes will be disadvantaged as shown in Figure 3.5. It can be seen that in comparison to Figure 3.4, when the site is sloping 5° to the north, the overshadowing effect is increased. The effect of this reduced solar access is to increase the energy consumption. This was revealed in a mathematical study of the effect of site slope on the space heating energy consumption of domestic buildings[3]. That study found that in comparison to a flat site a 5° northerly slope increased the energy consumption of a typical house by 400kWh/year, whereas a 5° southerly slope decreased the annual energy consumption by 150 kWh/year.

Good solar access to a site can be achieved by;
● spacing out and staggering the buildings so that they do not overshadow each other (Figure 3.6). This approach can create conflict with the economics of housing development that dictates that houses should be densely packed on the site to increase the number of units on the land unless the site is designed carefully
● roof pitches should be kept shallow, typically below 40°, to reduce ridge height but greater than 10° to avoid wind suction
● where the site has a mixture of building heights, keep high buildings to the north to prevent over-shadowing
● avoid placing minor buildings, such as a garage or store room, to the south of the main building.

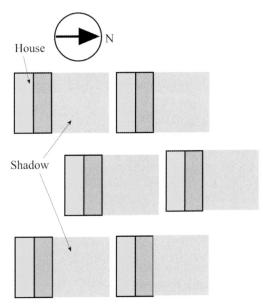

Figure 3.6. Housing layout for solar access.

The use of dark paved materials enhances the absorption of heat in the general vicinity of a building. Conduction of this heat to the surrounding air increases air temperatures. It must be remembered, however, that dark paving materials, due to their reduced daylight reflectiveness, may result in diminished daylight entry into the building.

The solar heating effect will be swept away if winds are allowed free access to the site. One way of trapping this pool of heated air is to form the buildings into a sun trap arrangement (Figure 3.7). The arms creating the sun trap should be kept short to avoid an unacceptable degree of overshadowing at the early and latter parts of the day.

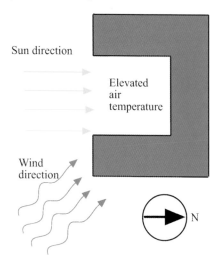

Figure 3.7. Building form to create a sun trap.

The effect of solar absorption by building materials and protection from winds increases average temperatures. This leads to reduced heat losses and pre-heating of infiltration air. The gross effect is clearly demonstrated in cities which are typically 0.5°C warmer on average than the surrounding countryside. This is known as the heat island effect.

Building enhancement

If a proposed building is to be sited in an area with lower than average outside temperatures, it will have a greater than average demand for space heating, resulting in higher costs. Part of these higher fuel costs can be saved by applying additional insulation to the building. The cost of this insulation will be recouped from the value of energy savings made. Having returned the capital cost, the savings will then continue for many years into the future.

Insulation is an excellent low technology method of saving energy. Following installation

it requires no monitoring or adjustments, unlike devices such as electronic heating controls.

An example of the usefulness of additional insulation can be seen when comparing the heat losses through 1m² of masonry wall constructed to a U value of 0.35W/m²K in Southampton and Aberdeen. In Southampton 10.3kWh of energy is required over a heating season to maintain 21°C inside against the outside temperature (see Table 3.1). The same wall in Aberdeen would require 12.1kWh of energy, an increase in energy requirement of 14% due to the lower outside temperatures.

The wall in Aberdeen would require additional insulation to reduce its U value to 0.31W/m²K to have the same heat loss as the wall in Southampton. This principle also applies to other external elements of the building such as roofs, floors and glazing.

Windspeed and direction

When wind hits a building it creates a pressure difference between the windward and leeward sides. This drives cool air into the building and draws warm air out of the other side (Figure 3.8). The energy used to heat the internal air is lost from the building. As the wind speed increases, so does the pressure difference across the building. This in turn increases the ventilation rate.

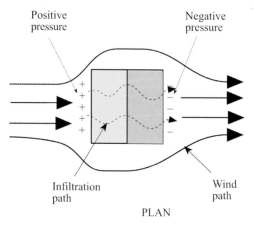

Figure 3.8. Wind induced infiltration.

Figure 3.9 shows how the ventilation rate of a low energy building increases as the wind speed increases. In addition, it can be seen from the ventilation heat loss equation (Figure 3.1), that the ventilation heat loss rate increases in direct proportion to the increased ventilation rate. All of this means that increased wind speed increases the ventilation heat loss rate.

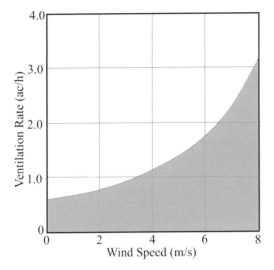

Figure 3.9. Increase in infiltration rate with increasing windspeed.

The direction of the wind has two effects. Firstly, its direction dictates the temperature of the wind. Typically easterly and northerly winds are coldest whilst southerly and westerly winds tend to be warmer. Because of this the prevailing wind direction will have a strong influence on the temperature of infiltration air entering the building. Secondly, the wind direction determines which faces the pressure difference acts across. If these faces contain openings such as doors, windows, cracks or service entries then infiltration will take place more easily. If the wind hits a well sealed facade such as a gable wall with no openings, then it will be more difficult for infiltration to take place and the effect of the windspeed on heat loss will be less severe.

Effects of wind on surface resistance

There is a layer of air attached by friction to the surfaces of all building elements. This still layer

of air adds to the thermal resistance of the wall. Inside the building it is known as the inside surface resistance (Rsi). Outside, on the exterior surface, it is known as the outside surface resistance (Rso) (see *'Thermal properties of construction materials'* in Chapter 5). The size of Rsi depends on the orientation of the surface - whether vertical or horizontal as this affects convective movement of the layer and it also depends on the emissivity and absorptivity of the surface. These are the ability of the surface to emit and absorb thermal radiation respectively. Rso is also affected by external weather conditions. If the surface is exposed then the still layer of air will be swept away and the thermal resistance it adds to the element will be lost.

Rso only contributes a small percentage to the total thermal resistance of a well insulated wall. For example a wall of U-value 0.35W/m²K has only 1.75% of this provided by the outside surface resistance. But for elements with a large U-value such as single glazing with a U-value of 5W/m²K, Rso contributes 20% of the total.

	Exposure category		
	sheltered	normal	exposed
Rso (m²K/W)	0.11	0.07	0.03
U-value (W/m²K)	5.00	5.60	6.00

Table 3.3. Effect of exposure on outside surface thermal resistance (Rso) and single glazing thermal transmittance(U-value).

The effect is seen when considering the variation of outside surface resistance and U-value of single glazing, in relation to changes in the exposure category of the glazing. From Table 3.3 it can be seen that the heat loss rate through single glazing increases by 20% as the exposure category changes from sheltered to exposed.

UK wind profile

The UK is one of the windiest places in Europe. Figure 3.10 shows average annual windspeeds for the UK. High windspeeds are typically experienced at the top of hills, coastal regions and at the edges of smooth terrain such as lakes and fields. The wind is slowed by friction when it passes over rough terrain and because of this windspeeds tend to be lower over inland and urban sites.

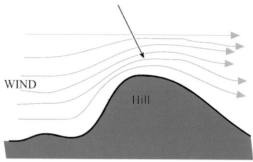

Figure 3.10. Average annual windspeeds (m/s) exceeded for 10% of the time.

At any given location wind speed increases with altitude. It is known that on average windspeeds increase by 7% for every 100m increase in altitude[4]. Tall buildings may be sheltered on the ground floor but experience high wind speeds on the upper floors. The increase in windspeed with height will be more extreme on hilltops due to the way in which the airflow is forced upwards and over the top by the impermeable hillside as shown in Figure 3.11.

Local topography can also modify wind speeds. For example, the wind can be channelled through a valley or between tall buildings. In this situation the same volume of air is trying to pass through a small gap, its velocity must

increase so that the volume flow rate is maintained.

ZONE OF HIGH WINDSPEED

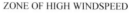

Figure 3.11. High windspeeds on hilltops.

Landscaping

Wind picks up speed when its travel is unhindered. Contact with any surface will create drag and slow the wind down. The more coarse the surface, the greater the drag and slowing effect. One of the roughest natural landscapes is coarse vegetation. We can utilise this effect to reduce wind speed by planting rows of trees, in-filled with shrubs around the trunk, to reduce the wind speed. This reduces windspeeds up to the height of the trees.

The effectiveness of a windbreak depends on its permeability. Permeability is a measure of how easily the air can pass through the windbreak. Values range from 0% to 100%, where 100% is no obstruction to the wind, such as that offered by an open field and 0% is an impermeable structure through which no wind can pass, such as a brick wall or earth mound. Most planted and fence type wind barriers have a permeability within this range depending on the number of air gaps through it. Figure 3.12 shows the impact of barriers with zero and 40-50% permeability on windspeeds.

The impermeable windbreak creates a small zone of zero wind speed close to the rear of the structure. This is useful if a small highly protected zone is required, such as a small yard or building entrance. Glazed walls are often used to protect outdoor swimming pools in this way. However turbulence created by the wind being forced up and over the wall creates eddies. This rapid, random air movement causes discomfort to people outside of the still zone and encourages leaf and litter collection in the turbulent wind vortices before and after the wind barrier. A windbreak with a permeability of 40-50% allows some wind through its structure making the airflow pattern less turbulent. The overall effect does not completely eradicate the wind but does create a larger zone of moderate wind speeds.

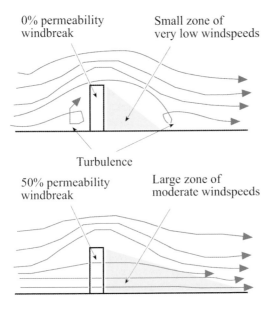

Figure 3.12. Effect of barrier permeability on airflow.

If a site wide windbreak cannot be accommodated, consideration should be made to planting at the corners of buildings where windspeeds are particularly high as they make their way around the building. Care must be taken to site any trees with sufficient separation from the building to avoid overshadowing it from the effects of solar gain. As a rough guide, a minimum gap of 4 -5 times the height of the trees is recommended between the building and windbreak. By choosing trees that lose their leaves in winter, solar access can be maintained even when the sun is at a low altitude. However the effectiveness of the windbreak will be dimin-

ished when out of leaf.

A tree belt, unless planted with mature trees and shrubs, will take a number of years to grow sufficiently high to be effective. The cost of land set aside for landscaping and the cost of the trees themselves will need to be recouped from the value of saved heating energy. However, there are non-energy advantages to shelter belts. These are; the enhanced aesthetics of sites planted with trees; the creation of habitats for wildlife, the sequestration of carbon dioxide and the increased comfort of persons using the outside spaces due to reduced wind speeds.

Building enhancement

Fabric improvements are available that reduce the infiltration rate at all wind speeds. These techniques are discussed more fully in Chapter 5 but the general principles are;

- seal the building envelope to remove any infiltration routes into and out of the building
- carefully position openings to avoid the predominant wind direction
- the main entrance doors should not be on opposite faces of the building as this would allow infiltration air to pass easily through the building from high to low pressure zones
- entrances should not be positioned at the corners of buildings as windspeeds will be greatest here as it moves around the building.

The form of individual buildings and the arrangement of groups of buildings can be designed to have minimal interaction with the wind. Generally this involves avoiding direct obstruction of the wind which would cause the wind to undertake sudden changes in speed and direction, creating large pressure variations. In effect it is advantageous to make the building more streamlined so the air flows across it rather than set up pressure differences. In addition the grouping of buildings should aim to slow windspeeds across the site rather than offer long channels through which the wind can build up speed. Table 3.4 lists the ideas used to reduce the sensitivity of individual buildings to the wind. Table 3.5 lists the suggestions for avoiding wind channelling around groups of buildings[5].

Individual buildings - low wind impact
Avoid 'flat' roofs with a pitch less than 10°
- wind passing over these roofs causes an upward suction which can draw air vertically out of the building
Step back successive storeys on high rise buildings
- the pyramid effect helps smooth wind flow around the building
Use hipped roofs with pitches of 30 - 45° on housing
- this encourages smooth airflow
Avoid long walls -
the shorter the extra path length the wind must travel to circumnavigate a wall, the slower it will travel

Table 3.4. Reducing the impact of the wind on individual buildings

Groups of buildings - low wind impact
Stagger buildings on the site - this removes clear pathways through which the wind could be channelled or pick up speed. If a long row is unavoidable limit its length to under 24m
Keep buildings heights similar
- if the wind passing over a building encounters a higher building, this could reverse the direction of wind flow causing turbulence
Arrange buildings into courtyards
- this creates a central sheltered zone. It is more useful if solar gains are also encouraged in the space
Avoid patterns that look like a funnel on plan
- wind will be channelled through funnel shaped arrangements. If there is a possibility of wind being collected leave gaps in the rows (>3m) to allow the wind to percolate out

Table 3.5. Reducing the impact of the wind on groups of buildings.

Driving rain

In the UK rain is a common occurrence and buildings are adequately served with rainwater drainage systems to deal with rain falling on the roof. However, when the rain combines with wind it can produce driving rain. Driving rain is rain that falls at an angle to the vertical and so can wet masonry walls.

The thermal conductivity of masonry materials depends on the density of the material. Table 3.6 shows how the thermal conductivity of materials vary with density.

Material	Density (kg/m3)	Thermal Conductivity(k) (W/mK)
Slate	2700	1.9
Sandstone	2100	1.3
Brick engineering	2300	1.0
Brick common	1790	0.72
Plaster	1570	0.53
Block (clinker)	1050	0.35
Plaster board	960	0.16
Pine	500	0.138
Plaster lightweight	448	0.115
Block aerated	400	0.08
Carpet	186	0.06
Glass fibre	12	0.04
Mineral wool	150	0.04
Expanded polystyrene	25	0.033

Table 3.6 Densities and thermal conductivities of common building materials.

The lower the density, the less heat is conducted out of the building. Low densities are achieved by having voids in the material that are filled with air. In driving rain the masonry becomes wet and the voids are filled with water, increasing its density. As a consequence the thermal conductivity increases. The thermal conductivity of brickwork with a density of 1700kg/m³ for 1% and 5% moisture content are 0.62 and 0.84W/mK respectively[6]. A masonry cavity wall constructed to have a U-value of 0.35W/m²K at 1% moisture content will have a U-value of 0.36W/m²K at 5% moisture content, an increase in U-value of 3%.

UK driving rain profile

Figure 3.13 is a map of the UK showing areas affected by driving rain, as indicated using the driving rain index. It can be seen that the west coast is particularly susceptible to driving rain. This is because south west and westerly winds tend to be warm but, having travelled over the oceans, carry a great deal of moisture which falls out as rain. By the time the winds have reached the east coast some of their velocity has been reduced by friction over land and the rain has already fallen. This generally makes the east coast an area of lower driving rain index.

ously under *'Wind speed and direction',* will offer some protection against driving rain. If the horizontal component of the windspeed can be reduced then the rain is less likely to impinge upon the vertical masonry surfaces.

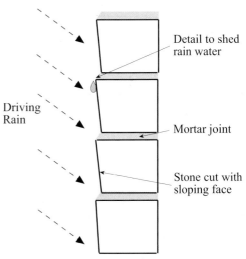

Figure 3.14. Traditional stone wall detail designed to clear rainwater from face of stone.

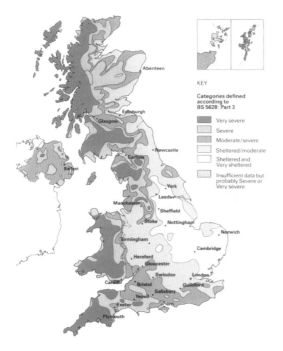

Figure 3.13. Zones of exposure based on driving rain index. Diagram from (GPG95). © Crown Copyright.

Building enhancement

Traditional buildings found in wet areas, such as the Pennines, utilised masonry methods which helped shed water from the masonry surface (Figure 3.14). In new buildings masonry materials should be water resistant or treated with water repellent coatings to prevent them becoming saturated. Any coatings should be permeable to water vapour to allow moisture within the masonry to escape. Reducing the U value of a masonry wall using additional insulation reduces the contribution made by the external masonry layer and so the effect of moisture content becomes less significant.

Landscape

The landscaping methods, mentioned previ-

Solar radiation

The two thermal effects of solar radiation that are important in energy consumption are the warming effect on the external air (see *'External temperature'* earlier in this chapter) and also contribution to space heating when it is deposited into the building. The other important component of solar radiation is daylight which, when introduced into buildings, can offset the need for electric lighting. *(Passive solar design is considered more fully in Chapter 2 and daylighting design in Chapter 6.)* This section will consider the availability of solar energy.

UK solar profile

Figure 3.15 shows the average solar irradiation (MJ/m^2) for the UK. It can be seen that the daily solar energy available on the north coast of Scotland is 8MJ/m^2 compared to 11MJ/m^2 on the south coast of England.

Landscape

Solar access requires the avoidance of overshadowing. The principal causes of overshadowing are tall trees and buildings situated on the south of the site.

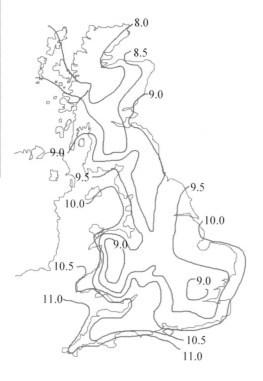

Figure 3.15. UK average solar irradiation map.

The majority of UK trees are beginning to come into leaf by mid April. By mid May they are in full leaf, with single trees typically allowing through only 18% of the solar radiation incident upon them. By mid September the majority of trees are beginning to lose their leaves. This process is complete by mid October. When out of leaf, the trees typically allow through 65% of the radiation incident upon them[7].

Buildings are usually opaque to light and so their spacing should be such as to allow good solar access over the roof pitch to buildings on the north. However, some degree of overshadowing is inevitable in all but the most open sites in mid winter when the solar altitude is at its lowest.

Transport

Buildings do not just consume energy for space conditioning. Figure 3.16 shows the energy inputs to a building throughout its life. These can be generally categorised as energy for production of materials and delivery to site, the construction process, energy in use, energy used in conveying the workforce to the building and finally energy to demolish and recycle or dispose of materials

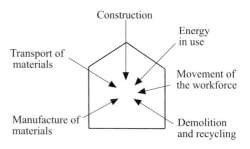

Figure 3.16. Building lifetime energy flows.

By far the greatest proportion of energy consumed is whilst the building is in use, i.e. energy to run building services and also to deliver staff and materials to and from the workplace.

In many cases the daily petrol energy used in cars during the journey to work can exceed the energy used by the building services. This has been illustrated in an energy usage survey of the offices of the Cheltenham and Gloucester Building Society where the commuting energy usage was 334kWh/m²/y. This compares with a gas and electricity consumption of 135 and 369kWh/m²/y respectively. It can be seen that the car fuel consumption is three times that of the building gas energy use and of a similar size to the electricity energy use[8].

Private cars use more fuel per passenger mile than public transport. To reduce transportation energy usage building planners can assess the closeness of their chosen site to suitable public transport systems. As with other energy issues a balance is required between this issue and the closeness to other determinants of location, such as closeness to intended markets for goods and proximity to the community using the services the building provides.

Conclusions

Here we have illustrated that the main concern of siting a building is the impact of the climate. Where space heating is concerned, this can be beneficial as in the case of solar access or detrimental as in the case of exposure to the wind. In both cases careful consideration of the topography, landscape and building reinforcement can reduce the worst effects of extreme climates on building energy consumption. However, it should be mentioned that all of the information previously presented could be undergoing change as a result of global warming. As stated in Chapter 1 the climatic effects of global warming are still being debated. Any change in the UK climate will require a change in the ways that buildings respond to it. Some of the predictions of climate change are;

Increased incidence of high windspeeds and greater intensity and frequency of storms - this will not only increase the wind induced heat losses described in 'Windspeed and direction' earlier but will require greater consideration of wind loading factors in structural design.

Hotter summers - most UK buildings do not require air conditioning for comfort since the summer cooling period is short. However, prolonged periods of high temperatures can disrupt passive cooling strategies that are based on exposed mass and night time ventilation (see *'Cooling the building'* in Chapter 10), leading to the need for mechanical cooling.

Colder winters - average temperatures encountered during the heating season may fall. Some predictions suggest that melting ice caps could reverse the gulf stream that keeps the UK warmer than comparable countries at the same latitude. This would result in a mini ice age. These extreme low temperatures would require a drastic increase in insulation levels to maintain comfort and minimise energy consumption levels.

Increased rainfall - predictions suggest rainfall rates could fall in southern European countries leading to drought. In the UK rainfall rates could increase leading to greater incidences of driving rain and flooding. ☙

References for Chapter 3

1. Building Research Establishment. BRE digest 350 Climate and Site Development Part : General Climate of the UK. p3. HMSO 1990

2. Energy Efficiency Office. Fuel Efficiency Booklet 7: Degree Days. HMSO 1993

3. Project Summary 045 Estate Layout for Passive Solar Housing Design. Ref ETSU S 1126 (1990)

4. Building Research Establishment. BRE digest 350 Climate and Site Development Part 1 : General Climate of the UK. p3. HMSO 1990

5. Building Research Establishment. BRE digest 350 Climate and Site Development Part 3: Improving Microclimate Through Design. p7. HMSO 1990

6. CIBSE Guide A Thermal Properties of Building Structures, pA3-5 CIBSE Publications 1980

7. Building Research Establishment. BRE digest 350 Climate and Site Development Part 3: Improving Microclimate Through Design. p6. HMSO 1990

8. Standeven, M., Cohen R. and Bordass W. PROBE 3 C&G Chief Office. pp 31-34. Building Services Journal, February 1996

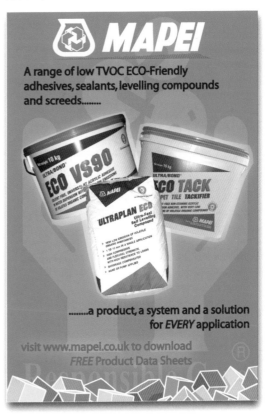

4 Building form

Introduction

There are many factors that have an influence on the form of a building. Cost is a major factor, simple cubical buildings are less expensive to construct than complex forms. Planning and design considerations may require the design of a building to be influenced by the form of its neighbours. Functional requirements and aesthetics also have an important role in deciding the form of a building. For example, some functions can only take place in large volumes, such as cinemas and certain manufacturing processes.

The internal and external form of a building has a significant impact on its energy consumption. Some of these impacts have already been discussed in Chapter 3 where methods were presented for reducing the impact of the wind on individual buildings by creating more streamlined forms (Table 4.1). There are also some aspects of form which will be discussed in subsequent chapters, one example of this is in Chapter 9 where the use of towers and sloping ceilings are described as a means of encouraging natural stack ventilation.

Individual buildings - low wind impact
Avoid 'flat' roofs with a pitch less than 10°
- wind passing over these roofs causes an upward suction which can draw air vertically out of the building
Step back successive storeys on high rise buildings
- the pyramid effect helps smooth wind flow around the building
Use hipped roofs with pitches of 30 - 45° on housing
- this encourages smooth airflow
Avoid long walls -
the shorter the extra path length the wind must travel to circumnavigate a wall, the slower it will travel

Table 4.1. Reducing the impact of the wind on individual buildings.

Changing the form of a building can reduce energy consumption in one area but increase it in another. Specifically these are that increased surface area increases fabric heat loss rates but also allows the capture of free energy flows. Secondly, increasing the volume of a building increases ventilation heat loss rates but also reduces ventilation and cooling energy consumption. Often a compromise has to be made to obtain an overall reduction in energy consumption. This compromise must be informed by the energy flows in the building as described in Chapter 1. For example, in domestic buildings there is a high demand for space heating and a low demand for ventilation and space cooling. As a consequence domestic room volumes should be kept small. In commercial buildings it is desirable to avoid air conditioning, one method of doing this is to increase room volumes.

This chapter describes the effect that modifying the internal and external form has on building energy consumption.

Surface area and fabric heat loss

The formula for the steady state heat loss rate through the fabric of a particular building element is shown in Figure 4.1.

$$Q_v = \tfrac{1}{3}.n.V.\Delta T$$

$$Q_f = \Sigma(U_x.A_x.)\Delta T$$

Figure 4.1. Equations for ventilation (Q_v) and fabric (Q_f) heat loss rate.

The equation shows that the fabric heat loss rate (Q_f) is directly proportional to the area of the element. Therefore, any changes to the form that increase the surface area will result in an increased heat loss rate.

This can be investigated further by comparing the surface areas of four detached buildings with the same volume but different floor plans, leading to different surface areas. Room heights, window area and total floor area are the same in all four shapes. The only difference is in surface area (Figure 4.2).

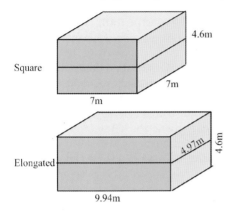

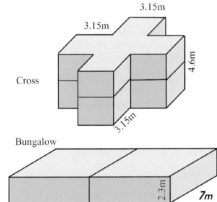

Figure 4.2. Buildings with different plan shapes.

Square. When combined with its height this form represents the smallest practical surface area for a given volume. The actual smallest surface area to volume ratio is obtained by a sphere but this form is not often used in practice.

Elongated. The square plan is stretched into a rectangle. The width of the building is reduced and the length is extended. This has resulted in 4% increases to the wall area in comparison to

the square as shown in Table 4.1.

Cross. This form is highly convoluted and results in a 35% increase in wall area

Bungalow. This is a single storey building. This form results in a 25% reduction in wall area in a manner similar to a semi-detached house, where external walls are eliminated. The floor and roof on the other hand have doubled in size.

Table 4.2 shows the total surface area of each shape and compares them to the square plan building that is taken as the standard. It can be seen from Table 4.2 that the elongated, cross and bungalow plan forms have 4, 20 and 29% more surface area respectively than the square plan.

Plan shape	Area of element (m²)		
	Wall	Floor	Roof
Square	129	49	49
Elongated	137	49	49
Cross	174	49	49
Bungalow	97	98	98

Table 4.2. Areas of building elements for various plan shapes.

Plan shape	Total surface area (m²)	Area relative to square
Square	227	1.00
Elongated	236	1.04
Cross	272	1.20
Bungalow	295	1.29

Table 4.3. Surface areas of the four building shapes relative to the square plan form.

However, the increase in surface area does not represent the increase in heat loss rate since different surfaces have different thermal transmittance values (U-values) (see *'Thermal properties of construction materials'* in Chapter 5). This means that the increase in heat loss rate will be greatest when a surface of high U-value increases in area. To take this into account we must weight each surface in terms of its heat loss rate, by multiplying the area of each element by a weighting factor. The weighting factors we will use are the typical U-values of each element as shown in Table 4.4. The outcome of this exercise is shown in Table 4.5.

By comparing the relative surface areas (Table 4.3) and weighted surface area (Table 4.5) it can be seen that the actual heat losses are lower than suggested simply by looking at total surface area increases. In particular the bungalow has seen a considerable improvement between total area increase and increases in heat loss. This is because the element with the largest increase in area is the roof and this has the lowest thermal transmittance of all the elements.

Element	Weighting Factor
Walls	0.35
Roof	0.16
Windows	2.00
Floor	0.25

Table 4.4. Weighting factors for each element of the building.

Plan shape	Weighted surface area (W/K)	Weighted area relative to square
Square	128	1.00
Elongated	131	1.03
Cross	148	1.16
Bungalow	148	1.23

Table 4.5. Heat loss factors for various shapes of buildings.

The conclusion is that any deviation from a square plan and cubical form will result in increased fabric heat losses. However the size of these losses can be reduced by adding additional insulation to the elements that have increased in area.

As well as adopting a cubical form a number of other techniques can be used that result in a reduced surface area. These are;
- use insulated ceilings rather than insulated exposed pitched roofs
- avoid projections and extensions causing deviation from a cubical form
- make external porches unheated or, if heated, make them internal halls
- attach unheated spaces such as a garage or conservatory to external walls to buffer it from the external elements
- use flat glazing systems as opposed to bay windows

Surface area to volume ratio

There is a difference in energy usage between housing and commercial buildings. In housing energy use for space heating dominates. In larger commercial buildings space heating still exists but lighting, ventilation and possibly air conditioning take on an increased importance. This is in part due to the different activities in the two types of buildings but is also due to the lower surface area to volume ratio found as buildings increase in size. This is illustrated in Figure 4.3 where our square plan building has been increased in size by 2, 3 and 4 times.

It can be seen that the surface area to volume ratio has fallen from 1.01 in the original domestic scale building to 0.25 in the larger commercial scale building. What this means in practice is that the internal space in the small building will be in greater contact with the outside world via the external surfaces. As such the spaces will experience fabric heat loss, but will also be able to take advantage of solar gains, natural light and ventilation.

In the large building less of the interior space is in contact with the outside world through the external walls. The core areas of the space will experience less heat loss but will, at the same time, be poorly supplied with daylight, ventilation and passive solar gains.

Since solar gains, natural ventilation and daylight are forms of free energy, deep plan buildings will be disadvantaged. The implications of this is pursued further in the following sections.

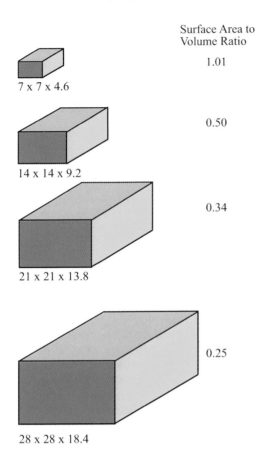

Surface Area to
Volume Ratio

1.01

7 x 7 x 4.6

0.50

14 x 14 x 9.2

0.34

21 x 21 x 13.8

0.25

28 x 28 x 18.4

Figure 4.3. Surface area to volume ratio decreases with increasing building dimensions.

Utilising natural energy

The dependence of a building on fossil fuels can be reduced by taking advantage of natural forms of energy. These are;

Solar gain can be utilised to replace energy consumption for space heating.

Daylight can be utilised to replace artificial lighting during the daytime.

Natural ventilation can be utilised to replace mechanical ventilation.

Examination of this list shows that each form of natural energy is obtained through the external skin of the building. It follows therefore that increasing the surface area will increase the possibility of taking advantage of these natural energy flows.

Solar gain

Considering the building forms shown in Figure 4.2 it can be seen that if the elongated form were to be oriented with its main axis in an east-west direction, then one of its large faces would face south. The building would, therefore, be able to collect a greater amount of solar energy than the cube. The amount of solar energy gained depends on the solar intensity on the vertical face, the ability with which this energy can enter the building (transmission coefficient) and the area of the glazing. Beyond optimum orientation of the building and exposing the site to sunlight we have little influence on the solar intensity. Similarly the transmission coefficient of the glazing is a factor of the glazing system, so to increase solar gains the area of glazing on the south facade must be increased. It is essential that this is achieved whilst reducing the glazed area on the north facade, so that the overall glazed area does not increase.

Various studies have estimated that careful passive solar design can provide up to 10% of the space heating energy needs of a domestic building. The net reduction in space heating energy use is less than this, since fabric heat losses would increase as the surface area increases, following extension of the southern facade. Continuing our consideration of the elongated plan shape, Table 4.5 indicates an increase in fabric heat loss rate of 3% giving a net reduction in space heating energy use of 7% as a result of elongating a cubical domestic building along its east/west axis. See Chapter 2 for more on passive heating.

Daylight

So far we have considered the various forms in terms of domestic space heating. In terms of lighting, most rooms in houses are sufficiently shallow in depth to be adequately served with daylight from appropriately sized vertical windows. However, if the building forms were used for large-scale commercial buildings then square floor plans would result in deep spaces.

The inner areas of which would then be distant from the windows, resulting in poor daylighting and the consequential use of artificial lights. As a rule of thumb, useful daylight penetration is considered to be available up to a depth of 2½ times the window head height from the windows into the room (approximately 5m).

In Chapter 1 it was pointed out that electricity is highly polluting relative to other fuels. For this reason its use should be avoided. One way of doing this is to use narrow building forms such as the elongated shape or the cross-shape indicated in Figure 4.2 previously in this chapter. Taking the cross plan as an example, the increased surface area results in 16% more fabric heat losses than a simple square plan. However, the plan depth will be reduced so that natural light can be used in preference to artificial light. Since electricity is almost five times as expensive as gas, any savings in lighting electricity will have approximately five times the value of space heating energy increases. A similar situation applies to carbon dioxide output arising from the use of the two types of fuel. Single storey buildings can have deep plans as they can be illuminated with daylight using roof lights. See Chapter 7 for more on daylighting.

Natural ventilation

As with daylighting, single sided natural ventilation of spaces is considered possible up to a depth of 5 to 6m from outside walls and for cross ventilation across a plan depth of 13m between two outside walls (Chapter 6). It can be seen that both the elongated and cross forms will reduce the plan depth, allowing natural ventilation to take place. This will avoid the energy consumption by fans used to drive ventilation air through ductwork to the core of the building. In this way energy savings of approximately 20kWh/m²/year can be made, which is a typical ventilation fan energy consumption. See Chapter 6 for more on ventilation

Application in practice

Much emphasis is now being placed on natural ventilation in office design by incorporat-

ing narrow plan depths as is illustrated in the Building Research Establishment Environmental Office of the Future, which has a plan depth of 13.5m[1]. This technique has also been applied to low energy hospital designs which have wards arranged in a cruciform shape around a central nurses' station[2].

Loss v/s gains energy balance

By optimising the above natural energy flows we are trying to obtain a net improvement in the energy consumption of the building. To be successful we need to achieve the following balance;

solar gains +
  reductions in artificial lighting +
    reductions in mechanical ventilation >
      increase in fabric heat losses.

As the size of the building increases and its energy flows become more complex, it becomes more difficult to make sure that we are achieving the required balance. This can be determined by modelling the energy flows in the building using computer techniques. This gives results with a reasonable accuracy dependant on the limitations of the data and model. The disadvantage is that it is time consuming to set up the model in the first instance. A simpler method that uses graphical techniques is the lighting and thermal (LT) method of design.

The lighting and thermal (LT) method of design

The LT method of design[3] is a technique that is used to make comparisons between the energy consumption of alternative floor plans. This is illustrated in the following example.

Reducing the energy consumption in offices is possible if we design-in better use of daylight, passive solar gains and natural ventilation. This can be achieved by reducing the depth of the floor plan.

To investigate this further we will consider the energy consumption of two alternative floor plans for a 2304m² mid floor of an office building. The two alternative floor plans are square (Figure 4.4) and L shape (Figure 4.5).

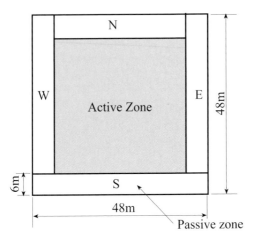

Figure 4.4. Square floor plan.

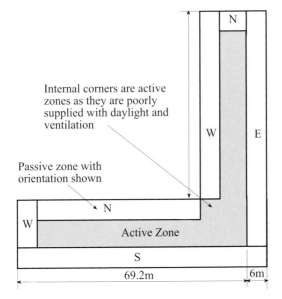

Internal corners are active zones as they are poorly supplied with daylight and ventilation

Passive zone with orientation shown

Figure 4.5. L shaped floor plan.

The following assumptions are made about each floor;
- assume a glazing ratio of 50%. This is the percentage of the total external wall which is glazed
- assume a transmission factor of 0.35. Within the LT method are three transmission

factors which describe the degree of over shadowing of the building. These are 1.0 no shading, 0.7 light shading and 0.35 heavy shading.

The first stage in the method involves dividing the building plan into passive and active zones. Passive zones are those which benefit from natural light, solar gains and ventilation. They are considered to extend from the perimeter to a depth of 6m.

The first analysis is to compare the areas of active and passive zones in the building, as shown in Table 4.6. The square plan shape has 48% more active zone area than the L shaped building. Since the active zones require the greater use of mechanical services this indicates that the square shaped building will use more energy to provide comfort conditions than the L shaped floor plan.

Plan shape	Area of passive zones (m²)	Area of active zones (m²)
Square	1008	1296
L shape	1442.4	861.6

Table 4.6. Areas of active and passive zones for two floor plans.

Plan shape	Zone energy consumption (MWh)		
	Active	Passive	Total
Square	294.19	131.98	426.17
L shape	198.17	188.37	386.54

Table 4.7. Predicted annual energy consumption for two plan shapes.

To put numerical values in terms of energy consumption on to this, an analysis must be made of the energy consumption of each zone using the LT method. The method is described on the next page and the outcome is shown in Table 4.7. It can be seen that the energy consumption of the square plan building is 10.3% more than the L shaped building.

Table 4.8 gives a breakdown of the total energy consumption for each plan shape in terms of lighting, heating and air conditioning. The savings in the L shaped building arise from reductions in lighting and heating loads. It could be anticipated that the narrow plan form would have a higher space heating requirement due to its larger surface area. However, this is offset by additional solar gains through the extended south face of the building. The largest energy consumption reductions occur in the lighting energy usage. The technique assumes full use of photoelectric lighting controls that turn lights off in response to the entry of natural light.

The technique is not intended to give an accurate value for the energy consumption of a proposed building. This is because it uses simplifications and assumptions which may not accurately reflect all buildings to which it is being applied[4]. However, its strength lies in its simplicity in allowing comparisons to be made between the energy consumption of alternative plan forms at the design stage.

General outcome

From the discussions above it can be deduced that buildings in which space heating is the predominant energy flow, such as housing and small commercial buildings, should aim for a cubical form. Buildings having a high demand for lighting, ventilation and cooling, such as hospitals or offices should adopt a narrow plan form.

The 10.3% savings in energy described in the above example represent a signifi-cant quantity of energy. However, it must be remembered that these savings are not free. Construction costs will be higher for a narrow plan building and a larger area of building land will be needed to accommodate the same floor area.

LT method explained

The annual energy consumption for the two floor plan shapes described previously can be determined using charts of energy consumption against perimeter glazed ratio. These charts are provided in copies of the LT method of design. The charts give annual energy consumption in terms of megawatt hours per square metre (MWh/m^2) broken down into lighting, heating

and ventilation/cooling energy use. Charts exists for the four orientations of passive zone in different building types, for example, resi-dential, office and retail. Two sets of charts are available one for warm regions (zone 2) and another for cooler regions (zone 1). An example of a chart for a south facing passive zone for an office situated in climatic zone 1 is shown in Figure 4.6.

In this example the building is assumed to have a 50% glazing ratio. Starting from this point on the x-axis, the energy consumption for each square metre of the passive zone for lighting, heating and ventilation and cooling can be determined. The red arrowed line in Figure 4.6 shows how the lighting energy consump-tion is determined to be $0.025MWh/m^2$. Since the area of the south facing passive zone is $288m^2$ the lighting energy consumption for all of the south facing passive zone is $288m^2$ x $0.025MWh/m^2 = 7.2MWh$.

The following features can be seen on the graph

- heating curve - dashed line. As the glazing ratio increases, solar gains increase and so the demand for space heating falls. Eventually, at about 60%, glazing ratio the space becomes saturated with solar gains. The space heating can only be reduced until it is off. Once this is achieved no further reduction in space heating energy consumption is obtained by increasing glazed area
- cooling curves - dot/dash line. As the glazing ratio increases, the solar gains increase and so the air conditioning system is activated, increasing the cooling energy consumption. Three curves are shown identified by different transmission coefficients 1.0, 0.7 and 0.35. These represent no overshadowing, moderate overshadowing and heavy overshadowing respectively. The greater the over shadowing the smaller the transmission coefficient and so less the gains
- lighting curve - dotted line. As the glazing ratio increases the energy used for lighting reduces as the lighting control

system responds to the available daylight and modulates the artificial light output downwards. At 60% glazed ratio, the passive zone is saturated with daylight and no further savings are made. This causes the curve to flatten out

- total energy curve - solid line. This set of curves is the total energy consumption against glazing ratio. It has a U shape indicating that initially energy consumption falls as use is made of natural lighting and solar gains. However when these benefits plateau out and energy used for cooling increases the curve rises once more. This curve therefore shows a distinct minimum total energy consumption at 40-55% glazing ratio depending on transmission coefficient.

for each square metre of the passive zone for lighting, heating and ventilation and cooling, can be determined. To reiterate, the arrowed line in Figure 4.6 shows how the lighting energy consumption is determined to be 0.025MWh/m². Since the area of the south facing passive zone is 288m² the lighting energy consumption for all of the south facing passive zone is 288m² x 0.025MWh/m² = 7.2MWh.

This process is then repeated for heating and ventilation/cooling. Following this the energy consumption of the other orientations of passive zones is determined using other charts of appropriate orientation. The energy consumption of the active zone is determined by considering it to have zero glazing ratio. i.e. values of energy consumption per square metre for heating, lighting and ventilation/cooling energy use are taken from the y axis.

As can be seen from Figure 4.6 these values are 0.045, 0.129 and 0.056MWh/m² respectively. Once again the energy consumption of the full area of active zone is found by multiplying the area of the active zone by the sum of the heating, lighting and ventilation/cooling values. Finally, the energy consumption of the entire floor is determined by summing the energy consumptions for all of the passive zones and the active zone together. These values were shown in Table 4.6 for both the square and L shaped floor plans broken down into active and passive zone consumptions. Table 4.8 shows these energy consumptions broken down into the component parts.

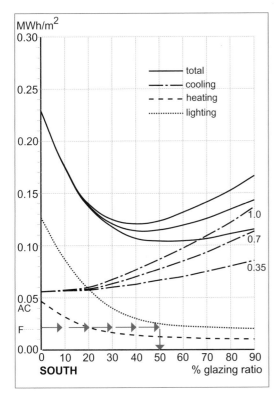

Figure 4.6. LT curve for a south facing office passive zone in climatic zone 1, assuming an illuminance of 300lx and a cooling load of 15W/m².

	Energy consumption (MWh)	
	Square	L shape
Lighting	204.62	164.45
Heating	84.53	81.82
Vent. and cool.	137.02	140.22
Total	426.17	386.54

Table 4.8. Breakdown of energy consumptions predicted by the LT method of design.

The building we are considering is assumed to have a 50% glazing ratio. Starting from this point on the x-axis, the energy consumption

The method includes factors for converting the energy consumptions into output of carbon dioxide. The conversion factors for heating, lighting and ventilation/cooling are 0.22, 0.19 and 0.22 respectively. Multiplying the values in Table 4.8 by the appropriate conversion factor, gives the annual carbon dioxide emissions in tonnes for each component.

The figures for carbon emissions for each plan form are shown in Table 4.9. It can be seen that the square plan form emits more carbon dioxide than the L shaped plan and that the biggest difference occurs in CO_2 output due to lighting.

Energy use	Carbon dioxide output (t)	
	Square	L shape
Lighting	45.0	36.2
Heating	16.1	15.6
Vent. and cool.	30.1	30.9
Total	91.1	82.7

Table 4.9. Carbon dioxide emissions.

Volume and ventilation heat loss

Inspection of the equation for steady state ventilation heat loss rate (Figure 4.1) reveals that ventilation heat losses are directly proportional to the volume of the building. Reducing the volume of heated spaces would therefore reduce the ventilation heat loss rate from the building.

Ventilation heat losses are not the only problem. Tall spaces experience stratification due to the ascent of warm air towards the ceiling. This creates a temperature gradient that increases between the floor and ceiling. The temperature at low level (up to 2m from the floor) may be in the range of 18-21°C. This is the occupied zone. Temperatures may increase to 28-30°C at heights over 4m (Figure 4.7). This effect causes additional energy consumption in two ways. Firstly, energy has been used to create high air temperatures in a space which is unoccupied. Secondly, the temperature difference across the roof structure is increased. This increases the rate of heat loss through the building fabric.

The first step towards minimising the

problem is to reduce ceiling heights where possible. The second is to use radiant heaters, if appropriate to the space, as these rely less on warm air for creating comfort. The third is to use destratification fans[5]. These are fans installed at high level within a space. They have an in-built thermostat which allows the fan to operate when temperatures at high level go over a certain threshold, say 28°C. The fan will drive the warm air at high level down to the occupied space.

If it is assumed that the plan size of a building has been fixed using functional criteria, then the deciding factor on room volume is the ceiling height. Typical for a domestic property is 2.3m. For larger spaces this ceiling height would create an oppressive 'feel' to the room. As horizontal dimensions increase vertical dimensions must also increase in proportion to avoid this perception.

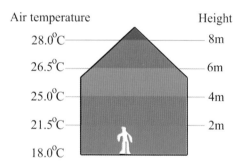

No destratification

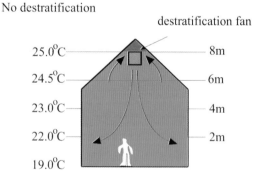

With destratification

Figure 4.7. Stratification of warm air in a tall space and destratification using a high level fan.

Various ratio relationships between horizontal and vertical distances in rooms have been considered but there is no definitive guidance on optimum room heights for a given plan area. This is possibly because psychology has an important role here, where perceived room heights are dependent on shade and colour of finishes, presence of windows and 'ceiling indicators' such as lines in the structure or finishes running horizontally around the room below the ceiling height.

Currently architects call upon their experience to determine appropriate room heights. However, for simple spaces this would be a useful area for further research. The outcome of which would produce useful design guidance.

Floor area to volume ratio

One way of determining if the space inside a building is under-used is to calculate a floor area to volume ratio. The larger the value of this ratio, the better utilised is the space. There are a number of ways in which this ratio might be increased. They are:

- make use of loft spaces in domestic buildings
- use mezzanine floors in large buildings
- when renovating old buildings, insulated suspended ceilings can be used to reduce the ceiling height and hence heated volume. However this remedial work is often criticised for its damaging effect on the aesthetics of the space.

Volume and cooling

In the previous section we discovered that increasing the volume of a building increases ventilation heat loss rates. However in this section we will find that increasing the volume of rooms that are prone to overheating can reduce temperatures in the occupied zone and so avoid the need for cooling energy use.

The cause of high temperatures in buildings is the heat gained by the internal air from sources other than the heating system. These sources are, in order of size, the sun, lighting, people and appliances (computers etc.).

In addition to the high air temperatures

further discomfort is caused by the presence of radiant heat sources within the room. The main source is the ceiling warmed by hot air rising to the top of the room. The human body is very sensitive to thermal radiation and will be affected by the radiation from the ceiling, especially about the head.

The higher air temperatures caused by these heat gains results in thermal discomfort. If the space temperature rises above 28°C for prolonged periods, air conditioning is considered necessary as a means of removing heat from the air and reducing temperatures. However the need for air conditioning can be avoided, or the length of time over which it operates can be reduced, by increasing the volume of the room. This is achieved by increasing the ceiling height.

Three effects come in to play as illustrated in Figure 4.8. Firstly, the increased head room allows warm air to rise upwards and out of the occupied space; secondly, the radiant effect of the ceiling is lessened due to its increased distance from the occupants. Thirdly, the high ceilings allow the inclusion of high level openable windows within the room.

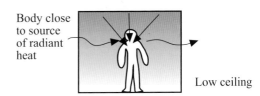

Body close to source of radiant heat

Low ceiling

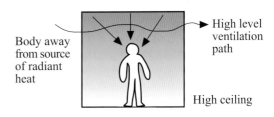

Body away from source of radiant heat

High level ventilation path

High ceiling

Figure 4.8. Increased room height as a means of improving thermal comfort.

This means that high level ventilation paths can be created which sweep the warm air out of the building without impinging on the occupants in the occupied zone. Low level ventilation routes directly affect the occupants causing draughts or movement of papers and so where provided should be under occupant control. It has been reported[6] that an increase in ceiling height from 2.5m to 3.5m in a medium weight office can reduce peak temperatures by 1.5°C. This reduction can mean the difference between needing and not needing air conditioning.

A balance must be made between increased ventilation heat losses and reductions in cooling energy use. As a general rule, room heights and hence volume should be kept low in dwellings and small commercial buildings where space heating is the dominant energy flow, and ceilings should be raised in medium to large commercial buildings where it is desirable to avoid air conditioning (see Chapter 9).

One problem with raised ceiling heights is that it increases the distance between ceiling mounted light fittings and the tasks to be illuminated. This increase in distance will reduce the light levels on the task. To counteract the reduction more light fittings would be required which in turn would increase the electrical consumption of the lighting system and add to the cooling load. To avoid this problem and reduce the number of luminaires required, pendant light fittings or task lamps should be used to illuminate rooms with high ceilings. This topic is discussed more fully in Chapter 7.

Internal planning

So far we have considered the shell of the building and the size of spaces contained within. However, energy consumption reductions can also be achieved by considering the planning and arrangement of the internal spaces of a building. There are two issues involved;

Orientation. External conditions differ on the north and south faces of a building. The availability of daylight and solar energy is higher on the south face of a building than the north. On average outside temperatures are higher on the

south face of a building than on the north face.

Cellular spaces. Different spaces in a building require different comfort and working conditions. To maintain optimal conditions in all spaces they should be isolated using partitions so that the heating, cooling and lighting systems can be controlled on a room by room basis to maintain desired conditions.

Orientation

Since solar gains are achieved on the south face of a building it is wise to place those spaces requiring the highest comfort temperatures on the south side of the building. Spaces requiring lower comfort temperatures, such as circulation routes, those in which physical activity is taking place, such as workshops and heat generating spaces such as kitchens, should be placed on the north side of the building.

There are exceptions to the above rules. For example, offices in which computers are being used require comfortable temperatures but would not benefit from south facing solar gains. This is because the computer equipment itself will be adding heat to the space. The addition of solar gains could cause the space to become too hot and require air conditioning. Computer suites should be considered as heat generating spaces and should be situated on the north side of the building.

Figure 4.9 shows floor plans for a low energy house. It can be seen that the main living spaces are on the south side of the building and kitchen, bathroom, toilets and circulation spaces are on the north side of the building. The rooms to the north act as a transition or buffer zone between the warmer south facing rooms and the cooler/darker conditions to the north. The following planning considerations should also be considered;
- cold zones in the centre of heated spaces should be avoided. One example is where unheated stairwells are placed in the centre of a block of flats. They should be placed on outside walls where they can act as a buffer to the external environment
- in housing, garages should be attached

rather than detached as they can act as a buffer between the occupied space and the external environment.

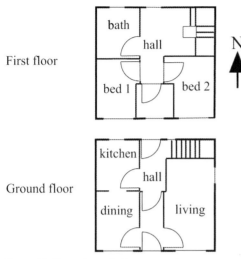

First floor

Ground floor

Figure 4.9. Floor plans of a low energy house.

Cellular spaces

Cellular spaces generally use less energy per square metre than open plan spaces. This is because a greater degree of control can be exercised over cellular spaces. Partitions should be placed between spaces requiring different conditions. For example, circulation routes only require 18°C comfort temperature compared to 21°C for working spaces. If the two spaces were combined, then the entire volume would have to be heated to 21°C. In addition, the recommended task illuminances will be different. For circulation spaces we need a task illuminance of 150 lux, for a work space 400 lux is required. On this occasion some difference can be maintained between the two spaces even if combined into a single open space by installing fewer luminaires in the circulation route. However, the difference cannot be too great or a noticeable contrast will exist between the circulation and office spaces causing the circulation route to appear dark.

The effect of separating spaces is illustrated by comparing the energy consumption of a naturally ventilated open plan office and a naturally ventilated cellular office[7]. The energy consumption breakdown is shown graphically in

Figure 4.10 and tabulated in Table 4.10.

It can be seen that the total energy consumption of the open plan office is 18% greater than the cellular office. Table 4.10 reveals that the biggest increases in consumption in the open plan office compared with the cellular office is for lighting and office equipment. The extra lighting energy consumption is due to the fact that the lighting cannot be turned off in unoccupied spaces as easily as it can in individual offices. This may be due to the lack of individual switches or the desire to avoid the gloomy effect created by switching off the lights in a section of a large open plan office.

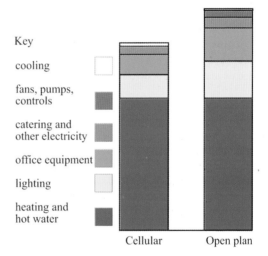

Figure 4.10. Energy consumption of naturally ventilated cellular and open plan offices.

Energy Usage	Cellular	Open Plan
Heating and hot water	79	79
Lighting	14	22
Office equipment	12	20
Catering and other electricity	5	7
Fans, pumps, controls	2	4
Cooling	0	1
TOTAL	112	133

Table 4.10. Energy consumption of naturally ventilated cellular and open plan offices.

The two internal arrangements have the same heating and hot water energy consumption. However, it could be anticipated that the space heating energy consumption in the cellular office could be reduced by individual temperature control of rooms. For example thermostatic radiator valves can be fitted to south facing rooms. Occupancy sensors or manual switches can be used to modulate down the heating in unoccupied rooms.

Grouping of buildings

A detached building of cubical form has six surfaces through which heat can be lost. By grouping buildings together the number of external surfaces can be reduced. This is illustrated by considering the heat loss rate from a detached house, a semi-detached house (one less external wall per dwelling), a mid-terraced house (two less external walls per dwelling) and a flat in the middle of a block of flats (4 less external surfaces per dwelling).

Table 4.11 shows the fabric heat loss rate for these types of housing and the fabric heat loss rate relative to the detached house. From this table it can be seen that the mid-flat, mid-terrace and semi-detached house have a fabric heat loss rate which is 43%, 22% and 12% lower than an equivalent sized detached house.

House type	Fabric heat loss rate (W)	Heat loss relative to detached (%)
Detached	2551	100
Semi-detached	2267	88
Terrace	1984	78
Mid flat	1455	57

Table 4.11. Fabric heat loss rate for various house styles (all have same window area).

The figures will differ for an end of terrace house and top or ground floor flats which have more external walls than a property that is more sheltered by other dwellings in the group. ☙

References for Chapter 4

1. Bunn, R. Building Analysis: Environmental Office of the Future. Building Services Journal, pp18-23. March 1997.

2. Corcoran, M. Building Analysis : Wansbeck Hospital. Building Services Journal, pp19-22, June 1993

3. Baker, N. V. and Steemers K. The L.T. Method 2.0: An Energy Design Tool for Non-Domestic Buildings. Cambridge Architectural Research Ltd. 1993

4. Burberry, P. LT Method of Energy Assessment. Architects' Journal, pp27-28, March 1994

5. Iles, P J, Destratification of Air in Industrial Buildings, BRE IP 9/95, HMSO, May 1995

6. BRECSU. General Information Report 31 Avoiding or Minimising the Use of Air Conditioning : A Research Report from the EnREI Programme, p19, HMSO, 1995.

7. BRECSU. Energy Consumption Guide 19: Energy use in offices. HMSO February 1998

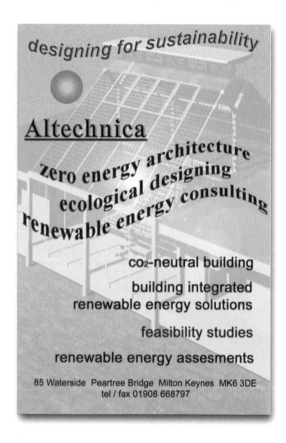
© Green Building Press

PEN Y COED INSULATION

WARMCEL

The insulation giving you the sustainable solution to energy efficient building

Southport Eco Centre

Six Bells, Bishops Castle

Pen y Coed Insulation are the most experienced company installing Warmcel throughout the UK. We have an extensive portfolio of work from large industrial projects, schools, housing developments to individual houses.

Development of Eco Houses in Castle Caereinion, Powys.
Built - Insulated - Sold by Pen y Coed Construction & Insulation Ltd

PEN Y COED INSULATION is a division of PEN Y COED CONSTRUCTION & INSULATION Ltd
a company that specialises in the design, detailing and construction of energy efficient buildings.

PEN Y LAN, MEIFOD, POWYS, SY22 6DA
TEL/FAX - 01938 500643
WEB:- penycoed-warmcel.com

5 Building fabric

Introduction

Heat is lost from a building by two routes. Conduction, convection and radiation across the building fabric, known as fabric heat losses, and by infiltration, known as ventilation heat losses. This chapter will concentrate on fabric heat losses. Ventilation heat losses will be considered in the next chapter.

To reduce fabric heat losses from a building the shell must be well insulated. A well insulated element has a low thermal transmittance (U-value). The thermal performance of the envelope is best when all of the elements of the building have similar U-values. However, it can be seen from Figure 5.1 that in practice some elements are better insulated than others.

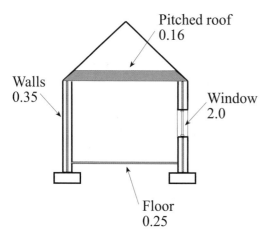

Figure 5.1. Typical U-values (W/m²K).

The reason for this is that some elements are easier to insulate than others. For example, pitched roofs have traditionally been well insulated. This is because it is relatively simple to install and accommodate large thickness of insulation in the loft space. Masonry cavity walls on the other hand are usually insulated by filling part or all of the cavity with insulation so a well insulated wall would require a wide cavity filled

with insulation. However, cavity width is typically limited to 150mm. Greater widths are difficult to achieve due to the limited length of wall ties and width of standard lintels.

Glazing stands out as being poorly insulated, having a U-value that is eleven times bigger than that of the roof. Windows are extremely useful multi-function devices giving views, ventilation, passive solar gains, means of escape and daylight. Unfortunately the high U-values of glazing systems are difficult to reduce and so windows remain the main source of heat loss from buildings.

This chapter will look at all of the elements making up the shell of a building but will give special consideration to glazing due to its thermal weakness. Finally it will consider the advantages and disadvantages of super insulation of domestic buildings.

Compliance

For both domestic and non-domestic buildings, compliance with the Building Regulations must be demonstrated, using a whole building method. This means that the method must consider:

- the building fabric
- ventilation systems
- the mechanical services, their efficiency and control
- hot water systems
- the fuel type (as this dictates CO_2 output)
- use of renewable energy such as passive solar gains.

The two methods used are; the Standard Assessment Procedure (SAP2005) for dwellings and the Simplified Building Energy Model (SBEM) for non-domestic buildings

Standard Assessment Procedure (SAP)

This method is based on the Building Research Establishment's (BRE) domestic energy model (BREDEM). Worksheets are available within the SAP specification document (http://projects.bre.co.uk/sap2005/) to carry out manual calculations, as are approved software packages which are available to purchase.

Inputting appropriate data into the spreadsheet or software gives the following outputs;

A SAP rating which is based on the cost of using energy in the building for space and water heating, ventilation and lighting, less the savings arising from renewable technologies. The SAP rating is normalised for floor area so the rating of a small building can be compared with a large building. SAP ratings are on a scale between 1 and 100, the higher the number the lower the cost to run the building. Buildings with a rating over 100 are net exporters of energy.

An environmental impact rating from 1 to 100, based on the annual amount of CO_2 emitted by the building due to its consumption of energy.

A dwelling CO_2 emission rate (DER,) which is the value used to demonstrate Building Regulation compliance. The is similar to the environmental impact rating described above, except that it is the annual CO_2 emissions per square metre due to all of the energy consumed in the building, less that generated by renewables, expressed in units of $kg/m^2/year$.

Compliance is demonstrated when the emission rate calculated for the dwelling (DER) is lower than a target emission rate (TER) which is 80% of the emission rate calculated for a notional building which is the same shape and size of the building being proposed but has a fixed set of criteria for the fabric heat loss, building services and fuel type. These values equate to a gas heated dwelling constructed to 2002 Building Regulations standards. Figure 5.1 shows the U-values to be assumed for the notional building.

Simplified Building Energy Model (SBEM)

The SAP method is for buildings under $450m^2$ in floor area. The SBEM method is used to demonstrate Building Regulations Part L2 compliance for non-domestic buildings. Free software is used for this, developed by the Building Research Establishment (www.ncm.bre.co.uk/). Like SAP, SBEM demonstrates compliance by calculating the annual energy use for a proposed building and comparing it with the energy use of a comparable 'notional' building. Both calculations make use of standard sets of data for different activity areas and call on common databases of construction and service elements.

Other accredited calculation software is available which uses the same databases but is interlinked or related to existing environmental design packages. These packages must be purchased but have the benefit that the information can often be shared by other modules in the package, allowing for example, for the building services to be designed to meet the energy requirements that were calculated. ◔

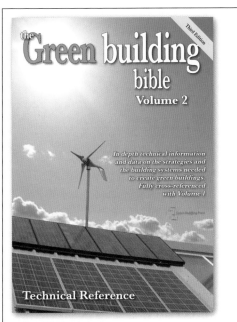

the **Green building** *bible*
Volume 2

Third Edition

In depth technical information and data on the strategies and the building systems needed to create green buildings. Fully cross-referenced with Volume 1

Technical Reference

Have you read Volume 1 yet? It is the companion to this book and in over 350 pages delivers an in-depth analysis of the green building industry in the UK. There are articles from over 40 industry professionals and observers.

Windows and doors

Windows are weak elements when it comes to keeping heat in the building. Glass is a highly conductivite material. The thermal performance of the windows can be improved by;
- increasing the number of layers of glazing
- increasing the size of the cavity between the sheets of glass
- replacing the air in the cavity with argon or krypton gas
- changing the spacer bars
- applying a low emissivity layer to one or more panes of glass.

   The other element in the window system is the frame. The performance of the frame can be improved by;
- choosing better, lower thermal conductivity frame materials
- creating thermal breaks in the frame.

Increasing the layers of glazing

As the number of sheets of glass increase, the U-value decreases. The U-values for single, double and triple glazing set in a timber frame are 4.8, 2.8 and 2.1W/m²K respectively. More than three sheets of glass can be used but the system starts to become impractical due to the increased cost, weight and dimensions of the unit. Similar performance to multiple glazing can be achieved using special coatings (see below). For example, double glazing, with a low emissivity coating, has a similar U-value to triple glazing with no coatings.

   The U-values for the multiple glazing given above are for sealed units with a 12mm air gap between. The air in the cavity is dried to avoid condensation forming on the outer sheet of glass. The dried air is kept in the unit and the separation between the panes maintained using an edge seal (Figure 5.2). This edge seal forms a cold bridge between the panes and so heat losses are greatest around the perimeter. The U-value of the double glazed unit, excluding frame can be given as a centre of pane value or an overall value taking into account the greater heat loss at the edges.

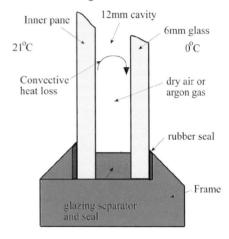

Figure 5.2. Sealed double glazed unit.

Increasing the cavity width

Increasing the width of the cavity between the sheets of glass reduces the U-value. This is demonstrated in Figure 5.3 which shows the centre pane U-value of double glazing decreasing as cavity width increases. It can be seen that beyond 16mm cavity width no further reductions occur. This is because the insulating effect of an increased layer of air is offset by increased convective heat transfer which can take place more easily across a wider air gap. The U-values of double glazed units with 6, 12 and 16mm air gaps set in a timber frame are 3.1, 2.8 and 2.7W/m²K respectively.

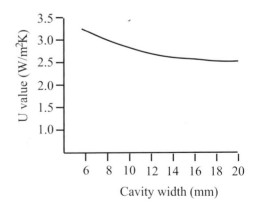

Figure 5.3. Graph of U-value against cavity width for double glazing (4mm air 4mm, no coatings).

Adding a cavity gas fill

Reductions in the U-value of double glazed units can be obtained by replacing the dry air in the cavity with gases such as argon. Argon has a lower thermal conductivity than air (162 and 241W/mK respectively) which will reduce conductive exchanges across the cavity. Argon is also more dense than air (1.784 and 1.293kg/m³ respectively) which will make convection currents more sluggish. The U-value of a double glazed unit with a 12mm cavity width and with air and argon fillings are 2.8 and 2.7W/m²K. With time the argon gas may escape from the glazing as the edge seals degrade. However, this will be replaced by moisture carrying air and so will likely be revealed as a failed unit containing condensation that would require replacement.

Using low emissivity coatings

All objects above room temperature emit energy in the form of thermal radiation. The thermal radiation is an electromagnetic wave and this exists in many different wavelengths making up a continuous spectrum. However, for an object at a particular temperature there will be one wavelength of radiation that is emitted more strongly than the others. Radiation from hot objects, such as the sun with a surface temperature of 5500°C, has a peak emission at the short wavelength end of the spectrum. As the temperature of the radiating object is reduced, the wavelength of the radiation peak increases. Radiation from objects at room temperatures emit mainly long wavelength thermal radiation.

The ability of an object to radiate energy is known as its emissivity. A perfect radiator has an emissivity of 1 and an object that radiates no heat has an emissivity of 0. Most building materials have an emissivity of 0.8 - 0.9. Light coloured and smooth objects have a lower emissivity. Polished aluminium foil for example has an emissivity of 0.5. Clear float glass has an emissivity of 0.9. However, by coating this glass during manufacture with a fine layer of metal oxide the emissivity of the glass surface is reduced.

Two types of 'low E' coating are available,

known as 'hard' and 'soft'. Hard coatings have emissivities in the range 0.15 to 0.2 and soft in the range 0.05 to 0.1. Coating the outer surface of the inner pane of a double glazed unit with a low E coating reduces the radiant transfer of heat from inside to outside (Figure 5.4).

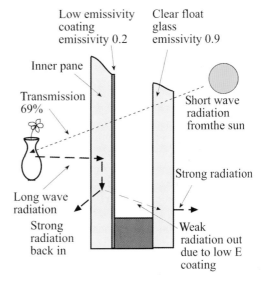

Figure 5.4. Low emissivity double glazing.

The low emissivity coating has minimal effect on the transmission of solar radiation from outside the building to inside. Total transmission of solar radiation for standard double glazing and low emissivity double glazing is 72% and 69% respectively. This short wave energy is absorbed by objects in the room and is re- emitted as long wave radiation. This is absorbed by the inner pane of glazing causing its temperature to rise. The heat contained in the inner pane is, in turn, re-radiated both into and out of the building. Radiation outwards is reduced because of the low emissivity coating. However, radiation back into the room occurs as normal. It is as if the inner pane is reflecting the long wave radiation from objects in the room back into the room. The effect of this is to reduce heat transfer through the glazing system. The U-value of 12mm double glazing in a timber frame for standard double glazing and low E (emissivity = 0.2) double glazing are 2.8 and 2.3W/m²K respectively.

Changing the spacer bars

As an alternative to traditionally used aluminium spacer bar (which fits between the panes of glass in a double glazed unit), 'warm edge' spacers can significantly reduce heat loss, particularly at the edge of the glass, where 80% of energy loss occurs. Super Spacer® from Edgetech, for example, is a 'warm edge' foam spacer, which is 950 times less conductive than aluminium spacer bar. These spacers can reduce the overall U-value of a window by 0.2W/m²k.

Most people will have witnessed the condensation that forms around the edges of double glazed units. Well, warm edge double glazing spacer bars (Figure 5.5) can significantly reduce this. For example, sealed units with 'Super Spacer®' or a similar product could reduce condensation by up to 70% compared to those with traditional aluminium spacer bar. Condensation may vary with a number of environmental factors as well as technical factors to do with the composition of the unit. Warm edge spacers can also reduce sound – up to 2 decibels compared to aluminium spacer bar.

The most significant savings using these types of spacer bar will be achieved on windows where small (Georgian) type glazing units are used due to the edge to area ratio. However, their use on all sizes of double glazing units will enhance the energy saving potential of the window.

Choosing a better frame material

Materials have different thermal conductivities depending on their density. The frame, made up of these materials, can form as much as 15% of the window opening. The thermal characteristics of the frame will therefore have a strong influence on the overall U-value. The thermal conductivity of the four most common framing materials are shown in Table 5.1. UPVC, hardwood and softwood have similar thermal conductivities, but softwood has the lowest value of the three. Aluminium on the other hand has a high thermal conductivity and if used would considerably increase the overall U-value of the glazing system. This is illustrated by the variation in indicative U-values of 12mm air gap double glazing system for various frame materials shown in Table 5.2.

Figure 5.5. This solar roof incorporates three panes of glass in a '2 + 1' configuration with the depth of the roof joist separating the single glazed outer pane (rainscreen) from the double glazed unit, filled with argon gas and edged with warm edge spacer bars.

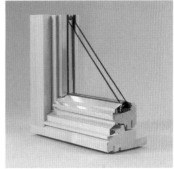

High performance timber & aluminium clad windows and doors

NorDan: Norwegian for quality

NorDan windows and doors offer superb quality, craftsmanship and design. Able to produce 1500 windows/doors daily, NorDan has the capacity of a major world exporter. Their five large factories have a work force in excess of 850 with computer controlled production lines. This enables manufacturing in volumes sufficient for the largest projects while remaining competitively priced.

Eco-friendly

More than 95% of the timber used in the manufacture of NorDan windows and doors is sourced from managed forests. For each tree that is used in the production, more trees are planted to meet future demands.

Energy saving

Although the NorDan standard U-value for the UK is 1.6 W/m^{2}K, NorDan can achieve a U-value as low as 1.0 W/m^{2}K with the added benefits of a secondary sash. With the facility to produce their own glazing units (circa. 400,000 per year) NorDan are more than capable of meeting your requirements.

Security

NorDan UK Ltd provide windows and doors to the police preferred specification of Secured by Design. Furthermore, NorDan also manufacture windows and doors to ISO9001 which guarantees the consistent quality of each and every product.

NorDan®

NorDan UK Ltd, Green Farm Business Park, Falcon Close, Quedgeley, Gloucester, GL2 4LY
T: 01452 883131
F: 01452 883739
E: info@nordan.co.uk
W: www.nordan.co.uk

POLICE PREFERRED
SPECIFICATION

Material	Thermal conductivity (W/mK)
Softwood	0.13
Hardwood	0.15
Aluminium	160
uPVC	0.17

Table 5.1. Thermal conductivities of different window frame materials.

Frame material	U value (W/m²K)
Wood	2.8
Metal	3.7
Metal (4mm thermal break)	3.4
Metal (12mm thermal break)	3.2
uPVC	3.0

Table 5.2. Indicative U-values of double glazing with different frame materials.

One way of improving the thermal performance of window frames, regardless of material, is to incorporate a thermal break into their construction. This is a barrier of low thermal conductivity material separating the inner layer of the frame from the outer. An example of a thermal break is shown in Figure 5.6.

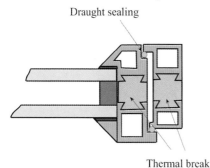

Draught sealing

Thermal break

Figure 5.6 Cross section of a window frame showing position of the thermal break.

The U-values shown in Table 5.2 indicate that the U-value of a metal framed double glazed unit is reduced by incorporating a 4mm thermal break from 3.7 to 3.4 W/m²K.

Lowest U-values are achieved by incorporating all of the above ideas. For example, triple glazing with a soft (E = 0.05) low-E coating with 16mm air gaps in a timber or uPVC frame has a U-value of 1.3W/m²K. or under.

Vacuum glazing

One idea for reducing the thermal transmittance of double glazing is to remove the conduction/convection path from between the outer and inner panes of glass. This involves removing the air in the cavity to create a vacuum[2]. Radiant heat exchanges would still occur but could be reduced by a low emissivity coating on the outer surface of the inner pane as described above.

The problem with vacuum glazing is that the air pressure on the outer and inner panes is not counteracted by internal air pressure and so would crush the glazing at mid pane and cause it to break. To overcome this the cavity is reduced to 1mm and small support pegs are moulded into the glass throughout its area as shown in Figure 5.7. This will create small thermal bridges but the cross sectional area of the supports are kept small to minimise this. Close inspection of the glazing would also allow the supports to be seen. Vacuum glazing is not widely available. It has a centre pane U-value of 0.8W/m²K.

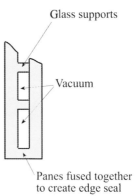

Glass supports

Vacuum

Panes fused together to create edge seal

Figure 5.7. Section through vacuum glazing.

Other transparent materials

Windows are multi-functional elements letting in solar gains, daylight and ventilation whilst allowing views out and contact with the outside world. If a view is not required, clear glazing can be replaced by transparent insulation material (TIM). TIMs have a low U-value and are actually translucent rather than transparent. This means light can get through them but it is diffused and so provides no view of the outside world. Limited contact with the outside world is retained by allowing changes in external daylight level to be perceived.

Locations where TIM can be used are rooflights and glazing panels above or below eye level. There are a number of different types of transparent insulation material including; multilayer polycarbonate sheets, aerogel and fibre glass panels.

Glass reinforced plastic

Glass reinforced plastic is a polymer sheet material that is reinforced using glass fibres. The sheets are 2mm thick and corrugated to give structural strength when spanning openings. Three sheets can be used to form a multi layer rooflight as shown in double layer form in Figure 5.8.

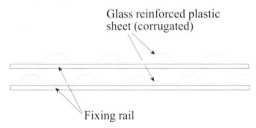

Figure 5.8. Rooflight composed of a double layer of corrugated GRP sheeting.

The light transmission of this is 50% and the U-value is 2.0W/m²K. This system is widely used in factory unit rooflights. The system can also be constructed using polycarbonate and PVC sheets, giving a choice of thermal and light transmission properties.

Glass fibre

In this system translucent glass fibres are used to fill the void between translucent glass or plastic sheets as shown in Figure 5.9. The glass fibre layer acts as an insulator but still allows light to pass through. Increasing the thickness

of the layer of insulation reduces the U-value but results in a reduced light transmission as indicated in Table 5.3.

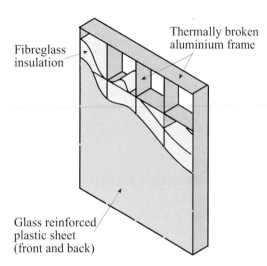

Figure 5.9. Structure of a translucent insulation panel.

Light Transmission (%)	U value (W/m²K)
20	2.74
15	1.25
10	0.99
8	0.78
5	0.56

Table 5.3. Light transmission and U-values for glass fibre translucent insulation panels.

Aerogel

The low thermal conductivity of most insulating materials arises due to the presence of air filled voids within the material. Aerogel is silicon dioxide (the main constituent of glass) that has been formed into tiny beads 2-6mm in diameter containing microscopic pores.

Because of the numerous air filled voids the material has a low thermal conductivity[3]. The product gets its name because it is formed by drying a gel of silicon dioxide. When it sets the porous structure is formed. Unfortunately contact with moisture after drying will destroy the porous and therefore insulating properties of the material. The framing/enclosure system in which it is used must protect it from contact with moisture.

The material is held in place within a sealed sandwich of glass sheets. The U-value of a 16mm double glazed unit with an infill of aerogel is 1.0W/m²K. Light transmission is approximately 50%. One concern with this substance is its tendency to settle within the glazing. This is due to movement caused by cycles of expansion and contraction due to intermittent solar heating.

Window energy ratings

U-values are used to compare the fabric heat loss characteristics of different window systems but an overall assessment, including ventilation losses and solar gains, is less common. However, the British Fenestration Rating Council (BFRC) (www.bfrc.org) has developed a voluntary energy labelling system for domestic windows. Independent assessors are used to assess windows using three performance criteria. Each window tested is a standard 1480 by 1230mm size with central mullion and single side opening configuration. The first factor is the windows thermal transmittance (U-value, W/m²K). The second is a solar factor (g-value, W/m²K) which measures how well the window blocks heat caused by sunlight. The value of g ranges between 0 and 1 where 1 is low shading and zero high shading. The lower the number, the less heat gain through that window system.

The final measurement is air leakage (L50 value, W/m²K) which assesses the air leakage (m³/h/m²) through the window when subject to a pressure difference across it of 50Pa. This is then converted into a ventilation heat loss rate. Individual values for the three criteria are presented on the rating label (Figure 5.10), as is an energy index (units kW/m²/year), which is derived from the three criteria using the formula; Energy Index = $218.6g - (68.5U + L50)$.

This energy index is then converted to a simple A-G energy rating using the scale shown in Table 5.4. This can then be used by specifiers

or customers to select energy efficient windows knowing that an 'A' rated window loses less heat than a 'G' rated window.

BFRC Rating Scale	BFRC Rating (kWh/m²/year)
A	Greater than 0
B	-10 to <0
C	-20 to <-10
D	-30 to <-20
E	-50 to <-30
F	-70 to <-50
G	Less than -70

Table 5.4. BFRC, A to G rating .

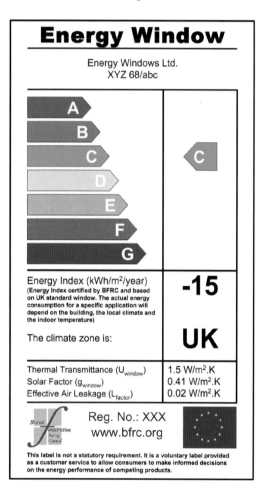

Figure 5.10 Example BFRC energy label (reproduced with permission from the BFRC).

Doors

Doors have traditionally been constructed out of solid timber with single glazed panels to allow light into hallways. Because of this they have a similar U-value to glazing. New developments in doors has seen the introduction of insulated timber doors with low emissivity double glazed panels having an overall U-value of 1.0W/m²K.

Care should be taken to ensure that doors are maintained properly and adequate seals are fitted as doors are one of the most commonly overlooked air leakage zones. Methods of reducing heat losses from doors and entrance areas are discussed in more detail in Chapter 6. ☯

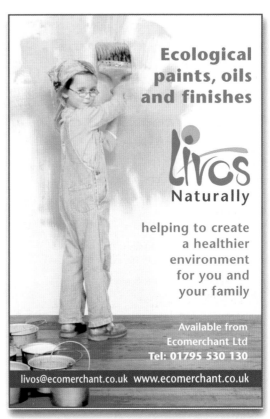
GREEN BUILDS

We are a small progressive housebuilding company building houses in the north Norfolk area.

Our future houses are to be super efficient in terms of insulation, energy and water usage and we would like to find potential purchasers who could be involved in the design process.

This would involve, for example, making decisions about whether to include features such as sheeps wool insulation, heat pumps, wind turbines, photovoltaics, solar panels and biomass boilers ... maybe more !

So....if you would like to be involved or you'd like to know more about our houses please call us on 020 7281 8497 or visit us at: www.developmentinsight.co.uk

Floors

Ground floors can be either timber boards supported on floor joists with a cavity beneath or concrete in contact with the ground. Suspended timber floors are insulated between the joists. The insulation must be supported in place using thin ply wood sheets or plastic mesh (Figure 5.11). Suspended floors are ventilated on the underside to prevent moisture build up and decay. The joists themselves should be hung from the inner leaf masonry using brackets so that they do not penetrate the inner leaf blockwork and create an air infiltration path. In addition to this an air tight barrier must be included in the floor to prevent draughts entering the room from the ventilated sub floor space.

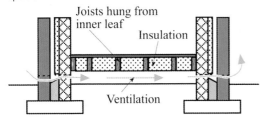

Figure 5.11. Suspended timber floor.

Heat losses through all parts of a suspended timber floor are uniform since conditions either side of the floor at all locations across it are similar. However, with solid floors in contact with the ground heat losses will be greatest along the edges adjoining the external wall (Figure 5.12).

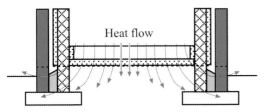

Figure 5.12. Heat loss is greatest at the perimeter of a solid floor.

This is because the ground underneath the centre of the floor will, over time, heat

up reducing the temperature difference that causes heat loss. At the edge of the building the ground will be cooler because it loses heat to the outside and so more heat will be lost through the floor at the perimeter. Vertical edge insulation helps prevent perimeter heat losses.

As a consequence of the different patterns of heat loss at the perimeter and centre of a large floor, the U-value of the entire floor will depend on the perimeter to floor area ratio. In large floors, such as those found in commercial buildings, the core area will dominate and so the average floor U-value will be low. In small floors such as in housing, the perimeter areas will dominate and so the average U-value will be high. The amount of insulation needed in a solid floor in contact with the ground to achieve particular U-values therefore depends on the perimeter (P) to area (A) ratio. This ratio is found by dividing the perimeter measured in metres by the floor area measured in square metres.

With small floors the size of the perimeter is comparable to the area and so the P/A ratio is large. Here a greater thickness of insulation is required. On large floors the size of the floor area is larger than the size of the perimeter and so the P/A ratio is small. Here a smaller thickness of insulation is needed to achieve a given U-value. This is illustrated in Table 5.5 which shows that the thickness of insulation (thermal conductivity 0.03W/mK) needed to achieve a U-value of 0.25W/m²K decreases as the P/A ratio decreases. ◉

P/A **Ratio**	**Insulation thickness (mm)**
1.0	91
0.9	90
0.8	88
0.7	85
0.6	82
0.5	77
0.4	70
0.3	59
0.2	39

Table 5.5. Thickness of insulation required in a solid floor in contact with the ground to achieve a U-value of 0.25W/m²K.

Walls

The type of construction used to form vertical elements of the outer shell varies depending on whether it is a domestic or commercial building. The basic requirements are, however, the same. The wall must be structurally sound, must have a low U-value and must prevent the ingress of wind and rain.

Masonry

The majority of house walls in the UK are masonry cavity walls (figure 5.13). They are a familiar, robust construction that are not easily damaged by prolonged contact with moisture. The cavity offers some insulating value but the majority of the thermal resistance has to come from insulation placed on the inner leaf of the cavity or from cavity filling. It is the width of the cavity that is the limiting factor in lowering the U-value. To reduce U-values the cavity must be widened to accommodate more insulation, or low thermal conductivity insulants must be used such as blown plastic foams which can be used in smaller sections but may be less ecologically acceptable.

Figure 5.13. Conventional UK masony wall construction with Insulation batts filling the cavity. Crown copyright.

Another advantage of masonry walls in low energy buildings is that they have a solid inner leaf that can provide some thermal mass in contact with the living space (though there has been much debate regarding exactly how much. See Volume 1 for a full story on this).

Thermal mass is useful for acting as a passive cooling mechanism in summer and prevents peaks in temperature. However, some of the insulating value of the masonry cavity wall is provided by low density aerated blocks forming the inner leaf. As described, these have low density and therefore provide less thermal capacity. In addition this is sometimes covered over by a dry lined plasterboard finish which, if used, would further isolate the masonry.

Timber frame systems

Conventional

Modern timber frame walls have the gaps between the frame filled with insulation (Figure 5.14). A large thickness is accommodated and so timber frame walls can have U-values as low as 0.15W/m²K .

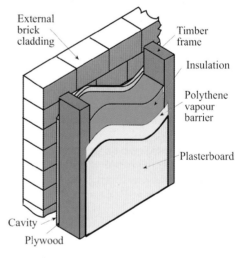

External brick cladding

Timber frame

Insulation

Polythene vapour barrier

Plasterboard

Cavity

Plywood

Figure 5.14. Conventional timber framed wall.

Brick is commonly used as an external cladding material held away from the frame on brackets creating a cavity to prevent rain penetration. A breathable water resistant barrier is also incorporated into the construction for this purpose.

Small commercial buildings can use masonry and timber frame walls but taller buildings use steel or concrete frames. Again, as with timber framed buildings, brick is commonly used as an external cladding with insulation behind or, as is the case with shed type industrial and out of town retail units, insulated cladding panels are used composed of insulation sandwiched between thin metal sheets.

Ecological walling systems

There are a number of ecological walling systems currently being tried out. These include straw bale, rammed earth (including chalk and lime), hemp and limecrete. Many of these are discussed at project or user level in Volume 1.

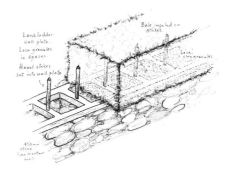

Figure 5.15. Straw bale building begins with a masonry plinth upon which the straw bales are laid in similar fashion to bricks.

Commercial ecological walling systems

EVT

A walling system, known as EVT (enhanced vapour transfer), walls from Excel Industries, comprise a 150mm deep stud framework, which is sheathed externally with 'Panelvent' sheathing board and internally with 'Paneline'. The core of the wall is insulated with 'Warmcel 500' insulation, which is manufactured from recycled newspaper and has very low embodied energy. The construction can deliver a U-value of 0.2W/m²K or better depending on thickness of insulation used.

NW1

Another ecological building products supplier, Natural Building Technologies (NBT), has introduced two, new build, ecologically sound external wall systems for timber framed buildings that meet, and can easily surpass, the requirements of the new part L Building Regulations. They offer U-values down to 0.16W/m²K, are easy to build and make airtight and can be rendered, or clad with a variety of materials. Timber frame is currently the fastest growing construction technique in the UK.

Straw bale

Straw bale building utilises normal sized agricultural straw bales which are used as construction blocks (Figure 5.15). The bales are often rendered on the outer skin, to provide protection from the rain, and plastered on the inside. Openings are framed by timber. This type of wall gives low U-values and is considered as a sustainable material since CO_2 is absorbed by the material as it grows and little energy is used to construct the walls.

Other 'natural' ecological walling systems enjoying a revival, include various traditional earthen methods of building, such as cob and adobe. Another form of earth building that uses tyres is a system known as earthships (Figure 5.16). Two earthship buildings have been constructed in the UK (see Volume 1). Systems such as these have been popular in the USA for some time and are likely to prove popular with eco-selfbuilders in the UK.

Figure 5.16. A tyre wall being built at Brighton, the home of the first UK Earthship.

Novel walling systems

More conventional and novel use of modern materials for walling include hollow polystyrene blocks filled with concrete; laminated timber structures and, of course, off site modular construction. ☯

Super insulation

It is possible to insulate buildings to such an extent that no heating system is required to maintain comfort conditions. A report from BRECSU[4] identified three categories of super insulated housing.

'Zero heating' or 'carbon neutral' house.
The house is so highly insulated and draught proofed that the space heating requirement is met from casual gains from the sun, occupants bodies, lighting, appliances and cooking. An electrical supply is needed for appliances and a minimal heating system is installed for severe winters, reduced occupancy or for sensitive occupants such as the young, ill or elderly. The U-values required for a zero heating house are low, as shown in Table 5.6.

This type of house can be upgraded into a carbon neutral or zero CO_2 house if the electricity and heating were to be supplied entirely from renewable sources. To be a zero CO_2 house it must create no net emissions of carbon dioxide over the course of its life. It can do this in two ways. Firstly (but least convincingly), it can utilise green electricity tariffs, which are derived from renewable sources (see Volume 1). Secondly, it can consume fuels and release CO_2 in the winter months but must pay this back by exporting the same amount of energy (based on CO_2 output) from renewable energy produced on site during other times in the year.

Element	U value (W/m²K)	How achieved
Roof	0.08	500mm celulose fibre
Floor	0.10	300mm expanded polystyrene
Walls	0.14	250mm full fill cavity
Windows/doors	1.7	Triple glazing with low E coating

Table 5.6. Elemental U-values for a zero heating house.

The autonomous house concept satisfies the requirements of the above two standards but must be entirely separated from mains services (Figure 5.17). This includes electricity, gas, water and sewage. A grid connection to the electricity system is permissible but the building must generate its own electricity and over the course of a year be a net exporter. Rain and grey water must be collected, stored, filtered and sterilised on site for the water supply. Sewage must be treated on site.

Figure 5.17. Hockerton Housing project near Nottingham is probably the most famous group of 'autonomous' houses in the UK.

Super insulation can eliminate the need for a space heating system. However, there are a number of technical risks associated with achieving this. These are;
- thermal bridging
- outer leaf damage
- rain penetration
- freezing of loft pipework
- thermal discomfort.

Each of these is discussed in more detail below.

Thermal bridging
Ideally a super insulated house will have a continuous coating of insulation applied to its entire outer skin. In practice this is difficult to achieve since dense, high thermal conductivity elements are needed to provide the structure of the building. These can create a thermal bridge between the inside and outside of the building. One example of this is shown in Figure 5.18, which shows a thermal bridge created at the junction between the wall and ground floor. The high thermal conductivity masonry must be continuous as it has to transmit the loads

it carries to the ground via the foundations. You could not link up the floor and wall insulation as the weight of the internal leaf would crush it. Figure 5.19 shows how cold bridging is minimised by overlapping the insulation[5]. This is achieved by taking the wall insulation down below the floor slab and bringing the floor insulation up at the edge of the floor slab. There is a continuous thermal path, but it has been made less effective by using low thermal conductivity blockwork. The insulation also makes the path narrow and tortuous.

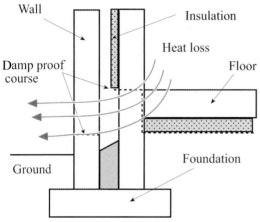

Figure 5.18. Thermal bridge between ground floor and wall.

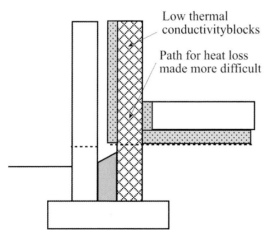

Figure 5.19 Elimination of thermal bridge.

Thermal bridging is also likely to occur at cavity closers, joins between intermediate floors and cavity walls and across lintels above windows and doors. The Building Research Establishment has produced a report[6] which describes thermal bridging in detail and the methods by which it can be avoided.

Outer leaf damage

Figure 5.20 shows the fall in temperature through a wall of U-value 0.35W/m²K from 21°C inside to -4°C outside. It can be seen that the temperature of the outer leaf is below freezing temperature (0°C). This is because one of the effects of highly insulated walls is to raise internal surface temperatures as heat is kept in the building, whilst at the same time reducing external fabric temperatures. This temperature will freeze any water in the masonry causing expansion and damage to the brickwork. It is essential that good quality outer leaf brickwork is used with sufficient water resistance and strength to avoid frost damage occurring.

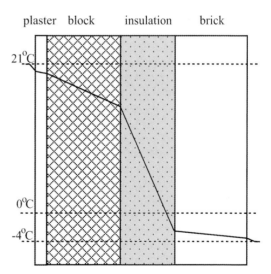

Figure 5.20. Temperature profile through a highly insulated wall.

Rain penetration

Achieving very low U-values in traditional cavity masonry wall construction requires that the entire cavity is filled with insulation. Table 5.6 showed that a super insulated house wall has a fully filled 250mm cavity. The main function of the cavity is to avoid the penetration of rain from the outer leaf to the inner leaf. Complete fills can introduce pathways for the rain to cross the cavity, wet the inner leaf, and damage finishes in the living spaces. There are three methods of avoiding this problem. The first is to maintain a cavity in areas that are at most risk from rain penetration. These are sites exposed to driving rain, as described below. The second is to apply impervious but breathable cladding to the outer leaf. The third is to use insulation materials which do not have continuous horizontal pathways throughout their structure running between the outer and inner leaves along which water can run. An example of this are mineral wool batts which are woven so that the layers of material run vertically down the insulation layer rather than across it.

In Chapter 3, the effect of driving rain was introduced and Figure 3.13 shows a map of the UK indicating the six driving rain exposure categories ranging from very sheltered to very severely exposed[7]. The categories are for walls facing the prevailing wind direction on an open site. The actual exposure can vary depending on building height and topography. Higher floors and peaks of gable ends may be more exposed, and buildings surrounded by trees may be in an exposure category one level below those indicated.

Freezing of loft pipework

The high insulation level in first floor ceilings reduces the roof U-value but can lead to freezing temperatures occurring in the loft space. The effects of this are two fold. Firstly, warm moist air travels upwards throughout the building and may enter the loft space through unsealed loft hatches. When in the loft the water vapour will condense back to liquid water due to the low temperatures. The liquid water can soak into and degrade insulation materials and encourage decay of structural timbers. The problem can be overcome by ventilating the loft space at the eaves and ridge so that any moisture laden air is swept out of the loft space. It is also advisable to seal the loft hatch.

The second concern of low loft temperatures is the possibility that water tanks and pipework

situated in the loft could freeze. This is avoided by insulating pipes and tanks individually or detailing the insulation to cover pipes and tanks rather than going under them (Figure 5.21). This keeps the water systems within the heated space.

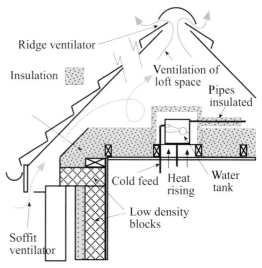

Figure 5.21. Loft Insulation to maintain ventilation and prevent pipework freezing.

Thermal discomfort

In a building that has a degree of heat loss through its fabric, space heating is required to maintain comfort. If extra casual gains occur, such as solar heating, then the heat output from the heating system can be reduced to maintain a constant total heat input. With super insulated housing that does not have a mechanical heating system there is no capacity for reducing heat input if the building gets too warm. Heat input is provided solely by casual gains. So modification of internal temperatures must be achieved by varying the size of the casual gains or by increasing heat losses. It must be assumed that heat gains from lighting, appliances and people are constant since it would be unacceptable to turn off lights and appliances or eject people if the building were to get too warm. Solar gains can however be reduced by lowering or adjusting blinds. This works but can cause the use of additional lighting and requires a high level of user interaction. The use of exposed mass within the building can help to even out temperatures. The mass absorbs excess heat when room temperatures are high and releases it when room temperatures fall again. Finally, free cooling can be used. If the outside air temperature is lower than inside then additional ventilation will bring in cool fresh air and exhaust excess heat out of the building. This is particularly important in rooms such as the kitchen where cooking can account for short duration heat input of a few kilowatts. Heat inputs would greatly exceed heat losses unless the heat released from cooking were to be extracted at source.

Workmanship

To achieve low U-values a high standard of workmanship and site supervision is required. For example, insulation products need to be installed as per manufacturers' guidelines so that there are no gaps present, and making sure mortar is not dropped on the top of insulation batts creating gaps and cold bridges. Additional instructions, supervision and working drawings may be needed where detail is important or installation procedures are complex[8].

On completion, the insulation and cold bridging of the external envelope can be checked using thermography[9]. Thermography is an imaging technique similar to photography except that the camera is sensitive to infra red radiation (heat) as opposed to visible light. A thermographic image of a wall would be made up of different shades or colours. The lighter the shade or colour the greater the heat loss. ✷

The thermal properties of construction materials

Heat moves naturally from a warm place to a cold place by a combination of the three heat transfer mechanisms; conduction, convection and radiation. Figure 5.22 shows these mechanisms in relation to an insulated cavity wall.

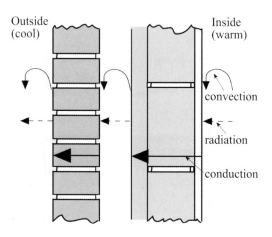

Outside (cool)

Inside (warm)

convection

radiation

conduction

Figure 5.22. Heat transfer mechanisms through an insulated cavity wall.

Conduction is the heat transfer process through the solid parts of the external envelope. Conduction can be thought of as heat being passed from one molecule of the material to the next in the direction of decreasing temperature. It follows that conduction will occur more easily in dense materials, i.e. those where the molecules are packed closely together. Conduction will be much more difficult in low density materials where the molecules are spaced further apart. This is witnessed in construction materials where dense products, such as concrete, conduct heat well and lightweight materials such as foamed plastics, conduct heat poorly. We tend not to call dense materials conductors,

but we do refer to lightweight materials as insulators. Most buildings are made up of a mixture of the two types of material. The hard dense materials providing structural strength and the light-weight materials preventing heat transfer out of the building.

Convection is the mechanism of heat transfer through gases. Air in contact with a surface hotter than itself will become warmed. This warm air will become less dense and rise up the surface, carrying energy away with it. If this airstream comes in to contact with a surface that is cooler than itself, then heat will be transferred from the air to the surface. It is by this mechanism that heat is transferred to and from surfaces in contact with air and across cavities in walls or double glazing systems.

Radiation does not require solid materials or air for heat exchange to take place. The exchange of thermal radiation takes place between the surfaces of a hot body and a cold body. The quantity of energy transferred depends on the temperature of the surfaces and the emissivity of the source surface and absorptivity of the receiving surface. Emissivity (E) is an indication of the ability of a surface to emit thermal radiation in comparison to a perfect emitter. The scale of values runs between 0 in which no energy will be radiated and 1 which indicates the surface is a perfect radiator. Most building materials have an emissivity of 0.9 indicating they are strong radiators of heat. Polished aluminium has an emissivity of 0.5. Absorptivity (A) is a similar concept but indicates the ability of a surface to absorb thermal radiation. For most building materials the value of the absorptivity is similar to the value of emissivity.

Radiation of heat is responsible for heat transfer from objects in a room, such as internal walls and furniture, to the inner surface of the external wall. It is also responsible for part of the heat transfer across cavities and loss of heat from the external surfaces. Radiative transfers are reduced in buildings by reducing the emissivity of surfaces. Two examples of how this is achieved are the use of foil backed insulation boards and low emissivity coatings on the inner pane of double glazed units.

Thermal transmittance (The U-value)

When designing low energy buildings we need to select constructional elements that minimise heat transfer and keep the heat inside the building. This can only be achieved if we have a method of comparing the heat transfer properties of different types of constructional elements. The method used is to compare their thermal transmittances. The thermal transmittance, also known as the U-value (Figure 5.23), is a measure of the speed with which heat is lost through one square metre of the element with 1K temperature difference across its faces. The units are W/m²K. The higher the U-value, the greater is the rate of heat loss through that element. Typical U-values for roof, walls, windows and floor are 0.16, 0.35, 2.0 and 0.25W/m²K respectively. The U-value incorporates the thermal characteristics of each layer in the element. The following sections describe these thermal characteristics and show how the U-value is calculated using a masonry cavity wall as an example.

ing two types of brick or a piece of polystyrene with a block of mineral wool, the similarity of the two types of material means we need more precise information to make a comparison. Standard terminology is used to allow us to compare the heat conducting properties of different materials.

For the comparison to be fair we require a fixed set of conditions under which the assessment of materials is made. The most basic measurement made is that of a material's thermal conductivity. Thermal conductivity (k) is a measure of the rate of heat conduction through one cubic metre of a material with 1K temperature difference across two opposite faces. This is illustrated in Figure 5.24.

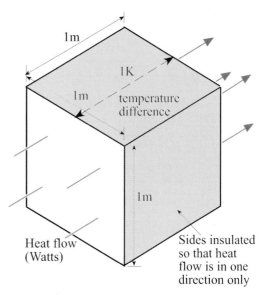

1m

1K

1m temperature difference

1m

Heat flow (Watts)

Sides insulated so that heat flow is in one direction only

Figure 5.24. Thermal conductivity.

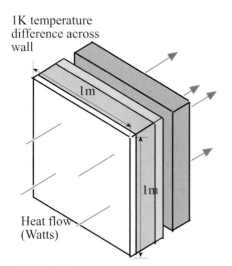

1K temperature difference across wall

1m

Heat flow (Watts)

1m

Figure 5.23. U-value .

Thermal conductivity

There are obvious differences between the heat conducting properties of a layer of brick and a layer of polystyrene. But when we are compar-

In reality measurements are carried out on small samples of material placed in a test cell. Four sides of the sample are insulated, one side of the material is heated and the rate of flow of heat through the sample to the opposite face is measured using thermometers. Some typical values of thermal conductivity are shown in Table 5.7. The larger the value of thermal conductivity, the greater is the speed by which heat flows through the material. The table also shows that generally thermal conductivity increases with increasing density.

Thermal resistance

Thermal conductivity is essential for comparing different materials but is based on a 1 metre cube! For actual construction thicknesses we use the term thermal resistance (R) (m²K/W). This is a measure of the ability of an actual thickness of material to resist the passage of heat. It is based on the thermal conductivity and the thickness of the material used in the construction. This is illustrated in figure 5.25.

Material	Density (kg/m³)	Thermal Conductivity(k) (W/mK)
Slate	2700	1.9
Sandstone	2100	1.3
Brick engineering	2300	1.0
Brick common	1790	0.72
Plaster	1570	0.53
Block (clinker)	1050	0.35
Plaster board	960	0.16
Pine	500	0.138
Plaster lightweight	448	0.115
Block aerated	400	0.08
Carpet	186	0.06
Glass fibre	12	0.04
Mineral wool	25	0.04
Expanded polystyrene	15	0.033

Table 5.7. Densities and thermal conductivities of common building materials.

Mathematically thermal resistance (R) is determined using the formula;

$$R = l/k \ (m^2K/W)$$

Where:

l is the thickness of the material (m)
k is the thermal conductivity (W/mK)

For example the thermal resistance of 50mm (0.05m) of expanded polystyrene ($k = 0.033$ W/mK)

is $\dfrac{0.05}{0.033} = 1.5m^2K/W$

To prevent heat loss from buildings the value of the thermal resistance should be as large as possible. From the above formula it can be seen that this is achieved by either increasing the thickness of the material or by reducing the value of the thermal conductivity (k).

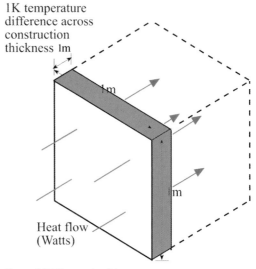

1K temperature difference across construction thickness 1m

1m

Heat flow (Watts)

1m

Figure 5.25. Thermal resistance.

Material thermal resistances are used to calculate the U-value of the element along with airspace resistances which are discussed next.

Cavity and surface resistance

Air gaps are present in many structural elements. In a masonry cavity wall the air gap is the cavity itself. One of the main functions of the cavity is to prevent the passage of rain from the outer to inner leaves. It also offers a resistance to the movement of heat. The other resistances to heat flow are caused by still layers of air attached to the inner and outer surfaces of the element by friction, known as the inside surface resistance Rsi and the outside surface resistance Rso. Heat transfer across air layers occurs due to convection and radiation. It follows that the size of the thermal resistance depends on the emissivity of the surface and the direction of heat flow (horizontal or vertical). Table 5.8 shows how the thermal resistance of a cavity decreases when the emissivity of the surfaces changes from low to high as radiant heat exchange is facilitated.

Surface emissivity	Thermal resistance (R_{cav}) m²K/W
Low	0.35
high	0.18

Table 5.8. Values of R_{cav}

The outside surface resistance is created by still air attached to the outer surface of the wall and so is affected by the exposure category of the building as shown in Table 5.9.

	Exposure category		
	sheltered	normal	exposed
Rso (m²K/W)	0.11	0.07	0.03
U-value (W/m²K)	5.00	5.60	6.00

Table 5.9. Effect of exposure on outside surface thermal resistance (Rso) and single glazing thermal transmittance(U-value).

Example calculation of a U-value

Most methods of constructing the external envelope result in the creation of repeated thermal bridges through the layer. A thermal bridge is a high thermal conductivity pathway through an otherwise low thermal conductivity layer. Examples of this are mortar joints across a low density blockwork internal leaf. and timber studs used to mount plasterboard spanning a layer of insulation applied to the internal surface of a wall. These thermal bridges can make up a substantial proportion of each square metre of the layer and so must be taken into account when calculating the U-value of the element.

The method used to calculate the U-value of elements with repeating thermal bridges is described in appendix B of part L1 of the Building Regulations (2002). It involves the following steps;

1. identify all heat flow paths through the element
2. calculate the upper resistance limit (R_{upper})
3. calculate the lower resistance limit (R_{lower})
4. calculate the total resistance (R_T) of the wall from: $R_T = \dfrac{R_{upper} + R_{lower}}{2}$

5. Calculate the U-value of the wall using

$$U = \frac{1}{R_T} \quad (W/m^2K)$$

This is best illustrated by means of an example calculation of the U-value of a brick and block cavity wall with insulation within the cavity as shown in Figure 5.26.

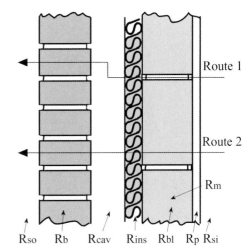

Figure 5.26. Heat flow paths through an insulated masonry cavity wall.

1. Identify all heat flow paths through the element

Figure 5.26. indicates the two possible paths that heat can take whilst flowing through the element. Note that the thermal conductivity of the brick and mortar are similar and so can be considered to be a homogenous layer. The paths in terms of thermal resistance as determined in Table 5.10 are:

Route 1.... R_{si}, R_p, R_m, R_{ins}, R_{cav}, R_b, R_{so}
Route 2.... R_{si}, R_p, R_{bl}, R_{ins}, R_{cav}, R_b, R_{so}

Route 1 paths make up 10% and route 2 paths make up 90% of the overall wall area.

2. Calculate upper resistance limit

The upper resistance limit is calculated using:

$R_{upper} = 1/(F_1/R_1 + F_2/R_2)$...(1)
F_1 = Fractional area of route 1
F_2 = Fractional area of route 2
R_1 = Total thermal resistance of route 1
R_2 = Total thermal resistance of route 2

Determine the total thermal resistances of the two routes by summing individual thermal resistances along the route as shown in Table 5.10.

$R_1 = 0.123 + 0.033 + 0.875 + 2.5 + 0.180 + 0.144 + 0.060$
$\boldsymbol{R_1} = 3.92 m^2 K/W$

$R_2 = 0.123 + 0.033 + 0.553 + 2.5 + 0.180 + 0.144 + 0.060$
$\boldsymbol{R_2} = 3.59 m^2 K/W$

Now calculate the upper resistance limit by substituting known values into equation 1 above.
$R_{upper} = 1/(0.1/3.92 + 0.9/3.59)$
$\boldsymbol{R_{upper}} = 3.62 m^2 K/W$

Layer	Thickness (m)	Thermal conductivity (W/mK)	Thermal Resistance (m²K/W)
Surface Rsi	-	-	0.123
Plaster Rp	0.015	0.46	0.033
Mortar Rm (route 1)	0.105	0.12	0.875
Block Rbl (route 2)	0.105	0.19	0.553
Insulation Rins	0.075	0.03	2.500
Cavity Rcav	-	-	0.180
Brick Rb	0.105	0.73	0.144
Surface Rso	-	-	0.060

Table 5.10. Values of thermal resistance for each layer.

3. Calculate lower resistance limit

The lower resistance limit is calculated by adding the thermal resistance of each layer together. However the bridged layer is considered in terms of the fractional areas of each material. So for the black/mortar (bl/m) layer

$R_{bl/m} = 1/(F_{bl}/R_{bl} + F_m/R_m)$
$R_{bl/m} = 1/(0.9/0.553 + 0.1/0.875)$
$\boldsymbol{R_{bl/m}} = 0.574 m^2 W/K$

Now calculate lower resistance limit using the resistance of the block/mortar layer.
$R_{lower} = R_{si} + R_p + R_{bl/m} + R_{ins} + R_{cav} + R_{br} + R_{so}$

$R_{lower} = 0.123 + 0.033 + 0.574 + 2.5 + 0.180 + 0.144 + 0.060$
$\boldsymbol{R_{lower}} = 3.61 m^2 W/K$

4. Calculate the U-value of the element

The U-value is found using:
$U = 2/(R_{upper} + R_{lower})$
$U = 2/(3.62 + 3.61)$
$\boldsymbol{U = 0.28 W/m^2 K}$

If there are air gaps or metal ties penetrating the insulation layer that create more than a 3% increase in U-value, then further corrections to the U-value will be necessary to take this into account. It can be seen in our calculation that the upper and lower resistance limits are almost the same. A much bigger effect will be noticed where there is substantial bridging of the insulation layer. One example is when structural members span the insulation in a concrete or steel framed wall.

Steady state heat loss rate

Heat is lost from a building through the envelope by conduction, convection and radiation and also by the escape of heated air from the building. These are known as ventilation and fabric heat losses respectively. Figure 5.27 shows the equations used to calculate the speed with which heat is lost by these two mechanisms known as the fabric heat loss rate (Q_f) and the ventilation heat loss rate (Q_v).

$$Q_V = \tfrac{1}{3}.n.V.\Delta T$$

$$Q_f = \Sigma (U_x.A_x.)\Delta T$$

Figure 5.27. Equations for ventilation(Q_v) and fabric(Q_f) heat loss rate (see following expanation)

Ventilation heat loss equation

The size of ventilation heat losses depends on the temperature of the internal air compared to outside air (the warmer the air the greater its energy content), and the quantity of it leaving the building. As such the following variables are used in the equation;

n is the ventilation rate measured as the number of air changes per hour (ac/h). This is the number of times all of the air in the space is completely exchanged with fresh air in an hour. So, for example, if all of the warm air in a room were to be replaced by cool outside air in an hour then the ventilation rate would be 1.0 ac/h.

V is the volume of the space measured in cubic metres (m³). The amount of energy lost will depend on the volume of warm air leaving the building.

$\triangle T$ is the difference in temperature between the air inside the building and outside the building, measured in degrees kelvin (K). Note a change in temperature of 1K is the same as a change of 1 degree centigrade (°C). We will use K here to be consistent with other texts. Temperatures in K are easily found by adding 273 to the temperature in centigrade. For example, the room temperature at 21°C is equivalent to 294K.

Fabric heat loss equation

Fabric heat losses depend on the thermal transmittance of the fabric and the area of envelope through which heat loss can take place. This changes for each individual element and so each element must be treated separately then added together. The one thing that is the same for each individual element is the temperature difference between inside and outside. As such the following variables appear in the fabric heat loss equation;

Σ is the symbol meaning 'add together'. It appears as the heat loss rate for each element must be calculated separately and then added together to give the heat loss rate for the entire envelope.

A_x is the area of element x (either window, wall, floor or roof) measured in square metres (m²).

U_x is the thermal transmittance of element x, also known as the U-value, measured in W/m²K (see earlier in this section). This is the heat loss rate in watts through 1 square metre of the element with 1K temperature difference across its faces.

$\triangle T$ is the inside - outside temperature difference as described above (K).

An example of how these equations are used to calculate the heat loss rate of a typical house follows:

Example calculation

Here the fabric and ventilation heat loss rates for the detached house shown in Figure 5.28 will be calculated.

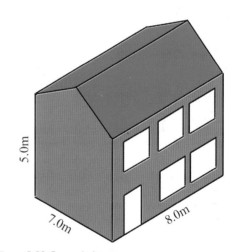

Figure 5.28. Example house.

Element	Area (m²)	U-value (W/m²K)
Floor	56	0.25
Roof	56	0.16
Walls	115	0.35
Window/door	35	2.00

Table 5.11. Example house data.

Fabric heat loss rate

The U-value gives the heat loss rate through one square metre of a building element for 1K temperature difference across its internal and external faces. To determine the heat loss rate through the entire element we must multiply the U-value by the area of the element and the actual temperature difference across its faces. If the internal temperature is 21°C and the external temperature 0°C, then the temperature difference ΔT, is 21 - 0 = 21°C.

For example the heat loss rate through the windows of the example house shown above is calculated from;

$$Q_{windows} = U_{windows} \times A_{windows} \times \Delta T ....(1)$$

where: Q = heat loss rate (W)
U = thermal transmittance (W/m²K)
A = area of element (m²)
ΔT = temperature difference between inside and outside air temp (K)

Substituting the given values for the windows from Table 5.11 into equation 1 above we get;

$$Q_{windows} = 2.0 \times 35.0 \times 21.0 \ (W)$$
$$Q_{windows} = 1470W$$

The heat loss rates for all of the elements are shown tabulated in Table 5.12. The final column shows the percentage contribution to the total fabric heat loss rate made by each element. Even though the windows have the smallest area they are responsible for over half of the fabric heat loss rate from the building. The table gives a final value for fabric heat loss of 2797.5W.

Element	U	A	ΔT	Q	%
Walls	0.35	115	21	845.3	30
Floor	0.25	56	21	294.0	11
Roof	0.16	56	21	188.2	7
Window	2.00	35.0	21	1470.0	52
			TOTAL	2797.5	100

Table 5.12. Elemental heat loss rates.

Ventilation heat loss rate

The volume (V) of the building is 280m³. We will assume some attention has been paid to draughtproofing and the average whole house ventilation rate (n) is 0.75ac/h. These values can be used in the equation for ventilation heat loss rate.

$$Q_v = \frac{1}{3} \times n \times V \times \Delta T$$

substituting the known values gives,

$$Q_v = \frac{1}{3} \times 0.75 \times 280 \times 21$$
$$Q_v = 1470W$$

The total heat loss rate from the house is $Q_f + Q_v$

i.e $Q_{total} = 2797.5 + 1470$
$Q_{total} = 4267.5W$

Choosing your optimum insulation thickness

Here, Mike George of the University of Glamorgan, advocates a new method for the assessment of optimum levels of insulation with the aid of the following 4 step procedure. The focus is to consider lofts and walls, primarily for retro-fit situations but also for new build.

The intention is to provide a tool for assessing the credentials of insulation to all of those involved in green building, from design professionals to 'do it yourself' enthusiasts. It is hoped that this tool will be particularly useful when specifying improvements to existing buildings for compliance with the new approved document L1B[10]. Floor insulation is considered only in the context of currently published information as the ready-reckoner method of assessment is not suited to floors. The 4 step procedure is as follows:

Step 1: consideration of available information
Step 2: dynamic thermal modelling
Step 3: the insulation ready-reckoner
Step 4: the eco-calculator - an internet based program to allow for greater accuracy and flexibility of construction choice.

Please note that this procedure is based on, and should be read in the context of, housing with space heating, something in common with the majority of the United Kingdom housing stock.

Step 1: consideration of available information

Loft insulation
In 1984 the economic optimum level of mineral wool for a typical dwelling was identified by the BRE[11] as 125-200mm. Comparisons were drawn from several years of research of two common house constructions with varying fuel types, interest rates, and payback periods. Later European research[12, 13, 14] has not revealed contradictory evidence. However, in a report published in 2000, entitled 'Reducing the greenhouse effect by domestic insulation', the UK mineral wool association (EURISOL) asserted, with reference to regulations of the day, that 'we are specifying thicknesses in lofts which are less than 16% of the environmental thickness'. They advocated 960mm as that being the optimum environmental thickness[15].

Cavity walls
Unfortunately, there is very little data available regarding the optimum insulation for cavity walls used for dwellings. This may be partly due to the variation of construction materials; and partly because of the difficulty and expense of installing any retrofit measures, should the chosen construction prove to be insufficient. The comparative studies[13, 14] relate to large buildings and the findings indicate an optimum range of 75-170mm. By contrast, EURISOL[15] advocated 700mm of mineral wool as environmentally optimum

Solid ground floor insulation
The calculation of heat loss through solid ground floors is historically the subject of much controversy. Macey[16], CIBSE[17] and Delsante et al[18] all exhort different theories and methods. It follows, therefore, that optimisation of insulation is similarly controversial and this may explain the lack of empirical substantiations. What is generally agreed is that the perimeter of a floor requires some insulation. In reality, builders generally insulate the whole floor to the same level. However, the effectiveness of this practice is currently the subject of some debate[19, 20].

Discussion
Optimum levels of insulation are extremely difficult to calculate with any accuracy and this is reflected by the lack of published research. Indeed, because of the many variables affecting economic and environmental assessment, opinions differ according to the level of

accuracy preferred by respective studies. For example, EURISOL[15] have chosen the purely mathematical optimum for roof insulation (960mm); while the BRE[11] recognised the negligible benefit accruing after 200mm.

What is clear is the BRE recommendations for roofs and cavity walls have been in the public domain since their publication in 1984. Not surprisingly, these values have largely been reflected in previous Building Regulation requirements. What is not clear is evidence which substantiates the need for the most recent changes[10] or indeed those proposed for the future[21]. In fact the recent sub-division of part L1 seems to have further confused an already confused construction industry. This is discussed in more detail in Volume 1 of the Green Building Bible. For the purpose of this assessment, the elemental method of U-value calculation and specification is relatively familiar to most building professionals and therefore utilised. Details of historical and possible future performance requirements are given in Table 5.13.

Step 2: dynamic thermal modelling

Methodology

This method of assessment is significantly different from previous studies as the optimum level of insulation is considered, not by any particular material, but by considering the optimum U-value of the complete construction element.

Results are based on a four bedroom detached dwelling located in Cardiff having a ground floor area of approximately 50m². Insulation is modelled at ceiling level and as part of a traditional cavity wall scenario, with the details of modelling geometry and parameters based on previous research[22]. The solid ground floor remains un-insulated for all models.

Any method of heating, fuel type or indeed boiler efficiency could have been chosen, as this is not important for the purpose of the comparison being drawn. This is because the percentage savings are based upon the annual energy use of an un-insulated building, compared to the percentage reduction realised

Title	Date	External wall (Wm² K)	Roof (W/m² K)	Floor (W/m² K)
SI 1676 Part F	1976	1	0.6	n/a
Part FF amendment	1978	0.6	0.6	n/a
SI 1685 Part L	1985	0.6	0.35	0.6
Part L	1991	0.45	0.25	0.6
Part L amendment	1995	0.45	0.25	0.45
Part LI	2002	0.35	0.16	0.25
Part L1A/B*	2006	0.35	0.16	0.25
EST Best Practice	2006+	0.25	0.13	0.2
EST Advanced standard	2006+	0.15	0.08	0.1

*compliance is no longer based on elemental values. See Volume 1

Table 5.13. Historical and possible future requirements of the Building Regulations.

Notes to Table 5.13. AECB standards are not included or discussed here as the U-values recommended within them are calculated differently and are part of a whole house strategy of measures akin to that of the Passivhaus standards in Germany.

by the incremental improvements to the building fabric. For example, an un-insulated building similar to that modelled may have an annual energy use of 18MWh at a cost of £400. Since cost is proportional to energy use, a 20% reduction in energy results in a 20% cost saving.

Regarding the simulation parameters, the model replicates a detached dwelling having the complete wall and roof surface areas exposed to extreme external temperature conditions. A CIBSE annual climatic data file, having particularly extreme winter temperature conditions is used for the simulations which are modelled for a period of 1 year. Because of these parameters, the findings can be considered to represent a worst case scenario and on this basis, can be used as an indicator for a large proportion of the housing stock.

Simulation results

The annual energy use values from space heating have been ascertained from the modeling of the incremental improvements shown in Table 5.13. Results are illustrated in Figures 5.29 and 5.30 which demonstrate the respective savings attributable to the roof and cavity wall structures. The upper and lower trend lines indicate the range of thickness required, depending upon the conductivity of the insulant.

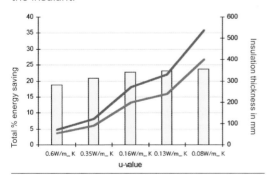

Total percentage energy saving

Thickness of low conductivity insulation

Thickness of high conductivity insulation

Figure 5.29. The annual % savings from ceiling insulation. The legend applies to both Figures 5.29 and 5.30.

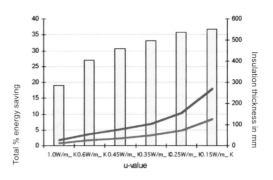

Figure 5.30. The annual % savings from cavity wall insulation.

Discussion

It is immediately clear from Figures 5.29 and 5.30 that the initial inclusion of insulation provides a good economic return, with a combined annual saving of 38% being made from the introduction of the original 1976 part F requirement[23]. Clearly, subsequent regulatory standards are also worthy of their introduction, even though savings are not as great. However, it cannot be deduced from the charts where the optimum level of insulation lies. In order to get some realistic idea of this, one must consider the energy saved by meeting a particular U-value, in light of the thickness of insulation required to make that saving. The assessment is complicated further by the wide range of materials available on the market, and with this in mind, Step 3 presents a ready-reckoner which can be used to consider the cost of incremental 'upgrades' against the savings they are likely to produce.

Step 3: the insulation ready-reckoner ©

To compare the thermal performance of different insulations, simply choose your design U-value and read across the adjacent row in Tables 5.14 (ceilings) and 5.15 (walls). Examples of typical thermal conductivities (k-values) of insulation are listed and the thickness of insulation has been calculated in accordance with each stated k-value. The importance of thermal bridging is discussed previously in this chapter and no allowance is made within the calculated

U-values. Anyone wishing for accuracy of this nature will invariably be utilising some form of part L validated software which takes this complicated assessment into account.

The energy savings modelled in Step 2 are also tabulated to enable a payback calculation to be made, as this will subsequently allow the reader to assess where the optimum level lies and therefore which performance requirement they wish to upgrade/design to. The design U-values are chosen in common with the simulated historic and current best practice standards previously shown in Table 5.13. All ready-reckoner values are calculated using the lowest conductivity ascertained but are examples only and are not specific to any manufacturer.

Calculating payback period

Calculating the payback period for any improve-

ments is a complicated procedure and depends upon many variables. Two simplified examples for DIY loft insulation are given below.

Example 1. Assume a pre-1976 un-insulated house with an annual heating bill of £400 and which is to have 250mm mineral wool insulation installed in the loft. Reading from the ready reckoner the expected annual saving would be around 23%. Calculate 23% of £400 = 400 x 23 ÷ 100 = £92 This is the annual saving. Estimate the total cost of the insulation and associated work, eg. DIY at £300, and divide this by the expected cost saving = 300 ÷ 92 = payback of approximately 3.3 years.

Example 2. Assuming a house with 50mm of mineral wool installed in the loft, which is to be upgraded to a total thickness of 300mm. The current annual heating bill is £332. Firstly calculate how much the fuel cost would be with no

U-value	Exfoliated vermiculite	Perlite beads	Hemp batts	Cork board and granules	Recycled cotton fibre flexible batts	Wood fibre semi rigid insulation batts	Cellulose batts/loose fill	Flax batts and rolls	Sheeps wool batts/rolls	Recycled newspaper	Cellulose/viscous flexible batts	Fibreglass batts and rolls	Mineral wool batts and rolls	Expanded polystyrene board and beads	Savings
	0.065	0.045	0.043	0.042	0.039	0.038	0.038	0.037	0.037	0.035	0.034	0.033	0.033	0.032	
0.60	108	75	72	70	65	63	63	62	62	58	57	55	55	53	18.7%
0.35	186	129	123	120	111	109	109	106	106	100	97	94	94	91	20.9%
0.16	406	281	269	262	244	237	237	231	231	219	212	206	206	200	22.8%
0.13	500	346	331	323	300	292	292	285	285	269	262	254	254	246	23.2%
0.08	812	562	537	525	487	475	475	462	462	437	425	412	412	400	23.7%

Thermal conductuvity of insulant (W/mK)

Thickness of insulation required in millimetres

*percentage savings indicate the expected reduction in annual energy use when compared to an un-insulated house.

Table 5.14. Ready-reckoner for ceiling insulation thicknesses. © Mike George 2006

insulation. From the ready reckoner, assess the expected saving from 50mm = around 17%. The annual fuel cost (£332) is equal to 100% -17% = 83% Therefore the total un-insulated fuel bill would be 332 x 100 ÷ 83 = £400

Using the calculation set out in Example 1, the annual saving due to the existing 50mm of insulation is £400 - £332 = £68 per year. Next calculate the expected saving from the total upgraded thickness of 300mm. Again reading from the ready reckoner, the expected saving would be around 23.5% and using the calculation set out in Example 1, the annual saving due to 300mm of insulation is 23.5% of £400 = 400 x 23.5 ÷ 100 = £94 per year

Estimate the total cost of the insulation and associated work, eg. DIY at £200, and divide this by the expected cost saving. The fuel cost saving from the upgrade is the difference between 300mm and 50mm which is £94 - £68 = £26 per year. Expected payback is 200 ÷ 26 = approximately 7.5 years

Calculating carbon dioxide savings

First divide the cost savings by the unit cost per kilowatt-hour (kWh). The model results are based on 2.2 pence per kWh.

Table 5.15. Ready-reckoner for wall insulation thicknesses. © Mike George 2006

U-values	Strawboard	Wood fibreboard	Hemp batts	Foamed glass slab	Recycled cotton fibre flexible batts	Wood fibre semi rigid insulation batts	Cellulose batts	Flax batts and rolls	Sheeps wool batts/rolls	Cellulose/viscous flexible batts	Fibreglass batts and rolls	Mineral wool batts and rolls	Expanded polystyrene board and beads	Extruded polystyrene board	Urethane rigid board	Polyisocyanurite rigid board	Phenolic foam board	Savings
Thermal conductivity of insulant (W/mK)	0.100	0.080	0.043	0.042	0.039	0.038	0.038	0.037	0.037	0.034	0.033	0.033	0.032	0.028	0.023	0.023	0.020	
Wall type : 400mm un-insulated random stone wall																		
0.45	179	143	77	75	70	68	68	66	66	61	59	59	57	50	41	41	36	31%
0.35	241	193	104	101	94	92	92	89	89	82	80	80	77	67	55	55	48	33%
0.25	357	286	154	150	139	136	136	132	132	121	118	118	114	100	82	82	71	36%
0.15	625	500	269	262	244	237	237	231	231	212	206	206	200	175	144	144	125	37%
Wall type 2: un-insulated heavyweight cavity wall																		
0.45	167	133	72	70	65	63	63	62	.62	57	55	55	53	47	38	38	33	31%
0.35	227	182	98	95	89	86	86	84	84	77	75	75	73	64	52	52	45	33%
0.25	337	269	145	141	131	128	128	125	125	114	111	111	108	94	77	77	67	36%
0.15	588	471	253	247	229	224	224	218	218	200	194	194	188	165	135	135	118	37%
Wall type 3 un-insulated lightweight cavity wall																		
0.45	147	118	63	62	57	56	56	54	54	50	49	49	47	41	34	34	29	31%
0.35	204	163	88	86	80	78	78	75	75	69	67	67	65	57	47	47	41	33%
0.25	323	258	139	135	126	123	123	119	119	110	106	106	103	90	74	74	64	36%
0.15	565	452	243	237	220	215	215	209	209	192	186	186	181	158	130	130	113	37%
Thickness of insulation required in millimeters																		

Total saving in kWh for Example 1, is therefore £92.00 ÷ £0.022p = 4181kWh.

The total carbon dioxide savings are based on fuel conversion factors stipulated in part L, in this case for gas, which is 0.194Kg/kWh[10]. Total carbon dioxide saving for example 1 is therefore 4181/x 0.194 = 811Kg. Total carbon dioxide saving for example 2 is £26 ÷ £0.022p x 0.194 = 234Kg.

Walls

The many possible variations of wall components make the comparison of walls a far more complex procedure as an allowance must be made for the thermal conductivity of each component part. In order to simplify this, such an allowance is calculated into the wall ready reckoner, although this is limited to three reasonably common construction types: random stone, heavyweight and lightweight cavity walls.

Payback assessment is, however, complicated further by the consequential complications of increasing insulation thickness. Foundation width, for example, will increase proportionally with cavity wall thickness beyond 300mm. This is an important consideration for superinsulated buildings and needs to be factored in to any payback calculations.

Further considerations when choosing insulation

Appropriate use

As touched upon previously in this chapter, the thermal conductivity values for materials vary in many ways. This is particularly true of insulation and some of the many influencing factors are purity of material, manufactured density, compactness, moisture content and hybridisation. It must be remembered that any type of insulation is only suitable for a specific application and it is essential that when designing or upgrading buildings, manufacturer's specifications and recommendations are strictly adhered to. It is equally important that the

material chosen is fit for the intended purpose. Suitability should always be judged by any form of certification held by the manufacturer and this is a good place to look for appropriate installation details. Examples include British Board of Agrément (BBA) and the European Standard CEN keymark.

Environmental impact

In environmental terms, one should consider how the product is derived, whether from organic, mineral or fossil sources. NGS Greenspec[24] is a good source of further information, which considers this in some detail.

Embodied energy

When designing for zero or low energy space heating, the embodied energy of a product becomes a more significant consideration, although calculating this is a very complex matter. The fact that energy saved by using insulation far outweighs that used in its production is unquestioned. However, there must come a point where this position is nullified. It is well known that many of the insulation manufacturing processes use large amounts of energy for production and it is inconceivable that adding insulation to infinity is an environmentally friendly exercise. An inventory of carbon and energy, which determines the embodied energy and carbon content of a large number of building materials, is available free as a pdf download from Bath University[25].

Step 4: the eco-calculator ◦

The Eco-calculator is an online programme, currently under development, which takes the ready reckoner a step further in terms of flexibility. It is primarily designed so that different insulation retro-fits can be compared for more varied wall constructions in terms of their thermal performance. Please check at the Green Building Bible website: www.greenbuildingbible.co.uk for further information. ◉

References for Chapter 5

1. The Building Regulations part L1 and L2 conservation of fuel and power. 2006

2. Roche L. and Collins R. Smart Glass. Building Services Journal.pp 27-29 August 1997

3. Field A. Super insulation from Sand. Building Services Journal pp45-46. October 1994

4. General Information Report 53. Building a Sustainable Future: Homes for an Autonomous Community.HMSO October 1998

5. Good Practice Guide 93. Energy Efficiency in New Housing: Detailing for designers and building professionals: Key detailing principles. HMSO. November 1993

6. Building Research Establishment. BRE Report 242. Thermal Insulation Avoiding the Risks. 2002

7. BS8104 Code of practice for assessing exposure of walls to wind driven rain. HMSO

8. Good Practice Guides. 99 to 110. Energy Efficiency in New Housing: Site Practice for Tradesmen. HMSO 1993.

9. Building Research Establishment. BRE Report 176. A practical guide to infra-red thermography for building surveys, 1991

10 . ODPM. 2006. Conservation of fuel and power, Approved Document L1B Work in existing dwellings. The Stationary Office, Norwich, UK

11. Pezzey 1984 BRE Report 58 An economic assessment of some energy conservation measures in housing and other buildings Glasgow. BRE publications

12. Erlandsson et al 1997 Energy and environmental consequences of an additional wall insulation of a dwelling. Building and Environment 32, No 2. Pergamon Press

13. Gorgolewski M 1995 Optimising renovation strategies for energy conservation in housing, Building and Environment 30, No 4. Pergamon Press

14. Henderson, G and Shorrock, L D 1986 BREDEM, BRE Domestic energy model- Testing the predictions of a two zone model Garston, BRE publications

15. EURISOL 2000 reducing the greenhouse effect by domestic insulation. Herts. Eurisol UK limited

16. Macey, H 1949 Heat loss through a solid floor. J Institute Fuel 2, pp.369-371

17. CIBSE 1999. Guide Book A, Environmental Design. Chartered Institute for Building Services Engineers, London

18. Delsante et al 1983 Application of fourier transforms to periodic heat flow into the ground under a building, Int. J. Heat Mass Transfer 26, pp121-132

19 . George, M.D.J; Geens, A J & Graham, M. 2006. Stimulating simulations. Building for a Future, Volume 15, No 4, Spring 2006 pp.28-32

20. George, M.D.J; Geens, A J & Graham, M. 2006 Solid floor insulation and energy use, does more equal less. Workshop presented to the conference for the Association for Environment Conscious Building (AECB) Genesis Project, Taunton, July 2006 Powerpoint presentation available at www.aecb.net

21. The Energy Saving Trust 2003 CE12: energy efficiency in new housing: Best practice specification / advanced design specification

22. George, M D 2004. Do small builders need more L? Unpublished Dissertation, University of Glamorgan, Pontypridd, UK

23. DETR 1976 Statutory Instrument no 1676: Building and buildings, part F. London. HMSO

24. Greenspec 2006 Insulation materials compared available at www.greenspec.co.uk/html/design/materials/insulation.html

25. Hammond and Jones 2006 An Inventory of Carbon and Energy, University of Bath available at: http://people.bath.ac.uk/cj219/

The method for calculating U-values is given in the following British Standards:

Walls and roof - BS EN ISO 6946:1997 building components and building elements - thermal resistance and thermal transmittance - calculation method

Ground floor - BS EN ISO 13370:1998 Thermal performance of buildings - heat transfer via the ground - calculation methods

Windows and doors - BS EN ISO 10077-1:2000 Thermal performance of windows, doors and shutters - calculation of thermal transmittance - Part 1: Simplified methods, and prEN ISO 10077-2:2000 Thermal performance of windows, doors and shutters - calculation of thermal transmittance - Part 2: Numerical methods for frames

6 Infiltration & ventilation

Introduction

A source of fresh air is a vital requirement for all buildings. It provides oxygen for breathing, dilutes and displaces pollutants, such as body odours and metabolic carbon dioxide, avoids condensation by removing moisture, keeps buildings cool by removing excess heat and allows combustion appliances to operate safely. Unfortunately, ventilation also removes warm air, representing a loss of heat from the building.

Two terms are used to describe the movement of air in to and out of a building; infiltration and ventilation. **Infiltration** is the natural movement of air through cracks, gaps and porous elements of the building envelope. The air movement is driven by pressure differences created by the wind and the buoyancy of warm air. **Ventilation** can be either 'natural', when it is the movement of air through purpose built openings in the fabric by naturally occurring pressure differences, or 'mechanical', when driven by fans through ducted openings. All of these processes are often simply referred to as "ventilation". Heat lost by both infiltration and ventilation is known as ventilation heat loss.

The speed with which air enters and leaves a building is known as the ventilation rate. This can be measured in litres of fresh air per second (l/s), or for particular rooms, as a number of air changes per hour (ac/h). This is the number of times the air in a room is completely replaced by fresh air each hour.

In the past buildings were draughty places, in part due to the presence of open fires which drew air from the room and up out of the chimney. Many existing buildings remain draughty. New building that are fitted with central heating, and room sealed appliances that do not require flues, are less draughty. In a house with no special attention paid to draught proofing, the ventilation rate will be

approximately 1.5 ac/h. If this was applied to the example house shown in *'Steady state heat loss rate'* in Chapter 5, it would give a ventilation heat loss rate of 2.9kW which is greater than the fabric heat loss rate as shown in Figure 6.1. The figure also shows the benefits of further reductions in ventilation rate. At 0.5 ac/h the ventilation heat loss rate is just over one third that of the fabric heat loss rate.

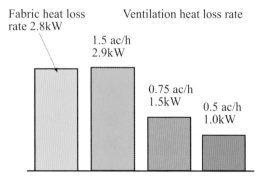

Figure 6.1. Fabric and ventilation heat loss rates.

Non energy issues

Reducing the infiltration rate can have many advantages beyond reducing heat losses these are;

- avoiding thermal discomfort arising from draughts
- preventing dust and pollution ingress on polluted sites
- ensures insulation, especially in cavities, is not short circuited
- allowing correct operation of mechanical ventilation systems
- in hot climates, preventing overheating
- reducing the capacity and hence cost of the heating and cooling system.

The role of occupants

One major factor that has an influence on ventilation rate is the role of occupants. Door and window opening can greatly increase ventilation rates. This is outside the control of the building designer. However, it may be possible to provide sensors on windows which, in conjunction with an energy management system, can turn off the heating or air conditioning system when windows are opened. This, however, is not easy to achieve in practice

This chapter will concentrate on the methods by which the air tightness of buildings can be improved, adequate ventilation can be maintained, heat can be recovered from exhaust air and natural ventilation can be provided in commercial buildings. ☯

Infiltration

The routes by which air enters and leaves a building are as follows;
- porous building materials
- cracks around service entries
- cracks in the join between window/door frame and the wall
- door and window opening
- suspended timber ground floors
- floor to wall junctions
- ventilated cavity routes around dry lining plasterboard
- loft hatch
- open flues and chimneys
- openings for fans through walls
- steel and concrete framed commercial buildings are prone to leakiness around curtain walling elements.

The air movement is driven by pressure differences built up by the wind and temperature variations between inside and outside the building (wind induced ventilation was described in Chapter 3). Ventilation caused by temperature differences is called stack ventilation because a height difference is also required. This is illustrated in Figure 6.2.

Air inside buildings is generally warmer than the air outside due to heat gains from the heating system or casual sources. Warm

air is less dense than cold air, so the air inside the building is less dense than that outside. Air inside the building will tend to rise and as it does, so it creates a low air pressure relative to outside. As the warm air leaves the building at high level, the low internal pressure draws fresh cold air in to the building through openings in the fabric.

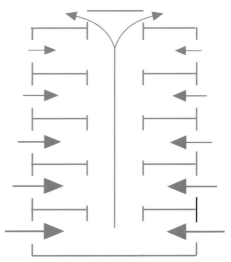

Figure 6.2. Stack ventilation.

The pressure differences set up by this mechanism increase as temperature differences between inside and outside increase and also as the height difference between exhaust and intake points increase. So if the outside and inside temperatures are constant, there will be a larger pressure difference between outside and inside on the ground floor than on the top floor. The pressure difference decreases with each successive floor up from ground level. In tall buildings this can mean that air movements on the ground floor are excessive and air movement on the uppermost floor is sluggish.

Where stack ventilation is being used to replace the use of fans (see '*Natural ventilation in commercial buildings*' later in this chapter), the system can be balanced by varying the size of an opening between the room being ventilated and the stack using a damper. If air movement is excessive the damper can be closed, when air movement is sluggish the damper can be opened. The height of the stack must be carried above the height of the building to maintain a height difference between the top of the stack and the topmost floor. Ventilation towers rising above the building are a necessary aesthetic of passively ventilated buildings driven by stack ventilation

In commercial buildings there are many routes that air can take in moving vertically up and out of the building. These include lift shafts, stairwells and vertical service ducts. Air movement in these routes needs to be controlled to ensure the effective operation of purpose built, vertical ventilation ducts.

Retaining heated air

There are two ways in which warm air can be retained in a building. These are firstly, ensuring internal air does not escape when doors are opened and secondly, closing cracks and gaps in the external shell of the building.

Door opening

Warm air can escape as people and goods enter and leave buildings. In domestic and commercial buildings the amount of warm air that escapes when entering the building can be reduced by creating a draught lobby (Figure 6.3). This is a zone at the entrance to the building, having two doors. The first is the external door. Entering this will allow the air within the lobby to escape but the air beyond the second doors is retained in the building. The size of the lobby should be sufficient to allow the external door to be closed before progressing through the internal draught lobby door.

Draught lobbies at the entrance to commercial buildings can restrict the flow of people. If this is a concern the two sets of draught lobby doors can be replaced by automatic doors which are normally closed but open when a person approaches them. When the flow of people is at its peak, such as at lunch time, it is possible that the automatic doors will be permanently open. To avoid this situation, revolving doors can be used. The nature of revolving doors means they form a permanent

seal across the opening at all times, whilst still allowing people to make their way in to and out of the building.

In factories and warehouses the main movement in to and out of the building is by raw materials inwards and goods outwards. These are often bulky, requiring fork lift trucks to move them. As a result factory doors are large. The concerns with large doors are their size and that they take a long time to open and close. This combination allows large volumes of warm air to escape during the door opening and closing process. A number of techniques are used to avoid this. The first is to replace the door with a flexible barrier. One example of this is the use of overlapping plastic strips hung vertically within the opening. When no movement is taking place the weight of the plastic strips causes them to hang together and seal the door. People and vehicles can push their way through the plastic strips creating an opening, which is only as wide as is needed. After passing, the plastic strips fall back into place to form a complete barrier. The plastic strips are not ideal as strong winds can force them to open causing draughts.

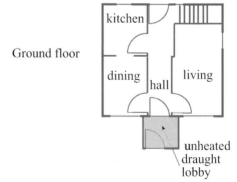

Figure 6.3. Simple draught lobby.

Alternative draughtproof doors are fast acting doors (Figure 6.4). These are reinforced plastic sheets covering the door opening. The plastic sheet is attached to a motorised roller. When a vehicle approaches the door it is detected using sensors, such as photocells or ultrasound, the motor is activated and this rapidly rolls up the barrier for the vehicle to pass. Once passed the barrier rapidly descends to cover the doorway again. The speed of opening and closing is up to 3m/s so a 6m high door will be opened in two seconds. The door is designed to prevent air loss and by the nature of its construction is not highly insulated. More highly insulated doors are available composed of hinged horizontal panels. The U-value of these doors is 0.4W/m²K, so heat is retained better than the fast, lightweight door when it is closed. However their speed of operation is reduced to 1.5m/s.

Figure 6.4. Fast acting door. photo from GPCS 294 Energy efficient refurbishment of industrial buildings (1995). Crown copyright.

The loading of goods on vehicles can take a long time with the loading bay doors open throughout the process. There are a number of ways heat loss through these doors can be avoided.

Design the loading bay door dimensions and threshold heights, so that when vehicles back up to the opening, a seal is created between the trailer and pads around the loading bay door. This system also saves energy when frozen foods are being loaded into a refrigerated vehicle (Figure 6.5).

Partition the space behind the loading dock so that the space where goods are stored and

people work for most of the time is heated but the loading bay area forms a separate zone and is unheated

Use an appropriate heating system that is not based on warm air. Radiant heaters (see Chapter 8) should be used as these heat people rather than the air.

Use sensors to turn the heating system off when doors are opened.

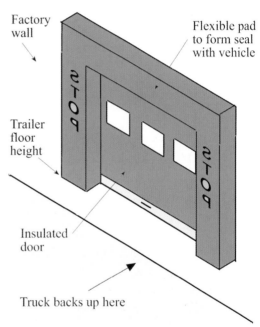

Figure 6.5. Loading door/vehicle seal.

Draught proofing

Draught proofing involves increasing the air tightness of the external envelope by closing air paths through it. These air paths were identified earlier in this chapter. The way in which they can be closed are:

Porous building materials. Construction materials have differing permeabilities to air. Materials should be chosen with a low air permeability, or the envelope should be sealed as described in *'Envelope sealing'* later in this chapter.

Service entries, masonry structure, joins between frames and walls. The air movement routes around and through these are cracks and gaps. Gaps appear when two materials are butted together. Cracks are formed when a rigid material is trying to move, for example due to settlement or shrinkage, but is prevented from doing so by being held in position by the rest of the structure. The stresses that build up in the material cause it to crack. These cracks should not be filled using rigid fillers since further movement will crack the filler material. Instead the filler must be flexible. In this way further movement can be accommodated and the seal created by the filler retained. Silicon rubber extruded from a tube is an example of this type of material (Figure 6.6).

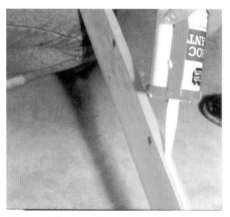

Figure 6.6. Flexible silicon sealant being applied to a skirting board. photo from GPG 93.2 Energy efficiency in new housing - detailing for designers and building professionals (1993). Crown copyright.

Doors, windows and loft hatches. Sometimes the gap to be sealed is one that needs to be opened and closed. In this case a permanent sealant adhering to the two opposite surfaces is inappropriate. A flexible material must be used, attached to one surface that will create a seal with the opposite surface. Rubber strips, in the form of tubes and short nylon brushes, are two examples of the materials that can be used. Rubber strips are usually held in position using self adhesive strips. The brush type seals require a more secure fixing and are usually held in place by screws.

Floor wall joints/dry lining. There are no clear air movement paths through continuous materials such as in-situ concrete. However, when two materials join or one material penetrates another, an interface is created through which air can travel. Within buildings there are numerous interfaces like this. One example is where floor joists are supported at their ends by penetrating the inner leaf blockwork. A second is where plasterboard terminates at the floor (Figure 6.7).

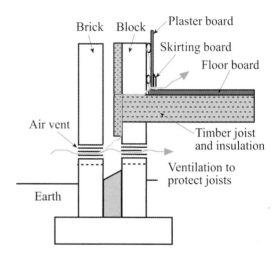

Figure 6.7 . Infiltration routes.

The method for dealing with these infiltration routes firstly involves identifying them then creating detailed design drawings and site instructions to eliminate or seal them. In the case of our two examples, joists can be hung from the inner leaf using brackets rather than penetrating it and silicon sealant can be used along the top and bottom edges of the skirting board to seal the infiltration route through the lower edge of the plasterboard (Figure 6.8).

Open flues and chimneys. Flues are designed to remove dangerous gases from the combustion appliance and deposit them safely outdoors. This is achieved by the natural buoyancy of hot combustion gases rising up out of the flue. Fresh air for combustion is drawn from the room in which the appliance is situated. If the appliance is powerful, then much air will be drawn from the room and purpose built ventilation openings are required in the room wall, or suspended floor, to allow air to enter the room to make up for the combustion air removed from it. This process naturally removes warm air from the room to be lost up the flue.

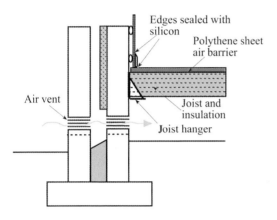

Figure 6.8. Infiltration routes closed using 'robust details'.

Ventilation rates in a typical house with and without an open fire are 4.0 and 1.5ac/h respectively. However, the presence of open flues is an essential safety feature and flues should never be restricted or combustion gases will spill into the room and asphyxiate the occupants. To avoid this source of ventilation the combustion appliances should be room sealed. This means they do not take combustion air from the room. Instead they have a small section of ducting alongside the flue which brings combustion air into the appliance from outside the building (Figure 6.9).

Draught proofing techniques, as described above, can reduce the ventilation rate of a domestic building to 0.5ac/h. If the ventilation rate is reduced below this level problems may occur with poor air quality and condensation.

Envelope sealing

In some very cold countries, such as Canada, there is a requirement to treat the external envelope of the building as an air tight barrier.

This means that as well as draught proofing to seal up cracks and gaps, the porous masonry materials must also be sealed. This involves building a continuous air tight membrane covering the entire outer skin of the building including walls, floor and upper floor ceiling. Good seals must be made between windows and doors and around service entries. As well as being continuous, the barrier must be durable so that any movement in the building will not create tears.

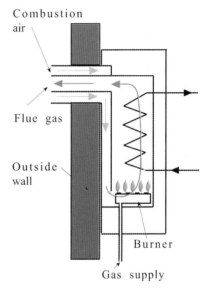

Figure 6.9. Room heater with balanced flue.

The type of materials used include plastic sheeting such as polythene. Great care must be taken with sealing joins between sheets. Liquid compounds can also be used, which are sprayed on to the masonry and which set to form a flexible airtight membrane. Finally, foamed plastic can be injected into the cavity between the leaves in masonry walls. This sets to create an airtight barrier and also offers thermal insulation. A thermographic study may be required to ensure the plastic foam is continuous.

Using sealing techniques as described above can reduce the ventilation rate of a domestic building to a value as low as 0.2ac/h. This low ventilation rate would produce unacceptable air quality and condensation problems within the building. To avoid these problems, purpose built, and therefore controllable, infiltration openings must be created in the building envelope. This form of ventilation must be used in conjunction with mechanical extract ventilation to remove heat, moisture and odours whenever they appear in high quantities.

Air-tightness testing

It is assumed that if a building is constructed using details which are known to give good air-tightness performance, then the envelope leakage will be low. However, the only way to confirm this is to test the air tightness of the envelope. This is usually carried out by pressurising the building using fans[1]. For domestic buildings the front door is replaced by a panel containing a fan as seen in Figure 6.10.

Figure 6.10. Adjustable blower door and fan in-place for carrying out an airtightness inspection.

The fan is run at a known speed until a constant internal pressure is achieved inside the building, usually 50Pa above atmospheric

pressure. (Pressure is measured in Pascals (Pa), normal atmospheric pressure is 101Pa but this is not noticed due to a balance between internal and external atmospheric pressures). At constant pressure the volume of air being moved into the building by the fan equals the volume of air escaping from the building through leakage routes. 50Pa is not a large pressurisation. This is useful as it means the building is performing close to normal pressures whilst masking temperature induced pressure variations. However, wind pressures can greatly exceed 50Pa and so pressure testing should not be carried out on windy days.

The value obtained from this test is known as the air permeability of the building, measured in cubic metres of air per hour, per square metre of envelope area ($m^3/h/m^2$). The air movement is divided by envelope area so that buildings of different sizes can be compared. The value represents the volume of air lost each hour through $1m^2$ of the building envelope. Table 6.1 below shows good and best practice values of air permeability obtained by pressurisation testing in commercial buildings[2]. Some buildings when tested have extremely high air permeabilities with values as high as $34.0m^3/h/m^2$.

Building Type	Air Leakage ($m^3/h/m^2$)	
	Good Practice	Best Practice
Office, air conditioned	5.0	3.0
Supermarket	5.0	3.0
Office naturally ventilated	10.0	7.5
Industrial buildings	15.0	10.0

Table 6.1. Good and best practice air permeabilities.

The value obtained for air permeabilities is fine for comparing the air tightness of different buildings, but to calculate the ventilation heat loss rate, the ventilation rate measured in air changes per hour (ac/h) is required. This can be measured by pressurising the building and carrying out a tracer gas test as described below. However, the ventilation rate at pressure is greater than under normal atmospheric conditions. Experience has shown that by dividing the ventilation rate at 50Pa by 20 an approximation of the ventilation rate at normal atmospheric pressures can be determined.

Measurements of air change rate at standard room temperatures and pressures can be carried out using tracer gas measurements. Here a known volume of tracer gas is injected into the room. When first released the mixture of tracer gas and room air will result in a maximum concentration. This concentration is measured using a gas analyser. As ventilation of the space takes place some of the tracer gas will leave the building and be replaced by fresh air. As time progresses the concentration of tracer gas will slowly fall. The rate of fall in concentration indicates the ventilation rate. Ambient conditions such as internal/external temperatures and external wind speeds should be measured at the time of the tracer gas tests.

The specific route by which air is escaping from the building can only be determined by visualisation techniques. Visualisation involves releasing fine dust or smoke into moving airstreams. The movement of the dust/smoke reveals the movement of air streams. Outside the building smoke may be seen escaping through various cracks and gaps in the envelope. A second technique involves thermal imaging. The air inside the building is heated. Thermography outside the building would reveal escaping warm air as a bright plume on the thermographic image.

Building Regulations

Ventilation is considered in the Building Regulations. The aim is to provide adequate ventilation in buildings to avoid problems with poor air quality, whilst reducing energy losses. Adequate ventilation is considered in part F of the regulations. Energy losses are considered in part L.

Air quality requirements

There is a general acceptance that infiltration rates should be minimised as this is uncontrollable, and that infiltration should be replaced by a three stranded strategy[3]. The approach is based on the principle of 'build tight and venti-

late right';
- provide purpose built openings for natural ventilation paths into the building which can be controlled
- provide openable windows for higher levels of short term ventilation
- extract moisture and odours at source using extract fans or passive stack ventilators.

Purpose built openings are often known as trickle ventilators. They are sleeved ducts running from outside to inside the building through the building fabric, often through the head of a window frame (Figure 6.11). A rain and insect proof terminal is attached to the outside. On the inside is a terminal which incorporates an adjustable damper.

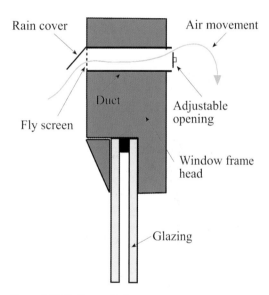

Figure 6.11. Trickle ventilator.

The damper allows adjustment of the unit to provide the correct level of infiltration through the device. Sometimes this damper is automatic. For example it could be a flap within the duct which is normally in the fully open position. As wind speed increases air movement through the duct increases. This rapid air movement would cause draughts and excessive heat loss but the air movement lifts the damper which partially close the duct, restricting the air movement. When the wind speed drops the damper falls back to the open position. Table 6.2 shows the recommended open area of trickle ventilator for various locations. In commercial buildings it is recommended to have 400mm² of openable area for each square metre of floor area[4].

	Ventilation requirements		
	window	trickle (mm²)	extract (l/s)
Kitchen	opening	4000	60
Habitable room	5% floor	8000	-
Bathroom	opening	4000	30
Toilet	5% floor	4000	6

Table 6.2. Ventilation requirements for various rooms.

Openable windows are used on occasions when trickle ventilation is inadequate. Examples of this are in summer when the room is warm and ventilation is required to remove heat. A second example is when odours such as cooking smells or paint fumes have entered a room and require clearance. The Building Regulations requirement is for an openable window area of at least 5% of the floor area for habitable rooms and the toilet. Kitchens and bathrooms have no minimum openable window size as the window ventilation is backed up by mechanical extract. Windows should be closed when the ventilation problem has cleared.

Extract fans are used where the source of moisture or odours is known, such as in kitchens, toilets and bathrooms. Fans consume electricity and remove heated air, so they should only be operated when moisture or odours require removal. Activation of the fan may be manual by switch, or automatic by linking to the bathroom light switch. Switching off the fan can again be manual, requiring the occupant to remember to switch the fan off, or it can be timed so that the fan runs on for a sufficient period of time to clear the residual moisture and odours. Another method is to use sensors, such as humidity sensors, that detect the moisture content of the bathroom air. When the moisture content rises the fan switches on. When the moisture content returns to normal the fan switches off. Table 6.2 lists the extract

rates specified for domestic buildings in the Building Regulations. Note, the kitchen extract rate can be reduced to 30 litres per second if an extractor hood is fitted as close as practically possible over the hob.

In well heated, well managed, dwellings controlled use of fans for moisture clearance is the most energy efficient method[5]. In less well heated homes passive stack ventilation (PSV) can be used (Figure 6.12). This is a continuous background ventilation system comprising a vertical duct running between the room requiring ventilation and the outside. The duct terminal should terminate at or above the apex of the roof to avoid wind induced down draughts. Air is extracted from the room by natural buoyancy up the stack. Recommended duct sizes are; kitchen 125mm, bathroom 100mm and toilet 80mm[6].

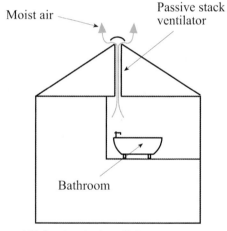

Figure 6.12. Passive stack ventilator.

In winter the temperature difference between inside and outside the building is at its greatest and so buoyancy in the stack will be increased. At this time a damper may be required in the stack to limit air movement. The use of a PSV removes the need for extract fans that typically consume electricity at a rate of 90 watts when extracting at 60 litres per seconds and 35W at 30 litres per second. However, it must be remembered that so long as the temperature is higher inside the building than outside, warm air will be lost from the building via the PSV.

Heat loss requirements

A domestic buildings can achieve compliance with the energy conservation aspects of the Building Regulations by the incorporation of 'robust details' that are known to reduce a building's air permeability. One example of this is the use of joist hangers attached to the inner surface of the blockwork leaf of a cavity wall instead of running joists though the blockwork wall into the cavity. Air-tightness testing is mandatory unless the development is a small number of new dwellings or is the same as a similar dwelling by the same builder that has been tested recently. The limit value is for the air permeability to be less than $10m^3/h/m^2$. Lower values than this may need to be achieved at the target emissions rate. If testing is not carried out an air permeability of $15m^3/h/m^2$ must be input to the SAP calculation. The effect of this would be a need to signinficantly improve other elements. ☙

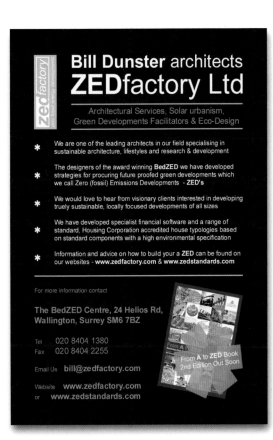
Ventilation

Ventilation of buildings can be carried out in two ways. **Mechanical ventilation** using powered equipment is very controllable but can consume vast amounts of energy. Mechanical ventilation can also be combined with heating and cooling measures but these are discussed in Chapters 8 and 9. The other and more ecologically acceptable method is **passive ventilation,** which relies on wind, pressure differential, or the natural convection of warm and cool air currents to achieve the desired goal. Like mechanical ventilation, passive ventilation can be combined with natural/passive heating methods, such as sun spaces or natural/passive cooling methods, such as earth pipes or hollow concrete floors to help warm or cool down buildings.

Mechanical ventilation

Mechanical ventilation involves the use of electrically driven fans to move air. The use of fans means that the amount of air delivered to, or removed from, a space can be closely controlled. The energy consumption of a mechanical ventilation system arises due to;

*   the electricity consumed by the fans. This depends on the efficiency of the electric motor, type of fan and the design of the air movement system as a whole
*   the heat lost from the building in the extract air. In some circumstances a proportion of this heat can be recovered using air to air heat recovery devices.

Fan energy consumption

The electricity used by fans is a substantial proportion of the total energy consumed in a mechanically ventilated and air conditioned building. This is illustrated in Figure 6.13 which shows the breakdown in energy consumption of a best practice air conditioned building. It can be seen that fans, pumps and controls together consume 17% of the total energy, equivalent to that used for lighting and over twice as much as that used in refrigeration.

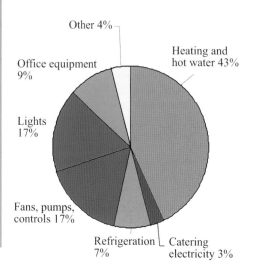

Figure 6.13. Breakdown of the energy consumption of a good practice air conditioned office.

and low loss windings which have an efficiency of 85%.

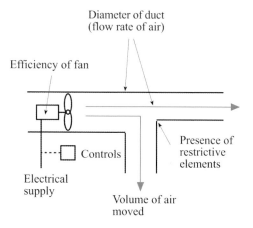

Figure 6.14. Factors involved in ventilation system energy consumption.

A fan consumes electrical energy in order to move air from one location to another. To do this the fan must be sufficiently powerful to overcome the resistance that the ductwork system offers to the flow of air. Figure 6.14 illustrates some of the elements that are involved in determining how much energy is consumed in a ventilation system. They are:

The type of impeller. The type of impeller has important implications for system efficiency. The most efficient types are backward curved centrifugal fans, followed by aerofoil section propeller bladed fans. Uniform cross section propeller fans are the least efficient.

The efficiency of the motor. The electric motor in a fan is a machine for converting electricity to rotational movement. Unfortunately, some of the electrical energy is converted to heat by friction in the bearings, magnetic induction in the metal and resistance in the windings of the motor. As a result the motor is not 100% efficient at doing its task. The waste, appearing as heat, may also need to be removed by an air conditioning system so adding to the cooling load. The efficiency of a typical 3kW motor is 81%. More expensive but higher efficiency motors are available with improved bearings

Speed of the fan. The greater the volume of air required to be moved, the faster the fan must rotate. Increased speed increases the electrical consumption of the fan and vice versa. Maximum volumes of air are not always required by spaces. For example, a lecture theatre may require maximum volumes when fully occupied but require less fresh air when there are fewer people in the audience. An air quality sensor can be used to detect the level of occupancy based on carbon dioxide (CO_2) concentrations breathed out by the occupants. When fully occupied the concentration of CO_2 will be high, When unoccupied the CO_2 concentration will be low. A controller can use this information to instruct a variable speed drive to adjust the speed of the fan to deliver the required volume of air to reduce CO_2 levels to normal.

Larger section ducting allows air speeds to be reduced from typical values of 4 to 10m/s to 1 to 2m/s. This is because the larger cross sectional area encloses a larger volume of air for each metre of air movement. Finally, consideration should be given to separating the heating and cooling process from the ventilation process. Air has a low energy carrying capacity and so much larger volumes are needed to heat or cool a room than is needed for ventilation only. The energy consumed by a combined heating/cooling and ventilation system is much more than a ventilation only system due to the smaller volumes of air required. When a ventilation only system is being used, heating or cooling can be provided by room based heating/cooling units.

System resistance. The fan can only move air if it can generate a sufficiently large pressure differential to overcome the resistance to air movement caused by friction in the system. The least friction is offered by straight lengths of smooth ducting. Other components offer additional resistance as illustrated in Table 6.3. The resistance factors shown relate to the resistance to airflow created by a straight 1m length of ducting. To reduce system resistance ducting should be; as short as possible, as straight as possible (where bends are used they should be gradual rather than abrupt), and the number of components used should be kept to a minimum. Finally, the system should be maintained regularly, for example removing dust build up and replacing blocked air filters.

Component	Resistance factor
90° bend (round)	0.65
90° bend (square)	1.25
Branch	0.90
Abrupt reducer	0.30
Smooth reducer	0.04
Open damper	0.30
Diffuser	0.60

Table 6.3. Resistance factors (relative to 1m of duct) of some common ductwork components.

Controls. The use of fans should be restricted to times when ventilation is needed. Various control systems are available that can achieve this aim. At its simplest this may involve a time switch that only allows the fan to operate during the hours of building occupancy. Better systems also monitor the requirement for ventilation. So if the ventilation is to remove moisture, provide ventilation for people or remove heat then relative humidity, air quality or temperature sensors should be used respectively. These

sensors provide the information for a controller to switch off the fan when acceptable air quality conditions have been achieved.

System power consumption

The method of specifying system power consumption uses the value of specific fan power, measured in W/l/s. This is the rate of energy consumption by the fan (W) divided by the rate of air flow in litres per second l/s. Table 6.4 lists values of specific fan powers against the system efficiency they represent. High efficiency systems should aim for specific fan powers less than 1.5 W/l/s with a best practice goal of 1.0 W/l/s.

System efficiency	Specific fan power (W/l/s)
High	<1.5
Medium	1.5 to 4.0
Low	>4.0

Table 6.4. Efficiency rating of specific fan powers.

Displacement ventilation

Displacement ventilation is a method of ventilating a space that incorporates many of the low energy features described previously. The energy savings arise from the fact that air is input to the room at a very slow speed, considerably reducing fan energy consumption in comparison to traditional high level ventilation systems (Figure 6.15).

With this system air is input to the room at very low velocity using raised floor terminals or low level wall terminals. The incoming air is usually tempered down to 18°C, which is a relatively high temperature when compared to all air cooling systems. The low airspeed and high temperature are necessary to avoid discomfort since the air is input directly into the occupied zone.

The supply air is cooler than the existing room air and so it pools in a layer along the floor. The presence of any sources of heat such as occupant's bodies, office electronic equipment or pools of sunlight on the office floor will heat this pool of air causing an upward convection current to develop at the site of the source of heat. As a result, fresh cool air is automatically brought to the heat source. Heat sources usually coincide with a source of pollution. Occupants, for example, give out heat, metabolic CO_2 and odours. The rising warm stale air from these sources is extracted at high level.

Because of the relatively high input, air temperature displacement ventilation cannot satisfy very high cooling loads and so it is often used in conjunction with a chilled ceiling or chilled beam cooling system (see Chapter 10).

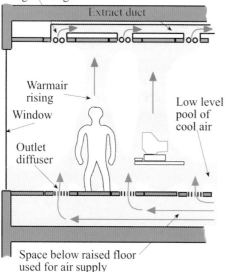

Figure 6.15. Displacement ventilation and chilled ceiling system.

Heat recovery systems

When air is extracted from a building it is carrying energy with it either in the form of heat or coolth. If possible some of this energy should be recovered and used to pre-heat or pre-cool the fresh incoming air. The way in which this is achieved depends upon the type of mechanical ventilation system being utilised. The three main types of mechanical ventilation system are;

Supply ventilation. Here a fan is used to supply air to a space. Air is lost from the space via cracks and gaps in the building envelope. This system does not allow heat recovery.

Extract ventilation. Here a fan is sited close to a source of pollution. The fan removes polluted air from the building. Supply air enters the building through cracks and gaps in the envelope. This system does not allow heat recovery.

Balanced ventilation. This system uses two fans. One to supply air to the space and one to extract air from it. This system can allow heat recovery to take place.

Domestic heat recovery systems

When ventilating single rooms, such as a kitchen, a small through the wall ventilation with heat recovery unit can be used (Figure 6.16).

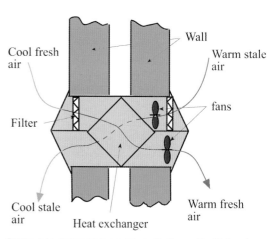

Figure 6.16. Through the wall ventilation unit with heat recovery.

The unit has two fans and two sets of ducting making it a small balanced ventilation system rather than an extract ventilation system. The fans cause incoming cool fresh air and out going warm stale air to pass through an air to air plate heat exchanger. The two air flows are separated by the thin metal or plastic sheets that make up the heat exchanger (Figure 6.17).

The temperature difference between the warm exhaust air and the cool supply air causes heat to flow to the incoming air stream raising its temperature. Figure 6.18 shows the heat recovery efficiency of the unit against rate of air flow. As the extraction rate increases, the efficiency falls off. This is because the air moves through the unit much quicker and so there is less time for heat exchange to take place.

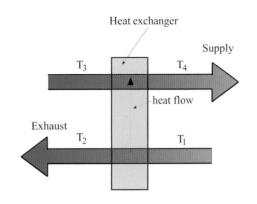

$$TE = \frac{T_4 - T_3}{T_1 - T_3} \times 100$$

Where;

T_1 = extract inlet temperature to heat exchanger (°C)
T_2 = extract leaving temperature (°C)
T_3 = supply inlet temperature to heat exchanger (°C)
T_4 = supply leaving temperature (°C)

Figure 6.19. Temperature efficiency parameters.

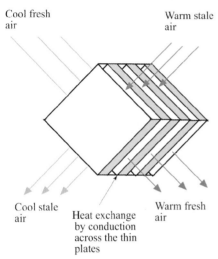

Figure 6.17. Air to air plate heat exchanger.

Whole house ventilation with heat recovery

In highly sealed domestic buildings all rooms will require ventilation to provide good air quality. To supply this a whole house mechanical ventilation with heat recovery (MVHR) unit can be used. Such a system is shown in Figure 6.20.

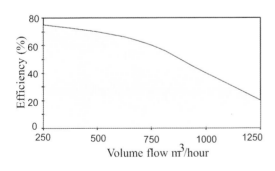

Figure 6.18. Graph of efficiency against extract rate for an air to air plate heat exchanger.

Temperature efficiency

The efficiency of air to air heat exchangers is usually expressed as a temperature efficiency. Figure 6.19 shows the parameters used in calculating the temperature efficiency (*TE*)

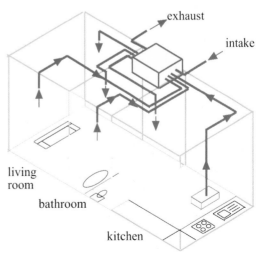

Figure 6.20. Whole house mechanical ventilation with heat recovery (MVHR).

The heat recovery unit is shown installed in the loft space. However, an alternative location is within a cupboard above the cooker extract hood (Figure 6.21). Heat recovery is carried out using an air to air plate heat exchanger as described previously.

The MVHR system can only operate effectively if the house is well sealed [7]. In this way heat is recovered from all of the extracted air. If the house were leaky then air could enter and leave the building without passing through the heat exchanger.

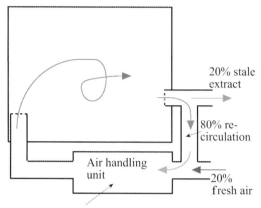

Figure 6.22. Recirculation of conditioned air.

In some rooms, such as in a public house where smoking is taking place, the air quality is always poor and so 100% fresh air should be used. In this circumstance air to air heat recovery should be employed.

Plate heat exchangers

Air to air plate heat exchangers, as described in the previous section, for housing are also used for commercial heat recovery. Their location in an air conditioning system is shown in Figure 6.23.

Figure 6.21. Heat recovery unit showing installation and finished appearance. Crown copyright.

Non domestic heat recovery systems

When ventilation is combined with air conditioning, the simplest form of heat recovery is to recycle a large proportion of the extracted air, say 80%, back in to the room (Figure 6.22). In this way 80% of the energy in the air extracted from the room is recovered. A small proportion of fresh air, 20%, is added to the recirculated air to maintain air quality. When the air quality is poor, contaminated with either odours or moisture, then 100% exhaust and 100% fresh air should be used. An indoor air quality sensor can be used to determine the proportion of recirculated air, varying from 80% to 0% as the room air quality changes from good to bad respectively.

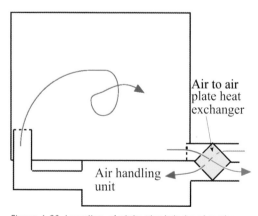

Figure 6.23. Location of air to air plate heat exchanger.

Plate heat exchangers have a number of advantageous features;
- they have no moving parts that require maintenance

- they keep the extract and supply air streams separate so that no cross contamination can occur
- no energy is required for their operation, though fan power will need to be increased to overcome air resistance through the unit.

Thermal wheels

Thermal wheels (efficiency 85%) are composed of a circular matrix of tubes through which air can flow (Figure 6.24). The wheel is positioned across the inlet and exhaust ducting so that supply air passes through the upper half of the wheel and exhaust air passes through the lower half. As the exhaust air passes through the wheel the matrix is warmed. The wheel rotates slowly bringing this heated section into the path of the incoming air stream. The incoming air stream is heated by contact with the warmed thermal wheel matrix.

The thermal wheel requires an electric motor to rotate it and so the energy consumption of this needs to be considered in assessing the heat recovery efficiency. Thermal wheels should not be used in areas where cross contamination of air flows would be a problem such as hospital operating theatres. This is because it is not possible to fully isolate the exhaust air from the supply air.

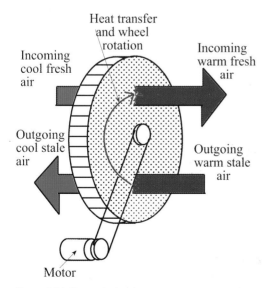

Figure 6.24. Thermal wheel.

Run around coils

Run around coils (efficiency 55%) are heat recovery devices that can be used when supply and exhaust ducts are not run alongside each other. A finned coil is situated in the path of the exhaust air (Figure 6.25). Air passing through the coil heats up a water and antifreeze mixture circulating in the pipe work. A pump circulates this heated solution to a similar coil installed in the supply duct. The supply air becomes heated by passing through this second coil. Topping up, electrical consumption and maintenance of the system will need to be considered in the economic analysis of this device.

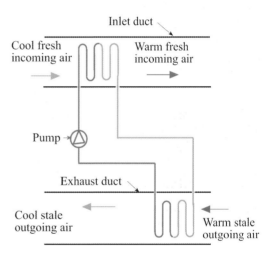

Figure 6.25. Run around coil.

Heat pumps

Heat pumps are similar to run around coils in that they can exchange heat between ducts that are separated by distance. They differ from run around coils in that they are filled with a refrigerant which evaporates in the coil situated in the exhaust duct. As the refrigerant evaporates, it absorbs heat. The refrigerant vapour then flows to the coil in the supply duct where it condenses and in doing so releases the heat it previously absorbed. The pipe work is fitted with a compressor and pressure reducing valve that enable movement of the refrigerant, and the evaporation and condensation of the refrigerant to take place.

Bypassing the heat exchanger

In summer it is desirable to cool a building by bringing in fresh cool ventilation air. This is known as free cooling. However, if this ventilation air has to pass over a heat recovery device it will be pre-heated before entering the building. It is necessary at times therefore, for incoming air to be able to by-pass the heat recovery unit. This requires some extra ducting and dampers to re-route the airstream. An additional benefit to by-passing the heat exchanger is the fact that it avoids the pressure drop in the system caused by the heat recovery unit. The pressure drop, for example, in a run around coil is approximately 60Pa, through a thermal wheel it is 120Pa. A pressure sensor and variable speed control unit are required for the system to detect that the heat exchanger has been by passed and to reduce the speed of the fan.

Economics of heat recovery

Heat recovery devices represent a capital cost that must be recovered in the value of energy savings made. For heat recovery devices to be economical;
- the capital and installation costs should be low
- the running costs should be low
- the amount and therefore value of energy recovered should be high.

There are a number of factors that affect the size of costs and savings;

Initial costs involve the capital and installation costs of the heat recovery device. However, some of this may be offset by savings arising from reductions in the size of boiler or cooling plant, made possible by the availability of recovered energy.

Running costs involve a debit in terms of electricity used by fans, pumps and motors and also maintenance costs. The credit is in the value of recovered energy. Running costs and credits are strongly dependent on the hours run by the system and availability of energy for recovery, and the efficiency with which it is recovered. For example, cost effectiveness will be greatest

in winter when differences between inside and outside temperatures are at their largest. Similarly the cumulative value of energy savings will increase in buildings where the ventilation system runs for a large number of hours each day.

Natural ventilation in commercial buildings

Since the operation of fans consumes energy it is desirable to avoid their use whenever possible. This is difficult in buildings with deep floor plans, as more of the floor space will be away from the perimeter where natural ventilation is available. One of the ways of reducing the need for mechanical ventilation is to keep floor plans narrow as described previously under *'Utilising natural energy'* in Chapter 4. Single sided natural ventilation, which arises due to wind turbulence, is illustrated in Figure 6.26.

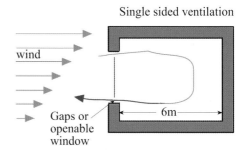

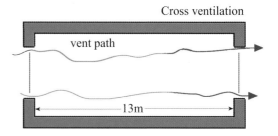

Figure 6.26. Single sided and cross ventilation.

The rule of thumb for single sided ventilation is that it is available up to a depth of 6m from the facade. Cross ventilation (Figure 6.26) is driven by pressure differences across the building due to the wind. The rule of thumb for cross ventilation is that it is effective across a plan depth of 13m. This is assuming there are no partitions across the space which would close the ventilation pathway. With both single sided and cross ventilation it is desirable to have high level ventilation openings as these can clear pollutants without the air stream impinging on the occupants and creating draughts.

A number of designers are achieving deeper floor plans than described above by providing ventilation stacks within the building. An internal stack shortens the distance over which the air must travel to reach an escape point, so cutting down on the resistance to movement. The stacks may be purpose built vertical ducts or an internal atrium. A good example of a duct/light-well system is the passively ventilated library at Coventry University [8]. This building has a 50m square plan shape. Air enters each floor via four corner lightwells. It is then drawn to either perimeter ventilation stacks or a central lightwell/ventilation stack. This creates a radial air distribution pattern which gives good air distribution across the space, see Figure 6.27.

Passive ventilation and cooling

Since comfort cooling was developed early in the last century, sealed and air conditioned office buildings have been seen by property consultants as the most sought after and there-fore easiest to let. However, the energy used for air conditioning and the damage caused to the ozone layer by leaking refrigerants, has seen a shift towards naturally ventilated and cooled buildings (see Chapter 9).

A central component of such strategies is the presence of ventilation openings such as openable windows. One barrier to the adoption of passive ventilation strategies is the presence of external air and noise pollution. A window that lets in noise and air pollution alongside the ventilation air will not be opened. As a result, designers of passive ventilation systems should ensure the site is not alongside sources of envi-ronmental pollution, such as factories or major roads. If the site is affected by these problems

then adjustment of the orientation and location of the building on the site is needed to place openings away from sources of pollution.

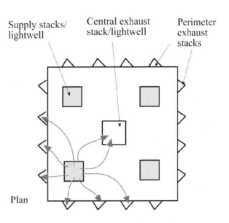

Supply stacks/lightwell   Central exhaust stack/lightwell   Perimeter exhaust stacks

Plan

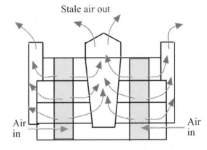

Stale air out

Air in   Air in

Schematic section

Figure 6.27. Stack ventilation at Coventry University library.

Natural ventilation is driven by the wind and stack effects, exposing the building to the wind by avoiding obstructions, such as trees, will encourage single sided and cross ventila-tion as long as the plan depth is kept small. The building should be well sealed so that the natural ventilation can be used when wanted by opening and closing purpose built ventila-tion openings, such as windows. Some building designs encourage the wind to pass over the building. Increased windspeed results in lower atmospheric pressures. Hence if the increased windspeed occurs over a ventilation flue, situated at the core of the building, then air will be drawn out of the centre of building. This would allow ventilation of deeper plan buildings than is possible with cross ventilation.

Passive cooling

Just as we try to raise external temperatures to reduce space heating energy consumption, depression of external temperatures will reduce cooling energy consumption. The two strands to this strategy involve shading external spaces from the influence of the sun and the introduction of evaporative cooling. Both of these functions can be provided by trees. Leaves on trees require sunlight to function and so have evolved to intercept the sun. This shades the spaces below. The movement of nutrients from root to branch occurs as a result of evaporation of water from the leaves. For water to evaporate it must absorb latent energy. In doing so it cools the air surrounding it.

Fountains and water features can also reduce ambient temperatures through evaporation. They also add an important psychological element with occupants feeling cooler in the presence of water features.

Modelling airflow and ventilation

As buildings become more complex, rules of thumb on aspects such as the effective distance of cross and single sided ventilation become less reliable. Large buildings are very expensive and house many occupants, so it is important that the theoretical airflows considered at the design stage are achieved in practice when the building is constructed. This aim is assisted using modelling techniques. Two methods are available; physical modelling and computer modelling. In the physical technique a scale model of a building or room in which airflow is important, is placed into a tank of saline solution. The saline represents the air. Wind can be modelled by causing the saline to flow using pumps.

Heat sources can be modelled using small heating elements placed at appropriate points in the model. When turned on these heaters cause a reduction in the density of the saline, making it rise and a convection current forms.

The saline (air) movement can then be visualised by placing a small amount of dye into the tank.

The computer modelling method uses a technique called computational fluid dynamics (CFD). In this a CAD model of the building or space is created. The volume within this is divided up mathematically into small elements which are assigned values of temperature, density and direction and speed of movement. The computer software then determines where these elements will flow to given the current dynamic situation. For example, warm air will rise and cool air will fall until the relative temperature between the element and its surrounding elements equalises. Using this technique it is possible to visualise, on a computer screen, where the air will flow in a complex space and with complex heat sources, including solar gains. The flow of each parcel of air is usually indicated graphically by an arrow the direction of which indicates the direction of airflow.

Computational fluid dynamics software requires specialist training. However, it is the prime method for modelling airflow in buildings. These techniques are useful for modelling ventilation airflow, movement of pollutants, such as smoke in a fire and also the effectiveness of passive cooling strategies based on the buoyancy of warm air. ❧

References for Chapter 6

1. CIBSE Technical Memorandum TM23 Testing Buildings for Air Leakage. CIBSE Publications 2000

2. Bordass, W. Envelope Airtightness. The Architects Journal. pp 48-51 13th April 2000.

3. The Building Regulations Part F: Ventilation HMSO 2006

4. Building Research Establishment. Digest 399: Natural Ventilation in Non-domestic Buildings. HMSO October 1994.

5. Wolliscroft, M. The Passive Approach Does it Stack Up? Building services, pp 28 -30. September 1994.

6. Building Research Establishment Information Paper 13/94. Passive Stack Ventilation. HMSO 1994

7. Stephen, R K. Domestic Mechanical Ventilation: Guidelines for Designers and Installers. BRE IP/18/88. HMSO 1988.

8. Field, J.Building Analysis: Coventry University Library. Building Services Journal pp18-22. December 2000.

Further reading

Good Practice Case Study 10: Llanerchydol Park, Welshpool. January 1990

General Information Leaflet 9: Domestic Ventilation. February 1993

Good Practice Guide 224: Improving Air Tightness in Existing Homes. 1994

Figure 6.28 and 6.29. Views of the famous cowls atop the BedZED project that are part of the heat extract and ventilation systems for the homes

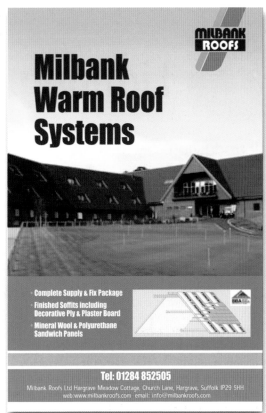
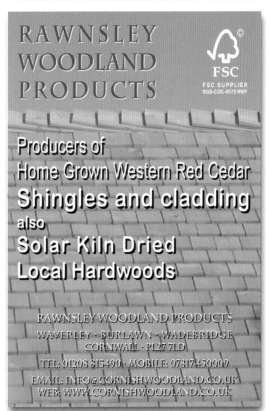

7 Lighting

Note: within this chapter daylighting is sometimes referred to as natural lighting and artificial lighting is also occasionally refered to as electric lighting.

Introduction

Before discussing lighting methods we will discuss some of the terminology used in natural and artificial lighting studies.

Luminous intensity (I) is the power of a light source when viewed from a particular direction. It is measured in units of candela (cd). This is a modern unit but is named after the old practice of comparing the luminous intensity of light sources against a standard candle.

Luminance (L) is a measure of the luminous intensity of light emitted or reflected in a given direction, divided by the area of the surface. Luminance is therefore measured in candela per square metre cd/m². It can be considered to be the brightness of a surface, although strictly speaking brightness is the human appreciation of the luminous intensity. There are two types of luminous surfaces. The first are self luminant surfaces, such as the sun and light bulbs. The second are surfaces that reflect light and therefore appear to be light sources themselves. Room surfaces do this, as does the moon which appears lit but is in fact reflecting sunlight from the sun on the other side of the earth.

The luminance of self luminant surfaces depends on the power of the light source, i.e. its ability to emit light and its surface area. So, for example, if the power is a fixed light source, a small surface area would appear brighter than a larger surface area with the same power. For example if a light bulb and a fluorescent tube had the same power, the tungsten bulb would appear brighter than the fluorescent tube because its light emitting power is concentrated into a smaller surface area.

The luminance of reflective surfaces depends on how much light is falling on the surface (see '*Illuminance*'), and how much of this is then reflected back into the observers eye. This latter factor depends on the reflect-ance of the surface. A perfectly reflecting surface would have a reflectance of 100%. A surface which absorbed all of the light falling on it would have a reflectance of 0%. Table 7.1 shows the reflectances of various surfaces. The two physical aspects of the surface that affect its reflectance are surface colour and texture. The reflectance of white painted plaster is greater than that of white painted concrete. This is because, for a given colour, the more coarse its texture the lower the reflectance. The reflectance of raw concrete is lower than that of white painted concrete. Here the texture is the same but the raw concrete has a darker surface and therefore absorbs more light.

Surface	Reflectance (%)
Raw concrete (grey)	40
White painted concrete	60
White painted plaster	80
Brown carpet	10
Light plywood	35
Brick	30
Gloss white paint	85

Table 7.1. Reflectances of various surfaces.

With a given amount of light falling on the surface, the higher the reflectance, then the higher the luminance of the surface.

Illuminance (E) is a term which describes how much light energy is falling onto a surface. The amount of light energy flowing through a particular volume of space is called the luminous flux (F) measured in lumen (lm). If this flux falls on an area (A) m², then the illuminance, E will be;

$$E = F/A \quad (lux)$$

Illuminance is the value given in lighting design guides to recommend the amount of light needed so that tasks can be carried out efficiently, safely and in comfort. Table 7.2 lists some recommended values of illuminance for various tasks. Generally the more complex the task, the more light that is needed and so a greater illuminance is required. When lighting is provided by an array of electric lights the illuminance will vary across the working plane. There will be a peak illuminance directly beneath the luminaires and a minimum in between the rows of luminaires.

Illuminance uniformity is a term based on the ratio between minimum and average illuminance that is used to describe the variation of illuminance across the working plane. Maintained illuminance is the minimum acceptable illuminance for a given task. This will be reached because the light output of lamps diminishes with age. At this stage the tubes must be replaced to raise the illuminance above the maintained illuminance level.

Task	Recommended illuminance (lux)
Circulation (stairs)	150
Classroom desk	300
Office desk	500
Laboratory bench	500
Electronics assembly	1000
Operating theatre	2000

Table 7.2. Recommended Illuminances for various spaces.

Colour rendering

The ability to see individual colours on an object depends on the spectral output of the light source. This is because in order to see a particular colour on a surface, that colour of light must be present in the light hitting the surface. Good colour rendering is illustrated in Figure 7.1. Good quality light such as daylight or a full spectrum electric light source is used to illuminate a blue surface. Blue wavelength light is reflected from the surface and enters the eye hence the surface appears blue. The other wavelengths are absorbed. Since the illuminating source contains all wavelengths, this light would allow the colour of all surfaces to be distinguished. However, Figure 7.2 illustrates a case of poor colour rendering. The surface is

illuminated by a tungsten bulb, which is strong in light output towards the red part of the spectrum but poor in light output in the blue part of the spectrum. Since there is little blue light to be reflected, the surface appears black. It is for this reason that it is difficult to distinguish between navy blue and black garments under tungsten lighting.

Surfaces that are white under full spectrum light appear to have a yellow tint under tungsten light, as they are reflecting the wavelengths that are hitting the surface. The human eye sees this as a 'warm' white light. The effect is exaggerated when taking photographs indoors without a flash. The photographs, when developed, have a strong yellow tint. The ability of different sources of light to reveal the colour of surfaces is specified using the colour rendering index (Ra). A value above 80 is good and above 100 excellent. In spaces where colour rendering is important, such as graphic design studios, lamps should be chosen with a colour rendering index above 90. ☙

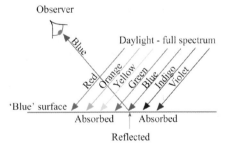

Figure 7.1. Full spectrum light source gives good colour rendering.

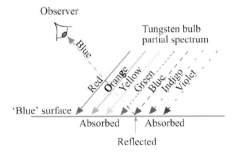

Figure 7.2. Limited spectrum light source gives poor colour rendering.

Daylighting

Daylight is the preferred form of illumination in buildings. The human eye has evolved using it, and its full spectrum output means it delivers the best colour rendering properties of any light source. It also gives building occupants contact with the outside world. Weather variations, and the passage of the day, are revealed in changing patterns of daylight. Of most importance to low energy design is the fact that, unlike electric lighting, daylight does not require electricity to create it. However, daylight is not entirely free. It is provided through glazing systems which are thermally poor and so there is a cost in terms of additional space heating energy consumption. This energy consumption is not solely due to the provision of daylighting but is also shared by the other functions of windows which are the provision of views and ventilation.

Daylight can only reduce the building's energy consumption if electric lighting is turned down or switched off in response to daylight entry.

An effective daylight strategy therefore requires;
● fenestration, plan shape, internal finishes and partition layout designed for optimum daylight entry and distribution
● reduction of heat losses through the glazed areas
● avoidance of glare
● avoidance of unwanted solar gains
● design and control of electric lighting in response to available daylight (see 'Artificial lighting' later in this chapter).

The potential for energy savings from daylight are large. Figure 7.3 shows that electric lighting accounts for 20% of the energy consumption of a typical naturally ventilated office.

Table 7.3 shows the percentage of the total energy consumed by lighting in a range of building types. It also shows estimated potential

savings arising from the adoption of a daylighting strategy[1].

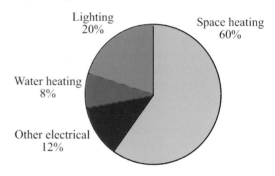

Figure 7.3. Breakdown of naturally ventilated office energy consumption.

Building Type	Proportion of total primary energy used for lighting (%)	Estimated saving from the uptake of a daylight strategy (%)
Multi residential	45	small
Offices	30-50	20-40
Shops	90	small
Education	22	10-30
Health	20-30	10-20
Factories	15	10-20

Table 7.3. Energy consumption by electric lighting and potential savings from daylighting.

The greatest savings in energy occur when;
● the electric lighting system has been wired into zones that can be controlled separately in response to daylight availability
● where there is a well motivated workforce or central control system switching off lights in response to daylight entry
● in spaces where illumination with daylight is preferable to artificial illumination.

Table 7.2 shows that the greatest potential for savings from daylight is in offices. This is because daylight is valued and wiring and control systems can be installed to make use of it. In shops the potential saving from daylight is small. This is because traders value electric lighting as a means of displaying goods to their best advantage. Multi residential buildings have a small savings potential, since each room is under individual occupant control.

Here we will look at how these savings can be realised, beginning with a study of how daylight enters a building. This knowledge will enable us to optimise certain elements, such as glazing and internal finishes, to improve daylight entry. We will then investigate the problems associated with daylighting including poor distribution in rooms, heat losses, glare and summertime overheating.

The properties of daylight

The sun is a large nuclear fusion reactor. Hydrogen and deuterium combine within the sun's outer layers to produce helium and large quantities of energy. This energy is radiated away from the sun as electromagnetic (EM) radiation. Electromagnetic radiation is emitted as a waveform. The EM radiation from the sun has many wavelengths, making up a range or spectrum of values. Each different waveband has different properties (Figure 7.4). The shorter the wavelength the more energy is contained within the radiation. The very short and therefore most energetic wavebands are cosmic rays, x- rays and gamma rays. The next group is the ultraviolet (UV) radiation.

Daylight is the band of wavelengths between 400 and 760nm that are visible to the eye. This band can be sub divided into individual wavelengths which the eye detects and the brain interprets as different colours. All of these wavelengths combined to give white light. It is this mixed light which makes up daylight. The actual spectral distribution in daylight varies, depending on weather conditions and time of day. An extreme example is the dominance of red wavelengths late in the day as the sun sets. Daylight consists of two components, sunlight and skylight.

Sunlight is light from the sun that passes through a clear sky. It is directional, which means it can create distinct pools of bright light within rooms, and causes objects to cast shadows. It also carries with it a large amount of infra red radiation (heat). This can be useful

in winter for solar heat gains, or problematic in summer by causing overheating. Overheating is a particular concern in commercial buildings as they already suffer from heat gains given out by equipment and high occupant densities. Where sunlight can enter a room, some form of adjustable sun screening is usually required so that glare and energy deposition can be controlled.

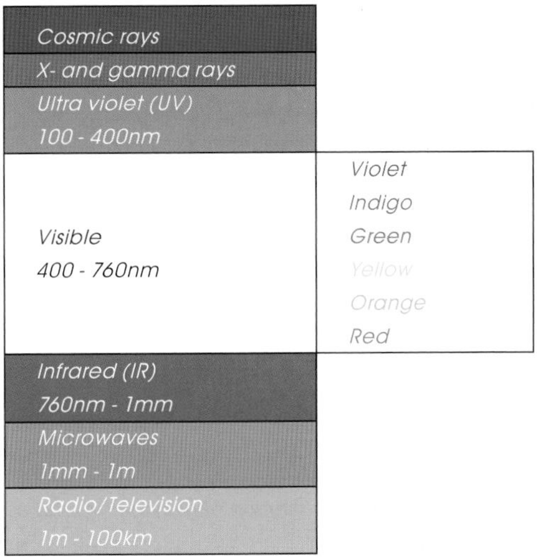

Figure 7.4. The electromagnetic spectrum.

Skylight is sunlight which has been scattered and diffused by moisture and particulates in the atmosphere. The more heavily overcast the sky the more scattered and therefore less directional the light is. Skylight provides less light and much less heat than sunlight. Even so, the amount of light provided by even a heavily overcast sky would easily satisfy most visual requirements if it were able to enter a building.

Standard sky models

The quantity of daylight is very variable depending on the time of day, atmospheric pollution and weather conditions. To help in daylighting design, a number of fixed standard sky models have been proposed so that people working on daylight designs can do so to a common standard.

Clear blue sky. This sky model is used for sunlighting design. As the name implies it is for summers in the UK or countries with hot climates where sunlight predominates. In the UK, daylighting design is carried out using overcast sky models, as this is the most common situation encountered here.

Uniform overcast sky. This sky model represents a heavily overcast sky. It is considered to have uniform luminance. That is to say it is equally bright, regardless of which direction you look in. It can be described graphically as a band whose uniform thickness represents the constant luminance in all directions (Figure 7.5). Uniform overcast skies are not often used for design purposes.

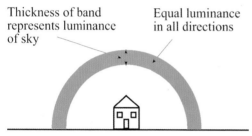

Figure 7.5. Luminance distribution of a uniform overcast sky.

Commission International de Eclarage (CIE) standard overcast sky. This sky model is intended to represent the variation in brightness of a less overcast sky than the uniform overcast sky. It has a defined luminance distribution that is considered to be three times brighter when looking directly overhead than when looking at the horizon. There is a gradual variation between minimum and maximum luminances as the angle of view increases from the horizon to the zenith (Figure 7.6). This sky model is the one that is used most frequently for UK daylighting design.

The illuminance provided by a sky varies depending on how overcast it is and the time of day. For design purposes it is assumed that standard overcast skies produce an illuminance of 5000 lux on the ground. This is a conservative figure since there is usually more daylight than this and so 5000 lux is exceeded for 85% of the working day (09.00 - 17.00 hours) by the actual sky throughout the year.

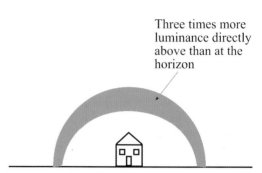

Three times more luminance directly above than at the horizon

Figure 7.6. Luminance distribution of a CIE sky.

The luminance distribution of these standard skies are built into various daylighting design methods which are described in more detail later.

Daylight factors

Because of the variability of daylight it is difficult to be specific about absolute quantities entering a room. Instead the amount of daylight at a particular point in a room is described by the daylight factor. The daylight factor is the proportion of the unobstructed external daylight illuminance that reaches a point inside the room. If the building were to be removed, the point of interest would receive all of the available daylight and so the daylight factor would be 100%. If the room had no windows the daylight factor would be 0%. The amount of daylight entering a typical domestic room is small and so the typical average daylight factor across a room can be as low as 3%. The daylight factor at any point in the room remains the same on both bright and dull days, even though the illuminance provided by natural light will be greater on a bright day than a dull day. An average daylight factor of 2% is needed across a room for it to appear well daylit[2]. The daylight factor at a particular point in a room can be determined from the formula;

$$DF = E_i / E_o \times 100\ (\%)$$

Where
DF = daylight factor (%)
E_i = illuminance at the reference point (lux)
E_o = external Illuminance (lux)

For example, if the external illuminance E_o

due to a standard overcast sky is 5000 lux and the average illuminance on a work surface near a window was 300 lux, then the average daylight factor over the surface would be;

$$DF = 300/5000 \times 100 = 6\%$$

Points of similar daylight factor within a room can be joined together to give a contour map of daylight distribution as shown in Figure 7.7. Measurements are usually taken at a certain level above the floor within the room, called the working plane height. This height is that at which the important visual task is taking place. It could be floor level in the case of circulation routes but in workplaces it is an imaginary plane passing through the top surface of the desks - typically 0.85m above the floor.

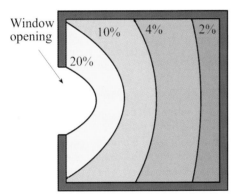

Figure 7.7. Plan of a room at working plane height showing daylight factor contours.

Figures 7.7 and 7.8 show the daylight factor contours on a plan and section of a domestic living room. It can be seen that the daylight factor is relatively high near the windows but this rapidly falls off towards the back of the room. This reduction in daylight, with distance away from the windows, is one of the issues that requires attention in daylighting design.

Components of the daylight factor

The daylight reaching a point in a room is considered to be made up of three components (Figure 7.9). The sky component (SC), which is daylight directly from the sky, the externally reflected component (ERC), which is daylight

reflected from external objects and finally, the internally reflected component (IRC), which is daylight reaching the point of interest having been reflected from internal surfaces. All of the components are described as a percentage of the available daylight that reaches a point within the room by the path taken. Summing all of the components together gives the daylight factor, i.e. $DF = SC + IRC + ERC$. An understanding of the factors affecting the size of these components can reveal how daylight entry to rooms can be improved.

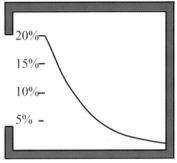

Figure 7.8. Section of a room with overlaid graph of daylight factor against distance in to the room.

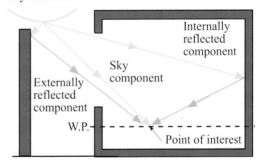

Figure 7.9. Components of the daylight factor

Sky component The size of this component depends on;
● brightness (luminance) of that part of the sky which is visible from the reference point. This depends on how overcast the sky is
● the size and location of the piece of sky seen from the point of interest. This

depends on the window dimensions. If we assume the sky is a CIE sky, a tall window will allow the reference point to see a larger and brighter area of the sky than a short window as shown in Figure 7.10

● obstruction of the sky by external objects such as trees or other buildings
● the daylight transmission factor of the glazing system. Glazing bars reduce the size of the window opening and glazing does not have perfect light transmission. Single glazing transmits 87% of the available daylight falling upon it, whilst double glazing has a transmission factor of approximately 77%. Window films or dirt build up reduces light transmission further.

in the range 60 - 80%. These are high values because the surfaces are usually painted light colours. Floors on the other hand have reflection factors in the range 20 - 30%. This is low because floors are often dark or carpeted to hide marks made by shoes.

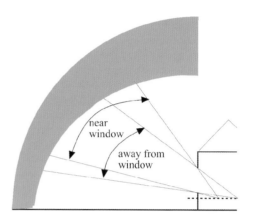

Figure 7.11. Area of sky seen by reference points near to and away from the window.

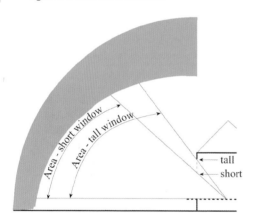

Figure 7.10. Area of sky seen by the reference point through tall and short windows.

Of the three components, the sky component is the most important, since it is not degraded by reflections. However, its importance diminishes as the point of interest moves away from the window. This is illustrated in Figure 7.11 which shows that a point away from the window sees a smaller, and on average lower luminance, area of sky than a point near the window.

Internally reflected component. The size of this component depends on all of the factors described above for the sky component with the addition of:
● the reflectance of the internal surfaces. Typical reflectance of walls and ceilings are

The internally reflected component is less significant than the sky component near the window but becomes more important at the back of the room away from the window. This is because most of the daylight reaching the rear of the room has been reflected there from internal surfaces.

Externally reflected component. The size of this component depends on all of the factors described above for the sky component, with the addition of;
● the size of the external object
● the reflectance of the external object. Most external objects have low reflectances, as illustrated in Table 7.4. This is because they often have dark rough surfaces, such as trees, masonry or concrete.

Because of the low reflectance of external objects, the externally reflected component is usually the smallest of the three components contributing to the daylight factor. If there are no vertical external surfaces near to the window, the ground may contribute an external component. However, this is unlikely to reach the working plane without being internally reflected also.

Surface	Reflectance (%)
Grass	12
Soil	15
Tarmac	10
Paving	40
Brick	30
Concrete	42

Table 7.4. Reflectances of some common external surfaces.

Improving daylight entry

From a knowledge of how daylight enters a room, derived from looking at the components of the daylight factor, we can make some recommendations for improving daylight entry. These are;

- avoid the obstruction of windows by external objects such as trees, climbing plants and buildings. Remove obstructions or maintain as much separation between windows and external structures as is possible
- make external surfaces opposite or beneath windows light coloured. Light coloured paving will reflect daylight upwards into the building
- tall windows increase the depth of daylight penetration in to the room
- Wide windows increase the spread of daylight across the room
- use splayed reveals to increase the area of sky 'seen' by points within the room
- use alternatives to reflective or tinted glazing as a method of reducing solar gains. These methods reduce daylight entry too. Consider using adjustable solar control such as venetian blinds which can be retracted on dull days to maximise daylight entry
- select glazing systems with the minimum of glazing bars
- keep internal surfaces light to improve internal reflections and distribution of light.
- keep the interior space open to daylight flow. For example, use glazed or spindle

balustrades. Allow deeper spaces such as corridors to borrow some daylight through glass panels within or above doors
- when the building is occupied, avoid placing obstructions such as furniture or plants etc. behind windows. There is a particular problem in schools where the windows are wrongly used as an additional display board with children's work obstructing the entry of daylight.

Daylighting problems

Increasing the height and width of windows increases the depth and spread of daylight. It also results in larger windows. Large windows create problems with increased heat loss, glare and solar overheating. Daylighting strategies are only successful if the three problems are considered and eliminated at the design stage.

Increased heat loss

The most effective method of reducing the amount of heat lost through glazing is to reduce its area. A compromise must be made between reasonable levels of daylight and acceptable heat losses. As window sizes increase there comes a point when the room is supplied with enough daylight for the activities being carried out in that space. Further increases in window area will not bring in any more useful light. This is illustrated in Figure 7.12 where increasing the glazed ratio beyond 40% in a south facing office begins to increase energy consumption rather than reduce it.

The second method of reducing glazing heat losses was discussed in Chapter 5. This involved reducing the U-value of the glazing by using multiple glazing, low emissivity coatings and cavity fill gases. Where a view is not required but daylight is, transparent insulation materials can be used. Movable insulation such as insulated shutters, blinds or curtains can be used to reduce heat loss through glazing during the hours of darkness. This also eliminates the unsightly 'black hole' effect that occurs when looking at windows in a lit room at night. If the internal surface of the movable insulation is light coloured it will also reduce the loss of electric light by reflecting it back into the room.

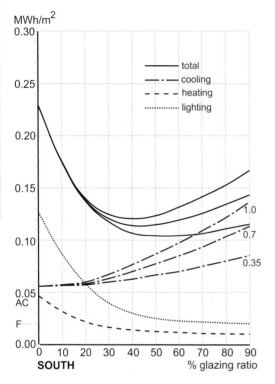

Figure 7.12. LT curve for a south facing office passive zone in climatic zone 1, assuming an illuminance of 300lx and a cooling load of 15W/m².

Reducing heat losses through glazing removes the associated problem of cold down draughts from the glazing and reduced surface temperatures, both of which can cause thermal discomfort.

Glare

Glare is the discomfort or interference with vision caused by a bright object appearing in the field of view. Glare occurs as a result of how the eye adapts to its visual environment. The eye can adapt to a very wide range of ambient light conditions from a 0.1 lux moonlit night to 100,000 lux bright sunlit day. It does this by adaptation and adjusting the size of the pupil. On bright days the pupil is small, restricting the entry of light into the eye. On dull days the pupil is large, facilitating the entry of light into the

eye. However, the eye does not accommodate all of this range at the same time. Instead it adapts to a small band of luminances within the large range as illustrated in Figure 7.13.

As the eye adapts to differing light conditions, the adaptation zone slides up and down the full range of luminances. The eye adapts to light changes relatively slowly. What this means is that if we assume the situation in Figure 7.13 represents adaptation to typical room luminances, then as the eye falls upon a large, bright window it will see luminances near to the bright day end of the scale. Too much light will enter the eye and discomfort or silhouetting of objects of interest will occur.

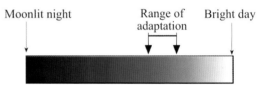

Figure 7.13. Adaptation of the eye to differing luminance levels showing the limited range at any particular time.

Glare can be reduced in two ways. Firstly by reducing the contrast between surfaces in the room and the window, and secondly by ensuring that windows are not placed in important fields of view. Reduction in the contrast between the walls and windows is achieved by reducing the brightness of the windows or increasing the brightness of the room generally. This latter point is achieved by providing surfaces with as high a reflectance as possible. Another method is to use splayed window reveals. This creates a smoother transition between the bright windows and relatively darker walls, as shown in Figure 7.14.

As well as increasing the brightness of the room surfaces, contrast can also be reduced by decreasing the luminance of the window. This can be achieved using blinds, such as translucent roller blinds or part closed venetian blinds. This will reduce available daylight but on bright days when glare is a problem the reduction may still produce acceptable daylight conditions.

© Green Building Press

Care should be taken to avoid leaving the blinds down when external daylight levels decrease as this could lead to an energy wasting 'blinds down, lights on' situation .

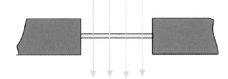

Square reveals creates sharp change in luminance

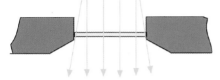

Splayed reveals reduces contrast between wall and window

Figure 7.14. Section through windows with square and splayed reveals.

Avoiding glare by keeping windows out of principal fields of view requires some knowledge of the functioning and use of rooms. One example is not to position windows at the front of classrooms, where the focus of attention lies. Computers, on which glare is created by reflections of windows, should be arranged so that the user sits side on to windows.

Avoiding overheating

The key to avoiding overheating, whilst still allowing in daylight, is to separate the heat component of the sun's radiation from the daylight component. This occurs naturally on heavily overcast days. The amount of heat entering a building with the skylight is small. North facing windows receive scattered skylight only. This means the heat input through north facing glazing is low. On the east, west and south facing windows, where sunlight can accompany the skylight, louvered blinds can be used to separate the heat from the light as shown in Figure 7.15.

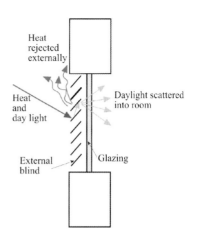

Figure 7.15. Blinds to prevent sunlight entry.

These blinds can be used internally or externally. External blinds are better at rejecting heat than internal blinds. Internal blinds trap a proportion of the sun's heat behind the glass. Unfortunately it is less easy to adjust and maintain external blinds and they are also susceptible to weather damage. Blinds should be retracted on dull days to maximise daylight entry. A fixed shading device that aims to separate sunlight from daylight is brise solail (Figure 7.16 and 7.17). This is an array of vertical plates fixed horizontally above a window. Direct sunlight is stopped but scattered daylight can still enter the window.

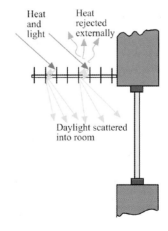

Figure 7.16. Brise solail.

Figure 7.17. Brise solail. Crown copyright.

Side lit rooms

The majority of rooms are daylit using vertical side windows. There is a problem with illuminating rooms in this way as daylight is mostly available near the window but finds difficulty in spreading to the points furthest from it.

Various methods have been proposed to improve the spread of daylight in side-lit rooms. They are; light shelves, louvres, prismatic glazing and prismatic films. Each of these methods change the direction of light flow so that, instead of pooling near the window, it is projected up to the ceiling and then reflected to the rear of the room. The general principle is shown in Figure 7.18 where an external light shelf is being used for this purpose. It can be seen from the overlaid daylight factor graphs that the total amount of daylight getting in to the space is actually reduced by the shelf. However, the amount at the rear of the room is slightly increased and the daylight spread has been made more even.

The uniform distribution of light within a space is particularly important in the psychology of switching on artificial lighting. What happens is that a person entering a room does not assess the overall amount of light in the room but compares where that person is stood, usually the door at a point away from the window, with the well lit area near the window. The person perceives it as being gloomy near the door in comparison to the window and so switches the light on, even though there may be adequate daylight for working. The effect of the light shelf is to make the spread of light in the room more even. A person entering the room now sees the entry point as being similarly lit as the rest of the room and so does not switch on the lighting.

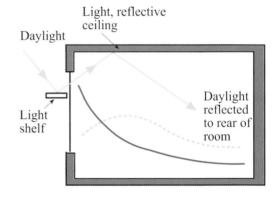

Figure 7.18 Daylight distribution in a side lit room.

Light shelves

Light shelves can be either internal, external or both. External shelves (Figures 7.18 and 7.19) have been found to have the most effective mix of daylight distribution combined with solar shading for the UK climate. There are a number of design issues related to light shelves;

● the shelf should be positioned above eye level to avoid obstruction of the external view
● the higher the ceiling above the shelf, the deeper will be the penetration of re-directed light
● the higher the reflectivity of the top of the shelf, the better the light redirection
● the underside of the shelf can also be

reflective to re-direct light from external paving into the room

- the greater the area of the shelf, the greater is the amount of light intercepted, and therefore shaded, and redirected.

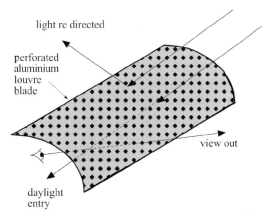

Figure 7.20. Perforated louvre blade.

Figure 7.19. Underside of external light shelf. Photo from GPCS19: South Staffs water company (1991). Crown copyright.

Louvres

Louvres are a form of multiple light shelf. Their benefit is that they can be adjusted to give optimum daylight redistribution throughout the day as the sun's position changes. This would, however, require the operator to adjust them at regular intervals throughout the day. The louvres can be retracted on dull days to allow maximum daylight entry. One of the problems with louvres is that they can obstruct views out of the window. To overcome this, some louvre systems form the louvre blades out of perforated aluminium sheet. This gives a combination of light re-direction, direct daylight entry and a view out (Figure 7.20).

Prismatic glazing

Prismatic double glazing includes a layer of glass which has had one of its surfaces formed into a series of prisms, the upper surface of which has a reflective coating deposited on it[3] (Figure 7.21). The glazing is no longer transparent and so is usually fitted above eye level in the glazed opening. Light hitting the prismatic glazing is reflected and refracted upwards on to the reflective ceiling.

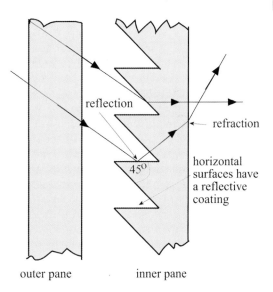

Figure 7.21. Prismatic glazing.

When white light passes through a prism, the individual wavelengths (colours) are refracted by differing amounts. This can lead to coloured fringes appearing around the pool of light redirected up on to the ceiling. This however is not usually a problem. Of more concern is that the optimum refracting angles in the prismatic glass are fixed. With sunlight, which is highly directional, this means that optimum refraction will only take place when the sun is at one particular angle of altitude. The problem can be improved by etching the glass to refract low angle sun on east and west facing glazing and higher angle sun on south facing glazing. An additional benefit of prismatic glazing is that it reduces the luminance of the sky seen through it. This helps to reduce glare. Prismatic glazing has a long history dating back to the late 19th century. However, it is not seen in modern buildings.

Prismatic film

A system which can accommodate multi directional sunlight is prismatic film. This is a plastic film which can be applied to glazing. The surface of these films has much finer prisms on it than prismatic glass. This means that in the space of one prism etched into glass a number of prisms can be etched into the film. Each prism has differing angles of refraction to accommodate changes in the sun's altitude throughout the day or different days of the year.

Performance of systems

A test comparing light shelves, prismatic glazing, louvres and prismatic films showed that prismatic glazing was the only system to increase light levels at the back of the room during periods of sunlight. However, it did this on only a few days in the year. On overcast days prismatic film and light shelves performed better[3]. All of the systems reduced the daylight in the room but improved its distribution. They also reduced the likelihood of glare in the room.

Roof lights

Roof lights are very useful for providing daylight to the core of single storey or upper floors of multi storey buildings. They are horizontal windows with the following benefits;
- they face the brightest part of the overcast sky (refer to Figure 7.6). As a consequence they let in three times as much daylight as the equivalent area of vertical glazing
- the daylight from roof lights is less likely to be shaded by external obstructions, such as trees and other buildings or by internal obstructions, such as posters stuck to windows or office furniture placed against windows
- daylight distribution below roof lights is in

the form of a symmetrical pool reducing in illuminance towards the edges.

The two negative aspects of rooflights are that heat losses in winter and heat gains in summer through them are high. The heat losses are greater than through vertical glazing as warm air rises up to them creating an elevated temperature difference between inside and outside. However, since a view is rarely required through rooflights, transparent insulation can be used (see *'Other transparent insulation materials'* in Chapter 5). The second concern, high heat gains, is traditionally overcome by tilting the roof lights towards the north to create a north light (Figure 7.22). This reduces the amount of daylight entering the rooflight but reduces heat gains and reduces glare.

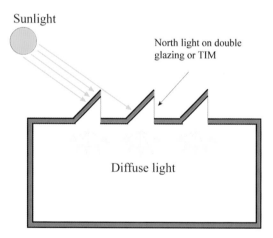

Figure 7.22. North light.

A second method is to attempt to separate the heat component of the solar radiation from the light. An example of this is shown in Figure 7.23. The rooflight is made out of vertical glazing protected from direct sunlight by overhangs.

Lightwells and atria

A lightwell is a vertical duct running through a multi storey building which is glazed on the top in a similar manner to a roof light. It also has vertical glazing in the form of internal windows throughout its length. The aim is to extend the rooflight idea to provide daylighting to lower floors. Lightwells perform best when they are short and wide, as opposed to tall and narrow. This is because windows on the upper floor absorb the daylight by allowing it to pass into the upper rooms adjacent to the light well. As a consequence there is less daylight available for the lower floors. One way of overcoming this is to reduce the size of windows on the upper floors and gradually increase them towards the lower floors. Any remaining structure should be smooth and painted white to ensure that light is reflected down the light well and not absorbed.

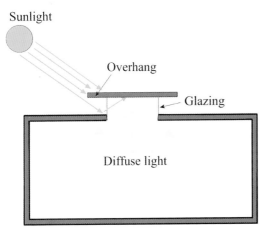

Figure 7.23 Rooflight protected from direct sunlight.

Lightwells are usually too narrow for useful occupancy to take place in them. However, they can have a dual function of acting as ventilation shafts for passive ventilation systems (Chapter 6).

Widening the lightwell so that its base can be used as an occupied space creates an atrium.

The atrium roof glazing system has a major impact on the amount of daylight entering the atrium. There are many devices which can obscure the sky. These include, structural elements, glazing bars, smoke dampers, ventilation dampers/fans, solar shading, fire detection equipment and acoustic absorbers (sound absorbers to reduce the high noise level arising from the hard, non absorbent, surfaces within the atrium). The effect of all of these can be to

reduce the available daylight by 50% between outside and inside the atrium roof.

Widening the atrium with successive floors improves the view that lower floors have of the sky and therefore improves daylight access (Figure 7.24).

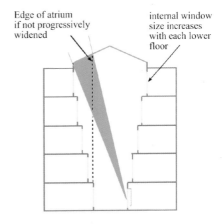

Figure 7.24. Stepped atrium design to improve daylight access to lower floors.

As with lightwells, the remaining internal structure should be finished in light reflective surfaces to encourage daylight distribution to the base of the atrium.

Atria come in differing patterns. Some examples are shown in Figure 7.25. The differences occur in the number of external surfaces through which daylight can enter the atrium and the arrangement between the atrium and the spaces adjoining it.

The side atrium, for example, will reduce daylight entry into adjacent rooms when compared to having no atrium. The street type atrium will add some daylight to the deep plan rooms next to it.

Light pipes

Light can be provided to interior spaces by guiding it along a light pipe. The actual system varies, depending on whether it is based on sunlight or daylight. Sunlight systems tend to be complex, as they are based on a mirror which tracks the position of the sun and reflects the sunlight down a light guide to the room in which it is required (Figure 7.26).

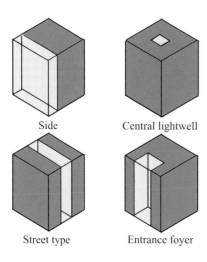

Side   Central lightwell

Street type   Entrance foyer

Figure 7.25. Various atrium positions.

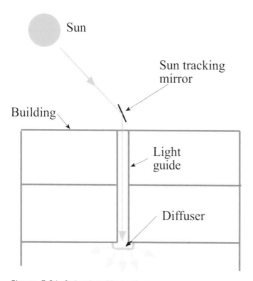

Sun

Sun tracking mirror

Building

Light guide

Diffuser

Figure 7.26. Solar tracking mirror.

The flow of light down the light guide is controlled using lenses. The light guide can be either a plastic rod, fibre optic bundle or a mirrored tube. A diffuser is fitted at the terminal of the light pipe to spread the light into the

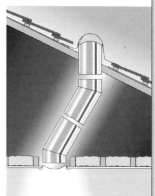

© Green Building Press

room beyond. The system is most appropriate to sunny climates and suffers from the need to have a solar tracking mirror, which has high maintenance costs.

A much simpler system, which can guide either daylight or sunlight, is based on a mirrored tube (Figures 7.27). The diameter is larger than the solar tracking system described above. A window is fitted to the top end of the tube and a diffuser to the bottom end. Light enters the tube and is guided to the space below by reflections from the tube walls. Lower spaces in the building can be served by connecting more than one length of light tube together. Bends can be included but should be avoided if possible as they reduce daylight transfer.

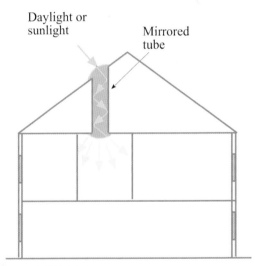

Figure 7.27 Light pipe.

Daylight assessment

There are a number of methods that can be used to assess daylight in buildings. The majority are based on the standard overcast skies described earlier in this chapter.

Artificial sky

A useful tool, because of its simplicity, is to use an artificial sky chamber (Figure 7.28). The chamber consists of a box, approximately 1.5m square on plan and 1.25m high. The walls of the box are lined with vertical mirrors. The roof of the box is fitted with lamps above a diffusing surface. When the lights are switched on reflections within the chamber produce a light distribution similar to a CIE sky. Scale models of the building under investigation are then placed at the centre of the chamber. The windows in the model are fitted with modelling materials with characteristics similar to those proposed in the full scale building. A light sensor outside the model measures the value of external illuminance E_o and an array of sensors inside the model measure the internal illuminance E_i over a grid of points. The data is fed into an analyser which compares the value of E_i at each point in the room with the value of E_o and outputs it as a daylight factor. Modifying the model by placing external obstructions, changing reflection factors of surfaces, type and size of glazing or adding lightshelves allows the effects of these changes on daylight distribution in the room to be assessed.

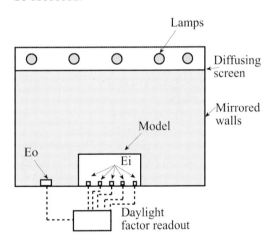

Figure 7.28 Artificial sky.

Daylight factor protractors

Daylight factor protractors are clear overlays, very similar to geometry protractors. They are used in conjunction with scale plans and sections of a room to determine the daylight factor at a particular point indicated on the drawings. Lines of sight are placed on the drawings between the point of interest and window reveals to determine the area of sky seen by the point of interest. The protractors have values of sky component based on the illuminance distribution of a CIE overcast sky printed on to them. Values of sky component are determined by reading off values where lines of sight from the point to the window opening on plan and section cross graduations on the protractor. The externally reflected component is determined using the same protractor and drawings. The variation is that the sight lines are drawn to the edges of the external obstruction and the values on the protractor are reduced by 80% to indicate the low reflectance of external obstructions. The value of the internally reflected component is obtained from tables.

The method is relatively simple, following basic instruction, but suffers from the fact that creating daylight factor contours requires the calculation of the daylight factor at many points in the room, and is therefore time consuming. It is also difficult to predict the daylight factors when the building has been fitted with novel daylighting systems, such as light shelves.

Computer modelling

The physical processes behind the movement of light in spaces and its reflection from specular and diffusing surfaces of various colours are well known. The limitations on the use of computers has been that a large amount of data needs to be processed. However, latest developments in computer hardware has made an analysis of how buildings interact with sunlight and daylight possible. The operator inputs data on the size, location and orientation of windows, glazing system light transmission factors, room dimensions and surface reflectances and colour. The computer then determines, by geometry, what proportion of the sky is seen by various points in the room and then calculates daylight entry and distribution within the room. The output can be in the form of daylight factor contours or 3D images rendered to show variations in daylight distribution within the space.

Daylight factor meters

A daylight factor meter is a light meter that has two sensors and so can simultaneously measure the illuminance at a point inside the building and outside the building. Internal circuitry then determines the size of the daylight factor from this data. The daylight factor meter is useful for determining daylight entry in existing buildings. It is not, however, very accurate as the value of external illuminance measured is rarely that of an unobstructed sky due to shadowing by nearby buildings.

Artificial lighting

Most of us would agree that daylight should be used where possible, because it has a range of psychological and visual benefits, in addition to removing the need for electric lighting. However, natural light is not without its problems as it can increase the risk of glare and, if not regulated to some extent, cause overheating of buildings. In addition, it cannot form a complete lighting strategy because it is variable and at certain times of the day disappears completely. At these times artificial lighting is required to supplement the natural light. Some spaces rely completely on artificial light. Examples are basement rooms and auditoria in cinemas and theatres. Others have a continuous requirement for artificial light, even if daylight is present. Examples are those buildings that have a specific requirement for display lighting, such as shops, art galleries or museums.

The advantage of artificial lighting is that it is available when required and in the quantities required. The disadvantage is that it requires electricity for its creation and, as described in Chapter 1, electricity is the most expensive and polluting form of energy. Note that artificial lighting is also referred to in this section as electric lighting.

Artificial light sources

There are three basic types of lamp; incandescent lamps, gas discharge lamps and fluorescent lamps. Each of them produce light by the excitation of atoms using electricity. When energy is input to an atom the electrons orbiting the nucleus rise to a higher orbit (Figure 7.29). At a later time the electron falls back to its original orbit and the energy is re released as a photon of light. The atoms that are excited may be material, forming the filament of a lamp, the gas inside it or a phosphor coating on the inside of the glass of the bulb.

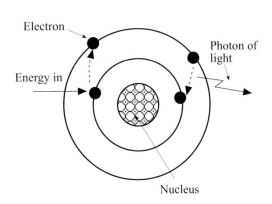

Figure 7.29. Excitation of atoms to create light.

Incandescent (GLS) lamps

Incandescent lamps are the common light bulbs found in most homes. They are also known as tungsten filament lamps or GLS (general lighting service) lamps (Figure 7.30).

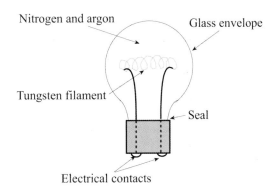

Figure 7.30. Tungsten filament incandescent lamp.

They consist of a glass envelope which is filled with argon (85%) and nitrogen (15%) gas. These gases are unreactive. Their role is to prevent the fine tungsten filament from burning out when it gets hot. A cap at the base of the lamp provides electrical contacts to allow the current to flow through the fine tungsten filament. The filament is made from tungsten wire as this is a metal which can get very hot without melting. As the filament heats up, it begins to glow with sufficient intensity that it emits light. This ability of hot objects to give out light is known as incandescence.

Tungsten filament lamps are very cheap to buy but are also very inefficient at producing light. Much of the electrical energy is turned to heat. This makes the bulbs hot to the touch. The luminous efficacy of a standard tungsten bulb is 13 lumen/W.

Tungsten halogen lamps are a special form of tungsten bulb. A halide gas, usually iodine, is added to the nitrogen/argon mix. Iodine combines with tungsten evaporating off the hot filament and returns it back to the filament. This extends the life of the filament, avoids bulb blackening and improves light output. This type of lamp is used in display lighting, usually in the form of spot lamps. Tungsten halogen lamps have a slightly improved efficacy when compared with a standard tungsten filament lamp at 17 lumen/W.

Gas discharge lamps

Gas discharge lamps work in a completely different way to filament lamps. Here a glass envelope is filled with gas at a low pressure (Figure 7.31).

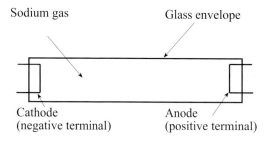

Sodium gas Glass envelope

Cathode Anode
(negative terminal) (positive terminal)

Figure 7.31. Gas discharge lamp.

The most common examples are sodium lamps which are the yellow lamps used for street lighting. A large voltage is placed across terminals either side of the tube. This causes electrons orbiting the gas atoms to be stripped off. The electrons move towards the positive terminal and the now positively charged gas atoms (ions) move towards the negative terminal. Collisions between the ions and electrons causes excitement of the gas atoms and the emission of light. Low pressure sodium lamps are very efficient at producing light but

unfortunately they only produce yellow light. This is acceptable for street lighting but cannot be used for lighting interiors. Low pressure sodium lamps are also known as SOX lamps.

By increasing the pressure of gas in the tube, the light emitted becomes more white. Unfortunately this also causes a reduction in efficacy. High pressure sodium lamps are known as SON lamps. They can be used in interior lighting, often as uplighters in offices and for lighting atria and tall spaces such as warehouses. Another form of gas discharge lamp for industrial use is the metal halide (MBI) lamp. It has a lower efficacy than the sodium lamp but better quality light output.

One aspect of gas discharge lamps and fluorescent tubes is that they require additional electrical circuitry to initiate and then control the current flowing through the tube. This is known as control gear. It first applies a large voltage across the gas, which is initially an insulator. The gas then breaks down and begins to rapidly conduct electricity. This rapid conduction would create a damaging surge of current if not controlled. Unfortunately, the control gear gets heated in the process. This heat is energy being wasted during the production of light and therefore control gear losses need to be considered when assessing the efficacy of the lamp.

Flourescent tubes

Fluorescent tubes are the lamps commonly found in workplaces, such as schools, colleges and offices. They are a special form of gas discharge lamp. The filling gas is argon, with a trace of mercury. When the gas discharge is created the gas does not emit useful visible light. Instead it emits ultra violet (UV) radiation. However, a phosphor coating applied to the interior of the tube absorbs the UV and re-emits this energy as visible light (Figure 7.32).

The phosphor coating is similar to that used on television screens. This means that by mixing the phosphors a cool blue, warm yellow or daylight white light can be produced. Fluorescent tubes have a high efficacy but less than that of the sodium gas discharge lamp.

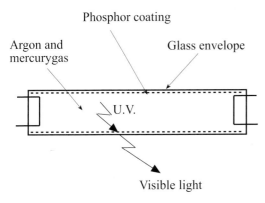

Figure 7.32. Fluorescent tube.

Forms of lighting systems

In domestic buildings the lighting system is based on individual lamps that create illumination within the room. Little attention is paid to lighting design in the home beyond aesthetic considerations. However, in commercial buildings there is greater emphasis on design to create the required light levels, avoid glare and generate a 'work like' ambience. The two main types of lighting found in commercial buildings are accent lighting and task lighting.

Accent lighting is used to create interest or a focal point at a particular location, such as a reception desk. It is based on individual or small groups of luminaires creating variations in the illuminance to draw the attention of the eye. A luminaire is a complete light fitting. It contains the lamp which creates the light from electricity, a power supply and the casing for the lamp. The casing has a number of functions. It supports the lamp, holds the wiring to supply it with power, protects the lamp from dust and physical damage and, using reflectors, prisms and diffusers, controls the spread of light from the lamp.

Accent lighting design is based on data supplied by the luminaire manufacturer. The data gives details of the direction and spread of light and the illuminance created by it at certain distances from the lamp. An example of this is illustrated in figure 7.33. This information

is known as photometric data. If the distance between the lamp and surface to be illuminated is known then the spread of light and the illuminance created on the surface can be determined from this information.

Accent and display lighting is often based on tungsten halogen spotlamps. These have a low efficiency and so should be used in a limited number of locations. Some retail installations use high pressure discharge lamps for accent lighting which are more efficient.

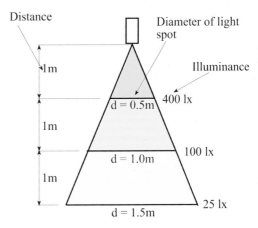

Figure 7.33. Photometric data for a display spot lamp.

Task lighting is used to provide adequate light for carrying out tasks. It can be provided by a desk lamp but is more usually provided in commercial buildings by a number of luminaires arranged in a uniform grid throughout the room (Figure 7.34). In this way the light output from each lamp combines to create reasonably uniform illuminance across the space.

Three other categories of lighting can be identified that generally consume less electricity than accent and task lighting but should still be considered.

Emergency lighting is to assist people to safely leave a building or close down dangerous processes in the event of mains power failure. The primary consideration with this system is therefore safety, although energy efficient systems based on LEDs are available.

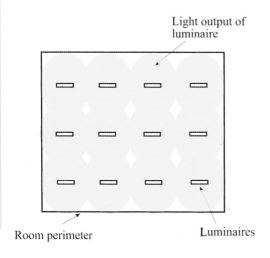

Light output of luminaire

Room perimeter

Luminaires

Figure 7.34. Uniform task lighting provided by an array of luminaires.

Outdoor lighting should use energy efficient lamps and be controlled so that it only operates as required during the hours of darkness.

Process lighting is used to illuminate individual processes/operations. One example is the provision of lighting in operating theatres. The limited use of process lighting means that the effective lighting of the process is the main consideration here.

To reduce the amount of electricity used for artificial lighting the following strategy must be adopted;
- optimise the use of daylight
- the lighting installation must be designed to give the required light conditions whilst consuming the minimum amount of energy
- the lamps must be energy efficient
- the lighting must be controlled so that it is on only when required and to the level required.

The first issue, optimisation of the use of daylight, was addressed earlier in this chapter. The remainder of this chapter will concentrate on the design of the lighting system, the lamps, luminaires and the control of the lighting system.

Task lighting

The lamps in a task lighting scheme consume electricity to provide light so, the more lamps that are required, the more electricity will be consumed. This section will consider the factors that determine the number of lamps required in a task lighting system. This is to identify those aspects of the lighting design that influence energy consumption.

The method used to compare the energy consumption of alternative lighting designs is to compare their installed loads. The greater the value of the installed load, the greater the electrical consumption of the lighting system when it is switched on.

The installed load is the rate at which electricity is consumed by the lighting system to illuminate each square metre of the room. It is determined by dividing the total power consumption of the lighting system (lamps, control gear and other items), measured in watts (W), by the area of the lit space, measured in square metres (m²). The units of installed load are therefore W/m².

$$Installed\ load\ =\ \frac{total\ power\ consumption}{floor\ area}\ (W/m^2)$$

Lamp rating is the rate at which a lamp consumes electricity is known as its rating. The rating is measured as the number of joules of energy that are consumed per second. The unit joules per second (J/s) is also known as the watt (W). For example the rating of a typical domestic tungsten filament bulb is 100W.

Control gear. One of the requirements of gas discharge and fluorescent lamps is that they require electrical circuitry known as control gear to initiate and then control the gas discharge. This circuitry consumes electricity in addition to that consumed by the lamp. For example, each mains frequency fluorescent tube rated at 58W requires control gear that consumes electricity at a rate of 12W during the operation of the lamp. The total rating is therefore 58 + 12 = 70W.

There may be additional power consumption by transformers in low voltage lighting systems and by power factor correction equipment.

As an example, if a room 7m by 16m was fitted out with sixteen luminaires, each having a total rating of 90W (including lamp and control gear). Then the installed load would be;

total power	*= number of luminaires x rating*
consumption	*= 16 x 90*
	= 1440W
floor area	*= length x width*
	= 7 x 16
	= 112m²
Installed load	*= total power consumption*
	floor area
	= 1440
	112
	= 12.9W/m²

A typical installed load to provide an illuminance of 500 lux in an office is 25W/m². A low energy installation would aim for an installed load of less than 12W/m². A low installed load has two benefits. Firstly, the electrical consumption of the lighting system is reduced and secondly, heat given out by the lamps is reduced so that the cooling load is reduced. This latter point is based on the understanding that most of the electricity consumed by the lighting system eventually appears as heat within the space.

Design considerations

The focus of task lighting is providing the recommended luminance on the working plane. However, it must be remembered that this is not the only criteria for producing a well lit room. For example, it is also necessary to ensure sufficient light falls upon the walls and ceiling of a room so that they do not appear gloomy, and that glare is avoided. The CIBSE lighting guides give more information on good lighting systems for buildings[4].

The number of luminaires, spaced out in a grid, required to give a uniform illuminance across a large work space is determined using the Lumen method of design. The method is based on the following formula;

$$N = \frac{E \, x \, A}{F \, x \, UF \, x \, MF}$$

Where:

N = Number of luminaires required
E = Illuminance required (lux)
A = Area of working plane (m²)
F = Total Luminous flux output of the lamps within each luminaire (lumen)
UF = Utilisation factor
MF = Maintenance factor

Since it is the lamps in the luminaires that consume energy we are interested in keeping the number of luminaires (N) small. It can be seen from the above formula that to do this we need to decrease the size of any of the terms on the top row of the formula or increase the size of any of the terms on the bottom row. The following sections will investigate each of the factors in turn and indicate how the lighting system might be optimised to reduce the number of lamps required, and hence the electricity consumed by the system.

Illuminance (E)

The value of the illuminance for any particular space is recommended in the CIBSE lighting guides[4]. The figures given have been chosen to provide an efficient, safe and comfortable working environment based on the complexity of the task and age of the occupants. Complex tasks require higher illuminances and therefore a greater number of lamps. One example is in the parts of factories that are dedicated to inspecting products. Identification of fine detail is required and so high illuminances are recommended and therefore more lamps are needed. This is illustrated in the photograph of an inspection area shown in Figure 7.35.

Reducing the value of illuminance as a means of reducing the number of luminaires is unacceptable, as this would result in poor lighting conditions. Our focus should instead be on the avoidance of over illumination as this does not create further improvements in working efficiency. This is illustrated in Figure 7.36, which shows efficiency of office working against illuminance. As the illuminance increases, the efficiency of working improves. However, the rate of improvement in efficiency with increasing illumination diminishes and illumination above 500 lux results in little further improvement.

Figure 7.35. Large number of luminaires in the inspection area of a factory. Photo from GPCS 174. Energy efficient lighting in factories (1993). Crown copyright.

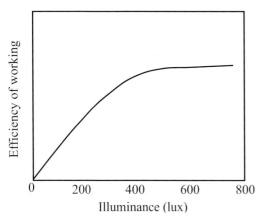

Figure 7.36. Graph of working efficiency against illuminance.

Recommended levels should be achieved in lighting design but not exceeded. Some spaces, however, accommodate mixed activities and therefore require more than one illumi-

nance level. One example is where there is an open plan office containing a circulation route (Figure 7.37). The illuminance required for an office is 500 lux. The illuminance required for a circulation route is 150 lux. Most lighting designs would provide 500 lux across the entire space. In an open plan office the lighting system cannot incorporate two very different illuminances as the contrast would be too great. The circulation route would appear very dull in comparison to the rest of the room. However, by partitioning off the circulation route the different illuminances could be achieved and therefore energy savings made.

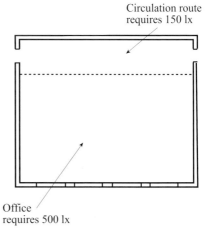

Figure 7.37. Open plan office incorporating a circulation route.

Background illumination and desk lamps. A method of reducing the number of luminaires whilst maintaining the illuminance on the task is to provide a lower level of background illuminance in the room to say 300 lux and then install individual desk lamps to provide the additional 200 lux required on the desk. If high pressure sodium uplighters are used to create the background illuminance and compact fluorescents used to create the task illuminance, then the installed load to provide 500 lux on the desks can be reduced to 8W/m².

Pendant light fittings. In rooms with high ceilings the luminaires are usually suspended from the ceiling to bring them closer to the working plane. This is necessary because the spread of light from a luminaire follows the inverse square law of illumination. This is where the illuminance falls by a factor of four for each doubling of distance between a point source of light and the surface it is illuminating. This is illustrated in Figure 7.38. It can be seen that as the distance is doubled, the area over which the light is spread is four times larger. This reduces the flux density or illuminance to one quarter of its original value.

The reverse is also true if you halve the distance between source and surface, the illuminance will increase by a factor of 4. Therefore, bringing the light fittings closer to the working plane increases the illuminance they create. This will also diminish the spread of light from each luminaire and so care should be taken in any designs that the uniformity of light within the space is not too uneven. Using pendant fittings can reduce the installed load necessary to provide an illuminance of 500 lux to as low as $11W/m^2$.

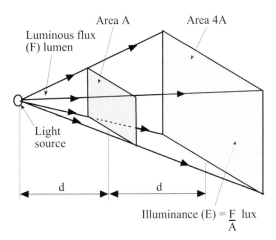

Figure 7.38. Inverse square law of illumination.

Area of working plane (A)

Luminaires have a limited area beneath them which they can illuminate. It follows there-fore that as the total area to be illuminated increases, the number of lamps needed to cover this area also increases.

Luminous flux output (F)

The amount of light given out by a luminaire is specified by its luminous flux output measured in lumen (see '*Introduction*' at the beginning of this chapter). The size of this is determined by the luminous flux output of the lamps and how much of this manages to escape out of the luminaire through the diffuser.

The light output of lamps is described in two ways. The first is the initial lumen output, which is a measure of the light output when nearly new (1 hour old for incandescents and 100 hours old for fluorescents). The initial lumen output of a 100W incandescent bulb and a 50W fluorescent tube are approximately 1400 and 1900 lm respectively. The second method of describing light output uses lighting design lumens. This is the luminous flux output of the lamp measured under standard test conditions to represent a more realistic 'in use' situation. This is necessary because the light output of lamps decreases with age, as shown in Figure 7.39. As the name implies, lighting design lumens are used in lighting design. It follows, therefore, that if the lamp light output depreciates quickly with time then a low value of lighting design lumens will be input to the formula and therefore more lamps will be required.

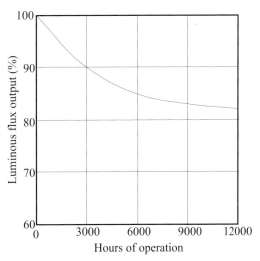

Figure 7.39. Decline in the luminous flux output of a fluorescent tube with age.

Not all of the light from the lamps leaves the luminaire. Some is reflected back into the tube itself and some is absorbed by the plastic diffuser (Figure 7.40) or dust on the surface of reflectors. The luminous flux output of individual luminaires fitted with different types of lamp is provided in trade literature produced by lighting manufacturers.

For energy efficiency, low lumen depreciation lamps should be selected as should luminaires without plastic diffusers.

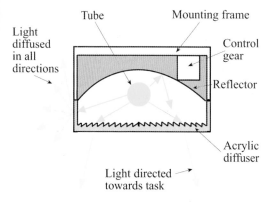

Figure 7.40. Section through a general lighting luminaire with plastic diffuser.

Utilisation factor (UF)

This is a factor that describes how well the light emitted from the luminaire is being used to create illumination. If all of the light were used perfectly the utilisation factor would be 1.0. In practice the utilisation factor is less than 1.0 indicating that not all of the light from the luminaire is being used to illuminate the surface. The lower the value of utilisation factor the greater the number of luminaires are required.

Light that reaches the working plane directly is utilised to the best advantage. Light that reaches the working plane after reflection from a surface is degraded. The size of the utilisation factor therefore depends on the pattern of light distribution from the luminaire, the reflectance of the room surfaces and the dimensions of the room as described below.

Light distribution. Luminaires vary in the way that they direct the light output from the tubes. Figure 7.40 shows a section through a general diffusing luminaire. The mirrored reflector at the top of the unit ensures that light moves predominantly downwards. The side diffusers scatter the light that hits it in all directions. This means that some light travels up away from the working plane. This creates a bright ceiling which results in a less oppressive environment. The prisms on the underside of the diffuser directs the spread of downward light into a well defined pool beneath the luminaire. For highest utilisation factor all of the light output should be directed downwards. Many modern luminaires have specular (mirrored) reflectors and no diffusers. Direction control of the light is carried out using polished anodised aluminium louvres below the tubes so that a maximum amount of light goes downwards. A softer downward light distribution, with some sideways scatter, can be achieved using a brushed aluminium finish.

The proportion of light output from the lamps that escapes from the luminaire is known as the light output ratio (LOR). The proportion of the LOR that travels downwards is specified by the downward light output ratio (DLOR) of the luminaire. For a general diffusing luminaire, as shown in Figure 7.40, the value of DLOR is approximately 75-80%. For a luminaire with a specular reflector, the value of DLOR is approximately 95%. It has been found during refurbishment that four tube diffusing luminaires can be replaced by three tube specular luminaires whilst still providing the same illumination level. This gives an energy saving of 25% for each luminaire. However, care must be taken to avoid creating too dark a ceiling and an uneven spread of light on the working plane.

In situations where visual display terminals are being used, it is recommended that the luminance of luminaires and the direction of light output is controlled to prevent light falling onto the screens and causing glare. However, this is not the only criterion for good lighting design and more information on this is presented in the CIBSE lighting guides.

Surface reflectance. Light which is reflected from a surface is degraded in two ways. Firstly, the quantity of luminous flux leaving the surface is reduced. For example, the amount of light leaving a wall with a reflectance of 70% will be reduced by 30%. The second degradation occurs due to surface colour. In this case some of the incident wavelengths of light will be absorbed and light predominantly in the wavelength of the colour of the wall will be reflected onto the working plane. This will only cause a problem when highly coloured room surfaces are used. Smooth white surfaces are therefore important in increasing the value of the utilisation factor. It should be remembered that high surface reflectance also assists in the utilisation of daylight.

Dimensions of the room. The width and length of the room are important as is the height between the working plane and the luminaire. When the luminaire is high above the working plane and the room dimensions are small, there is more chance that wall reflections will occur, reducing the utilisation factor. To maintain a high utilisation factor;
- choose a luminaire that directs most of its light downwards (with due regard to avoiding dark walls and ceiling)
- keep surfaces light (high reflection factor)
- keep luminaires as close to the working plane as possible (with due regard for head clearances and glare problems from lighting in the field of view).

Maintenance factor

This is a factor that tells us the average state of cleanliness of the luminaires and surfaces in the room. In dirty environments luminaire reflectors and diffusers will become dirty and therefore light absorbing. The reflectance of dirty room surfaces will also be lower. Typical maintenance factors are 0.9 for a regularly cleaned and maintained office, 0.8 for an office that is not regularly maintained and 0.6 for a factory.

Lamp efficacy

Lamps are devices for converting electricity into light. Lamps are not perfect at this task

as some of the electricity is turned to heat. The efficiency of a lamp is described by its luminous efficacy which is found by comparing its light output in lumens against the electrical input in watts. Circuit efficacy, on the other hand, includes the power consumption of the lamp plus associated control gear. The units of luminous efficacy are lumen per watt (lm/W).

$$Lamp\ efficacy = \frac{Light\ output\ (lm)}{Electrical\ input\ to\ lamp\ (W)}$$

$$Circuit\ efficacy = \frac{Light\ output\ (lm)}{Electrical\ input\ to\ lamp\ and\ circuit\ components\ (W)}$$

The actual luminous efficacy varies depending on the type of lamp and also the rating of individual lamp types (see *'Artificial light sources'* earlier in this chapter and *'New light sources'* later in this chapter). Table 7.5 shows the typical luminous efficacies of various types of lamp. The greater the luminous efficacy the better the lamp is at converting electricity to light.

Lamp type	Efficiency (lm/W)
Tungsten filament, GLS	13
Tungsten halogen	17
T12 - 38mm Fluorescent tube	55
T8 - 25mm Fluorescent tube	65
T5 - 15mm Fluorescent tube	96
High pressure sodium, SON	102
Low pressure sodium, SOX	130

Table 7.5. Luminous efficacy of various type of lamp (including control gear losses)[5].

The efficacy of fluorescent tubes has been continually improving since they were commercially developed during the 1940's. This is illustrated in Figure 7.41 which shows increases in tube efficacy over the past sixty years. In 1945 the maximum efficacy was 32 lumen/W by 2002 this had increased to 105 lumen/W.

High frequency control gear

There are three types of control circuits which can be used to initiate and then control the light output from fluorescent tubes.

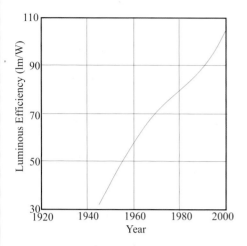

Figure 7.41. Improvements in fluorescent tube luminous efficacy over time.

- The control gear losses are reduced from 12W to 11W.
- the electronic circuit can control two lamps, whereas a wire wound circuit is needed for each lamp
- the lamps can be dimmed with an almost linear light output to energy consumption relationship, i.e. as the light output falls the electrical consumption falls in proportion (Figure 7.42). This is not the case with mains frequency fluorescents that reduce their power consumption when dimmed but to a much lesser degree. Dimming with comparable power saving is essential for incorporating the lamps in circuits that increase or decrease light output in response to daylight (see *'Lighting control'* later in this chapter)

Switch start. This is the simplest and cheapest circuit consisting of a magnetic copper/ iron ballast, a capacitor and a glow starter unit. Currents flowing through the coil create a magnetic field which induces a new current flowing in the opposite direction to the first. This prevents current surges because the stronger the current through the coil, the greater is the induced current flowing in the opposite direction. It is here where the control gear losses take place.

Electronic start. This uses electronic starting which is flicker free. It does this by slowly warming the tube for a fraction of a second before starting. This reduces the discolouration of the end of tubes, increases life and reduces lumen depreciation.

High frequency (HF) electronic starting.
A modern development in control gear is the introduction of electronic circuitry which replaces the control gear systems described above but uses the same tubes. The electronic circuitry operates at 20,000Hz, whereas wire wound control gear operates at the normal mains frequency of 50Hz. The energy benefits of this system are;
- high frequency lamps operate at a higher luminous efficacy than mains frequency lamps

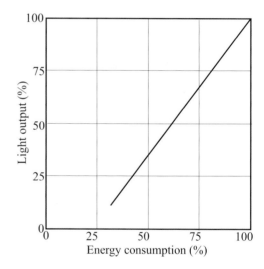

Figure 7.42. Reductions in energy consumption with falling light output due to dimming.

- high frequency lamps have instant starting characteristics. This means that almost immediately after switch on, they achieve maximum light output. Mains frequency fluorescents slowly build up light output after switch on. This means that high frequency lamps are better in occupancy controlled lighting installations. When occupants return to the room, light levels can quickly be recovered as the lights switch

back on again
- the lumen depreciation, when operating lamps at high frequency, is lower than operating lamps at mains frequency. This is illustrated in Table 7.6 which shows the luminous flux output of a high frequency and a mains frequency fluorescent tube at various ages.

| Age (hours) | Percentage of initial flux output (%) | |
	mains freq.	high freq.
100	100	100
2500	90	97
5000	85	92
7500	83	90
10000	82	89

Table 7.6. Reductions in luminous flux output with age for HF and mains frequency lamps.

The main energy implications of the above are illustrated in Table 7.7 which shows that the combination of reduced control gear losses and higher luminous efficacy of the HF tube result in a 21% energy saving for a twin tube luminaire when compared to a mains frequency one. Further savings will then be achieved if the HF lamps are part of an occupancy and daylight controlled lighting system.

| | Rate of energy consumption | |
Item	Mains Frequency	High Frequency
Tubes	2 @ 58W	2 @ 50W
Control gear	2 @ 12W	1 @ 11W
total	140W	111W

Table 7.7 Energy savings arising from the use of high frequency control gear.

A non-energy benefit from using high frequency lighting is that it eliminates the flickering and mains hum associated with mains frequency fluorescents. The frequency of operation of HF tubes is above that which can be detected by humans. This may give benefits in reducing the incidence of sick building syndrome where lighting has been identified as a possible contributory factor.

T5 tubes

The diameter of fluorescent tubes is identified by a T number. 38mm tubes are T12's, 26mm tubes T8 and 15mm tubes are T5's. The latest and most efficient tubes are T5 tubes with a luminous efficacy of 106 lumen/W.

The improvements in fluorescent tube efficacy have arisen as a result of;
- improved manufacturing techniques which maintain consistent quality and tolerances.
- modifications in the dimensions of the tube. This keeps the tube wall near its optimum operating temperature of 45°C. Note it is important that luminaire design helps to maintain this temperature and avoids heat build up
- developing improved phosphor coatings. The cheapest and least efficient phosphor coating is halophosphate. This is used to coat older 38mm tubes. The most efficient coating is the triphosphor coating made up of red, green and blue rare earth phosphors
- changes to the gas filling. T8 and T5 tubes use a krypton gas filling along with the mercury.

Compact flouresent lamps

Tungsten bulbs benefit from being cheap and small. However, they have a very low luminous efficacy. They are still widely used in domestic properties and for minor roles in commercial buildings, e.g. stairwells, lift lighting, hotel room lighting and the lighting of small rooms such as toilets and stores. They can however be replaced by fluorescent tubes that have been reduced in size and coiled so that they are only slightly larger than an equivalent tungsten bulb. These are known as compact fluorescent lamps (CFL). A 60W tungsten bulb can be replaced by a 15W CFL which has a similar spectral output. This exchange reduces the energy consumption by 75%.

One of the problems with CFL's is that the control gear for the fluorescent discharge is contained in the base of the lamp. The life of the control gear is much longer than that of the tube. This means that when the tube fails the control gear must also be thrown away. This wastes resources and is costly. This is difficult to avoid in domestic lighting when the CFL is replacing a standard tungsten bulb. In commercial buildings new light fittings should be installed that have separate control gear within the fitting itself so only the tube is replaced on failure (Figure 7.43).

Figure 7.43. Compact fluorescent lamp (CFL) with cover on and off. Photo from GPCS 86 Low energy lighting in the community areas of housing. (1993). Crown copyright.

New light sources

In addition to the three main categories of light source described in '*Artificial light sources*' earlier in this section, there are some significant new entries to the lighting market. Some are already commercially available and others are still under development.

Induction lamps

Induction lamps are a development in the way that energy is input to the lamp to create light. The traditional method is to use metal electrodes which either penetrate the lamp via a sealed metal cap or through a seal in the glass itself. The problem with this is that the seal is a weak element in the tube. Heating and cooling

of the tube creates mechanical stresses that can result in cracking around the seal, leading to failure. The induction lamp has no electrodes penetrating the glass envelope. Instead, an external coil is used to create a magnetic field that induces current flow within the filling gas of the lamp. The lamps, which are commercially available, have a high efficacy and an extremely long lifetime. This makes them very suitable for locations which are hard to reach or difficult to access, such as high places and subway lighting.

Light emitting diodes LEDs

One of the most efficient sources of artificial light is the light emitting diode (LED). They use approximately 10% of the energy needed by an equivalent tungsten bulb. We are familiar with red and green LED's as indicator lamps in electronic equipment but white versions are now available. Individual LED's are inadequate for lighting interiors as they are too small. However, they can be built up into arrays to produce accent and display luminaires[6]. They can be used to replace traditional lamps where limited lighting area is required. The most important example is in emergency lighting systems where LED's are used to illuminate exit signs. One of the main benefits of LED's is their long life. The typical lifetime of a LED light is 100,000 hours.

Electro-luminescent plastics

Certain specially developed plastics have been found to emit light when a voltage is applied across them. These plastics are only available in small quantities and are not commercially available for general lighting purposes. However, it may be possible in the future to coat a large area of the ceiling with this type of material to act as a source of light. This would give a much more even light distribution in the room than using an array of individual lamps that create peaks of illuminance beneath themselves and lower illuminances in between the luminaires.

Economics of high efficacy lamps

All higher efficacy lamps are more costly than the equivalent standard unit. Amongst the reasons for this is that both the improved triphosphor coating of high frequency tubes and the krypton gas filling are more expensive than the basic coatings and gases used. A standard luminaire, with twin 85W 26mm tubes, would cost approximately £58. An equivalent fitting with high frequency tubes would cost approximately £83, i.e. an extra cost per fitting of £26. The extra cost involved must be recovered in the value of energy savings made before additional financial savings can accumulate.

The payback period of energy efficient lighting depends on the number of hours over which it is run. The greater the number of hours the shorter the payback period as shown in Figure 7.44, which shows the fall in simple payback period of high frequency fluorescents with hours of use. However, it should be remembered that ultimately lighting energy savings are achieved by switching it off. The way that this is achieved is discussed in the next section.

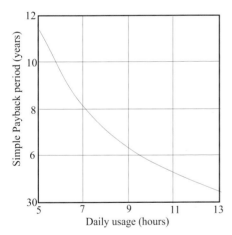

Figure 7.44. Reduction in payback period with hours of use.

Lighting control

No matter how efficient the lamps are, electricity is being wasted if the lamps are on when they are not required. The general rule is that 'lighting should be on only when required and to the level required'. What this means in detail is that;
- when the space is unoccupied the lighting should be off
- when there is sufficient daylight the lighting should be off
- when there is some daylight but not enough, the artificial light output should be varied to supply supplementary lighting up to the required illuminance.

There are a number of control methods that can be utilised to achieve these requirements, including manual switching, simple time control, occupancy detection and daylight sensing.

Zoning of lighting systems

Before considering control in more detail it is worth considering zoning of the lighting system. Zoning is the wiring up of lights to switches and control devices so that they can be turned off or on within certain areas independently. The two reasons for switching off lights are for lack of occupancy and the presence of adequate daylight. This indicates that zoning requires a consideration of how natural light flows into a room and patterns of occupancy. Table 4.10 in Chapter 4 shows that the energy consumption of an open plan office was greater than a cellular office. This, in part, was due to the ability to switch off lights in individual rooms without affecting the remaining occupied spaces. If this were to occur in an open plan office gloomy zones would be created, leading to lights being turned back on again.

A small room with a single luminaire is treated as a single zone. However, as the room becomes larger and requires two luminaires it is worth having the two luminaires switched separately. This means that the luminaire nearest the window can be switched off if there is sufficient natural light, so saving 50% of the room's lighting energy consumption. Figure 7.45 shows a lighting system zoned to take advantage of daylight.

It is known that light flows into a room from the windows and diminishes in quantity with depth from the windows. The lighting system should be zoned along the direction of diminishing light flow as shown in the diagram. In this example it may be possible to have zone

1 lamps off, zone 2 lamps at 50% of their output and zone 3 at 100%. If the room were switched as a single zone, these savings would not be possible. Zoning requires the installation of additional wiring and switches/sensors which increases the capital cost of the system. However, since electricity is a costly fuel, these additional costs are quickly recovered in the value of electricity saved.

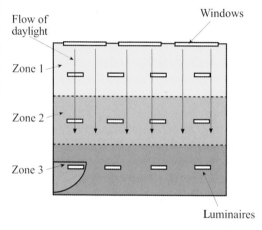

Figure 7.46. Lighting system zoned to take advantage of daylight.

Manual switching

The simplest and most cost effective method of switching off lighting is by manual switching. This is very effective in domestic properties where the occupants have responsibility for the fuel bills, but less effective in workplaces where lights are readily turned on in response to gloomy conditions but are not turned off again as the daylight returns. The situation can be improved by workplace awareness schemes. These use in-house magazines, posters and stickers by light switches to encourage occupants to switch off lights when they leave rooms. Unfortunately it has been found that the good practices encouraged by these awareness schemes soon wear off and the occupants return to their old habits within a month or so. For this reason it is necessary to continually repeat the awareness message throughout the year.

Simple time switching

Above it was stated that the occupants of work places readily turn lights on but do not turn them off again as daylighting improves. One way of overcoming this behaviour is to use simple time switching control. In this situation all of the lights in the building (where there is natural light) are turned off at certain times of the day. The building occupants must then decide if they want to turn the lights back on again or not. If daylighting has improved then it is likely that the lights will remain off. In addition, there is evidence that the probability of switching lights on, regardless of the amount of available daylight, diminishes towards the middle of the day and then slowly increases again towards the end of the day as shown in Figure 7.46.

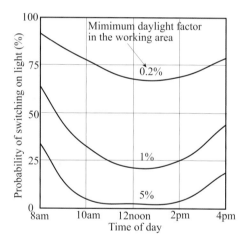

Figure 7.46. Graph of probability of switching on lights with time for various daylight factors.

This may be due to the fact that there is an expectation that lighting is required at the start and end of the day. A feeling which is retained regardless of actual daylighting availability.

Typical switch off times are morning break, 10:30am and lunchtime 12:00noon. A mid afternoon switch off time should be treated with care since the probability of switching back on is starting to increase once again (Figure 7.46). Experiments have been carried out with switching off at short intervals, such as hourly throughout the day. However, this simply creates annoyance amongst the building occupants who then tamper with it or demand that the control system be removed.

It is possible that the simple timers switch off lights on a gloomy day when they are needed. In this case the lamps can be turned back on using wall switches, pendant cords hanging from the luminaires or hand held remote controllers. In some elaborate systems it is possible to turn the lights on over your desk by dialling your own internal phone number. In addition dialling in a further digit between 0 and 9 allows you to vary the light output of the lamp above your workstation between minimum and maximum outputs.

Occupancy detection

One of the problems with simple time switching is that the lights can remain on between switching intervals, even when there are no occupants in the space. One way of overcoming this is to use occupancy detectors as part of the control system that switches the lights off when the space is vacant. The type of detectors used are passive infra-red (PIR) detectors that sense body heat or ultrasonic detectors that sense movement. Both of these detectors can give a false reading that the space is unoccupied. If the person is at their desk but not moving or are sat outside of the detection area of the PIR then the lights may be extinguished. Occupants can then be seen waving their arms about to re-activate the lighting system. This creates dissatisfaction with the system. One way of avoiding false absences is to build a delay in to the unit so that the lights remain on for a further 15 minutes after an absence is detected. This usually gives sufficient time for any stationary occupants to be sensed and the lights will remain on.

Rapid switching of fluorescent tubes should be avoided as the regular heating/cooling of the cathode and tube reduces the life of the lamp. As a rule of thumb each start reduces the life of a tube by two hours. When limited to reasonable switching (less than 8 times per day) this does not have a significant effect on tubes for

which the recommendation is that they should be replaced every 11 to 12,000 hours.

Some domestic versions of occupancy detectors are now available which are a replacement light switch incorporating the detector. These are limited in that the occupancy sensor cannot be positioned for best detection but is fixed at the existing light switch position. However there are also units that can be mounted in an appropriate detecting position (Figure 7.47).

Figure 7.47. Domestic, indoor occupancy detector. This type of detector can be placed in suitable locations to detect the widest possible movements. Ideal for locations like hallways and lobbies.

Daylight sensing

One of the problems with occupancy detection is that the lights can remain on during occupation even when there is sufficient daylight entering the space. Daylight sensing uses photocells (Figure 7.48) to detect the combination of daylight and artificial light within a space. Control takes two forms, the simplest is when the lights are turned off when the quantity of light detected goes over a certain threshold. The switching is sudden and is more noticeable. This could lead to the lights being turned back on as a reflex reaction. It is usually recommended, therefore, that the lights should only be switched off when the total light level exceeds the required illuminance by at least a factor of two. The second method varies the artificial light output so that a constant illuminance is maintained. This means that as the daylight levels increase, the artificial light output is reduced and vice versa. This is illustrated in Figure 7.49 where a constant room illuminance of 350 lux is maintained against reducing daylight levels.

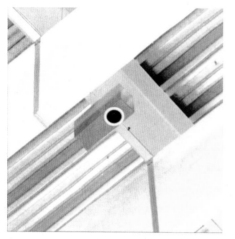

Figure 7.48. Internal photocell. Photo from GPCS158 Energy efficient lighting in factories 1993. Crown copyright.

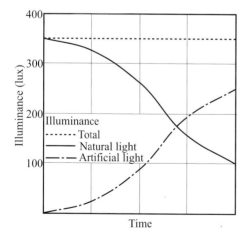

Figure 7.49. Control of artificial light output by daylight sensing.

Systems

A lighting control system requires sensors, wiring, a processor to determine actions from the sensed information, and actuators to switch on/off or modify the light output of the lamps. There are a number of ways in which these components can be arranged.

The simplest system is to install all of the control components into the luminaires themselves, occupancy and light sensors being built in to one end of the luminaire. This simplifies and reduces the cost of wiring but requires a larger number of sensors and processors as one is required for each luminaire.

Another method uses one daylight and one occupancy sensor for each zone being controlled. Each zone feeds information to a wall mounted processor and control unit. The processor is accessible so that commissioning and changes to control strategy can be easily made. The number of sensors is reduced but more control wiring is required, running from each sensor to the control unit and then back to each bank of luminaires.

A third method is similar to the second in that single zone sensors and a wall mounted controller are used. However, the signals from the sensors and to the luminaires are carried by mains signalling. This is where a signal is carried in the mains electrical cable to each luminaire. Each luminaire has an in-built control unit with a unique address so that the luminaire only responds to control signals that are meant for it. ✆

References for Chapter 7

1. Crisp, V.H.C., Littlefair, P.J., Cooper, I. and McKennan G. Daylight as a Passive Solar Energy Option: An Assessment of its Potential in Non Domestic Buildings. Building Research Establishment Report 129. HMSO 1988.

2. CIBSE Lighting Guide: Daylight and Window Design. CIBSE 1999

3. Aizlewood, M.E. Innovative Daylighting Systems: An Experimental Evaluation. Lighting Research and Technology. 25(4) pp141-153. 1993

4. Chartered Institute of Building Services Engineers. CIBSE Code for Interior Lighting. 1994

5. Philips Lighting. Indoor Lighting Catalogue (CI/SfB

(63) X. page 145. 1995.   Telephone 0181 686 1966

6. Richard Forster. The Challenge of LED's. Light and Lighting. pp14-15 September 1999.

Further reading

Good Practice Guide 245 - Desktop guide to daylighting for architects.1998

General Information Report 35: Daylighting for sports halls - Two case studies. 1997.

CIBSE. CIBSE Applications Manual AM1: Window Design. 1998

The British Standards Institute. BS8206 Lighting for Buildings, Part 2: Code of Practice for Daylighting, 1992

BRE. BR209 Site Layout Planning for Daylight and Sunlight: A Guide to Good Practice. 1991

BRE. BR288 Designing Buildings for Daylight. Professional Studies in British Architectural Practice. 1995

BRE. Daylight design in Architecture. 1998

BRE. BRE Digest 309 (part 1) and BRE Digest 310 (part 2) Estimating Daylight in Buildings. 1996

GPG 160: Electric Lighting Controls - A Guide for Designers, Installers and Users. 1997

GPG 272: Lighting for People Energy Efficiency and Architecture - An Overview of Lighting Requirements and Design. 1999

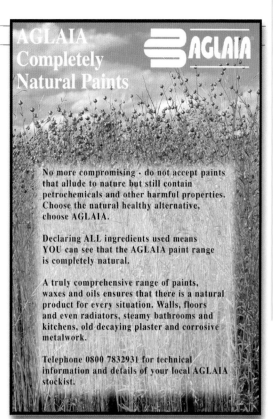

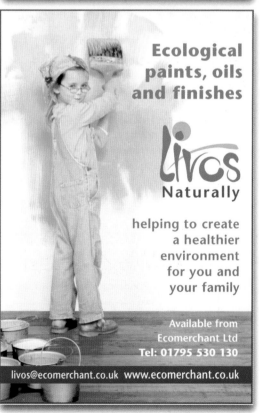

8 Heating

Introduction

Heat (thermal energy) is released when fuels are burned or when electrical current flows through resistive elements. This thermal energy is used in buildings for space heating and to heat water for cleaning purposes. Hot water is required all year round but space heating is only required during the winter months.

To achieve a reduction in the amount of energy used by combustion based space heating systems, the following aspects require consideration;

Fabric. Insulating the building and taking advantage of casual gains reduces the length of the heating season. Figure 8.1 shows that a poorly insulated building requires more energy and for a longer period than a well insulated building.

Combustion efficiency. The fuel must be burned efficiently so that all of the energy contained in it is converted to heat.

Boiler efficiency. The heat liberated during combustion must not be allowed to escape from the boiler. For maximum efficiency as much energy as possible must be collected and sent to the heat emitters.

System efficiency. The heat emitters must be selected so that they release heat into the occupied space effectively and without wastage.

Control. The heating should be on only when required and to the temperature level required.

Direct and indirect heating

There are generally two types of space heating device. The first are direct heaters. These are appliances situated in the room to be heated. The second are indirect or central heating systems that create heat centrally but use room based heat emitters, such as radiators, to supply heat to rooms. Direct heating systems have advantages and disadvantages in terms of energy efficiency. The main disadvantage is the difficulty of controlling their heat output centrally, although in-built controls provide effective local control. The main advantage is that they can be used to provide localised heating, such as the use of a radiant heater to provide comfort over a workstation in an otherwise unheated space.

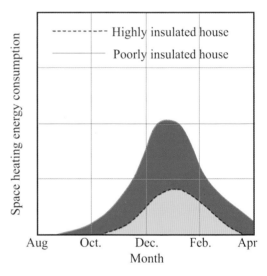

Figure 8.1. Space heating requirements of a highly insulated and a poorly insulated dwelling.

A note on electrical heating

The efficiency with which electricity is used for heating in the building is 100%. When heating is provided by electricity, combustion is dealt with remotely at the power station. As was stated in Chapter 1, power station combustion efficiencies are very low, typically around 35% for coal fired power stations and 43% for gas fired power stations. However, the low efficiency in generation means that space heating using electricity should be avoided. It is theoretically possible to increase the utilisation efficiency by

250 - 300% using a heat pump but in practice this is difficult to achieve using an air to air heat pump. The system can be made to have comparable carbon efficiency to a gas heating system if a ground loop heat pump is used (see Chapter 2).

Commissioning

One of the key elements in the energy efficiency of mechanical systems, whether heating, hot water, lighting controls, ventilation or air conditioning, is the commissioning of the system. Commissioning is the setting up and adjustment of both the hardware, such as valves, dampers, pumps, boilers etc and software, such as control strategies. Examples are that the combustion efficiency of boilers should be tested and thermostats should be confirmed to be turning off heating appliances and that BMS control strategies perform as expected. Badly commissioned heating, ventilation and air conditioning systems will be wasteful in energy and cause thermal discomfort. The Building Regulations part L require that a certificate should be issued on completion of the building stating that the commissioning has been successfully carried out. This certificate, including a record of system settings, should be included in the building log-book at hand-over (see Chapter 10). ☯

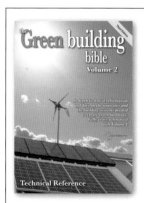

Boilers

Boiler efficiencies

The efficiency of a boiler is a measure of how well it transfers the heat liberated during combustion into the heating system. It therefore involves combustion efficiency and heat transfer efficiency. The quantification of boiler efficiency is illustrated in Figure 8.2.

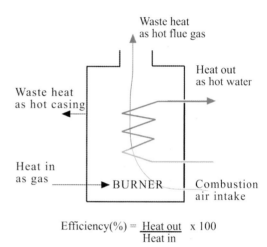

$$\text{Efficiency}(\%) = \frac{\text{Heat out}}{\text{Heat in}} \times 100$$

Figure 8.2. Boiler efficiency.

Boiler efficiency is a comparison between the heat input to the boiler and the useful heat output. Boiler heat input is in the form of gas or oil. When this is burnt the aim is to transfer all of the heat it contains into the heating circuit. A system that achieved this aim would be 100% efficient. However, for safety reasons, harmful waste combustion gases must be cleared from the boiler. This is achieved in natural draught boilers by allowing the natural buoyancy of the hot flue gases to carry them up and out of the flue. Unfortunately the heat contained in these gases is lost to the system. As a result all flued combustion appliances operate below 100% efficiency.

The energy content of the fuel is determined from its calorific value. Calorific value is usually measured in mega joules per cubic metre (MJ/

m³) for gas and mega joules per litre (MJ/l) for oil. Heat output from the boiler is determined by measuring the temperatures of the water flowing out of and returning to the boiler, and its flow rate. The volume of water flowing, and the temperature by which it is heated, allows the heat input to be determined. It can be seen from Figure 8.2 that the key energy flows from the boiler are;

When firing
- Heat lost in the hot flue gases leaving the boiler
- heat lost out of the boiler casing
- heat transferred into the heating system.

When not firing
- Heat from the burning pilot light which is lost by convection up the flue
- Heat lost from the warm heat exchanger as cool air moves through the boiler by convection.

The balance of energy flows changes depending on whether the boiler is firing, has recently stopped firing or has been standing for some time. When the boiler is firing most of the heat enters the heating system, approximately 22% of the heat is lost from the flue and 3% lost from the casing. When the boiler has just stopped firing, heat input to the heating system stops. Residual heat in the heat exchanger is lost by convection of warm air up the flue, along with any heat given out by the pilot light. To avoid wasting all of the residual heat in the heat exchanger, some control systems require the heating system pumps to run on for 15 minutes after firing stops to remove the residual heat from the boiler. When the boiler is standing, convective and casing losses slowly decrease as the heat exchanger cools until only pilot light energy losses occur.

Combustion efficiency of gas boilers

The aim of combustion is to convert all of the energy contained in the gas to heat. To achieve this the burner must mix the gas with the correct quantity of oxygen, known as a stoichiometric mix. It is based on the fact that combustion is a chemical reaction and there-

fore the exact quantity of oxygen needed to combine with the gas can be determined. Insufficient air (the source of the oxygen) would result in incomplete combustion. Carbon monoxide would be produced and dangerous unburned gas would build up. Too much air and the combustion gases will be diluted and cooled. It is the function of the burner within the boiler (Figure 8.3) to mix gas and air to give the most safe and efficient combustion possible.

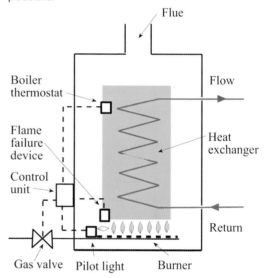

Figure 8.3 Generic parts of a gas boiler.

In practice burners are set up to run with slight excess of air. This results in safe, complete combustion but at a slightly lower efficiency than maximum. To optimise the settings, flue gas analysis can be carried out. Here a probe is placed into the flue during combustion and a quantity of flue gas removed for analysis. The quantities of carbon dioxide, carbon monoxide and oxygen indicate the completeness of combustion and hence the efficiency of the burner. The burner can then be adjusted until the composition of the flue gases indicates optimum and safe combustion is taking place.

Boiler load and efficiency

The efficiency of a boiler varies with the load upon it, as this determines whether the boiler is firing or not, and the rate of cycling between these two states.

High loads are when the boiler is being asked to do a great deal of work. An example of this state is first thing in the morning, when the building and domestic hot water are both cold. To satisfy the demand for heat the boiler will fire continuously and the flue and casing losses will be small, when compared to the heat being input to the rooms and dhw system. The efficiency at high loads will therefore be high.

Low load is when the boiler is being asked to do less work. An example of this situation is at the end of the day when the building has warmed through and the tanks are filled with hot water. The boiler will be cycling, that is firing for short periods then stopping to keep heat levels topped up. In this situation it is possible that more heat will be lost by convection up the flue than is given to the heating system. Because of this efficiency will be low.

The load on a boiler changes throughout the day and season of the year. High loads predominate in the winter months and low loads in the summer. On a daily basis, high loads are more likely to occur in the morning and low loads in the evening. Figure 8.4 shows a graph of efficiency against proportion of full load for three boiler types including a standard boiler (dotted line).

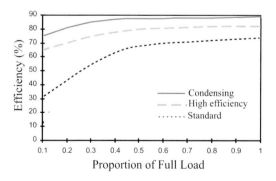

Figure 8.4. Graph of efficiency vs load.

It can be seen from the graph that whilst standard boilers are effective when operated at high loads, their efficiency falls off to as

low as 30% when the load on them decreases. From the same graph it can be seen that high efficiency and condensing boilers have better efficiency against load profiles. The features of these boilers that cause the improvement are discussed below.

Common types of boilers
High efficiency boilers

These boilers are more costly than standard boilers because they include additional features to reduce wasted heat and therefore improve efficiency (Figure 8.5).

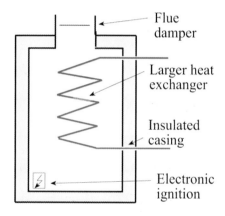

Figure 8.5 Features of a high efficiency boiler.

The features of a high efficiency boiler can include;
- extra casing insulation and smaller physical size to reduce casing losses
- larger heat exchanger to remove more of the heat from the flue gases. This means more enters the heating system and less is lost up the flue
- spark ignition to replace the pilot light. This removes the heat wasted by the pilot during weekends, night time and other occasions when the boiler is not firing.
- Flue damper which is open during firing to allow flue gases to escape but is closed when the boiler is standing to retain residual heat within the heating system
- Low thermal capacity heat exchanger that

heats up and cools down quickly and so is responsive to changes in demand and does not contain large amounts of residual heat when firing stops.

As a result of these features the seasonal efficiency is improved to approximately 85%, with a reduced fall off in efficiency at low loads.

Condensing boilers

These boilers have all of the features of the high efficiency boiler but have an even bigger heat exchanger (Figure 8.6). This extracts the vast majority of the heat from the flue gases increasing the efficiency of the boiler.

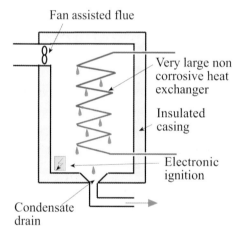

Figure 8.6. Features of a condensing boiler.

There are a number of consequences arising from this increased extraction of heat;
- the first is that water vapour in the flue gases is cooled so much that it condenses onto the heat exchanger (hence the name). This further increases efficiency by up to 8% because the latent heat of vaporisation that is released as the water vapour condenses is absorbed by the heat exchanger. In this way the heat exchanger recovers both sensible and latent heat from the flue gases. However, this can only be achieved if the return water temperature is below 55°C and peferably in the range 30-45°C
- the condensate is slightly acidic due to the products of combustion; nitric oxides and carbon dioxide being disolved in the water

and so the heat exchanger must be made out of a non corrosive material, such as stainless steel
- the condensate must be collected and drained from the boiler
- the flue gases, having been cooled, lose their buoyancy and so must be removed from the boiler using a fan.

The additional features add about 50% to the cost of a condensing boiler in comparison to a standard boiler for the same rating. However, their peak efficiency is as high as 92% with only a small fall off in efficiency with decreasing load (see Figure 8.4). This makes them economical with extra capital costs typically being recovered in the value of energy savings made within three years.

Combination boilers (combi)

A 'combi' boiler is a combustion device that has two heat exchangers, one for the space heating system and one for the domestic hot water (Figure 8.7). Cold water is fed into the unit directly from the mains. Turning on the hot tap allows cold mains water to flow through the boiler. The pressure changes cause the burner to fire. Hot water is therefore generated as needed. There is little or no stored volume of water which eliminates the standing heat losses associated with a storage cylinder full of unused hot water.

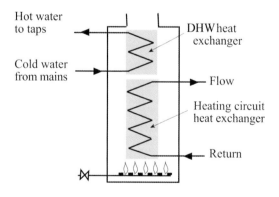

Figure 8.7. Combination boiler.

The major benefit of this system is that it is simpler and less costly to install than an indirect cylinder system with a feed and expansion tank. An indirect cylinder and cold water storage tank are not required. Condensing combi boilers are available, and these should be specified in preferance to standard models.

Efficiency ratings of boilers

In recognition of the role that boiler efficiency has to play in reducing the energy consumption of buildings, all boilers sold in Europe must operate to minimum efficiency standards. The classification used to compare boiler efficiencies is known as SEDBUK, seasonal efficiency of domestic boilers in the UK. Boilers are tested under standard conditions at full load and 30% load. The efficiencies found are used to calculate a seasonal efficiency based on typical load profiles. Boilers are then classified into one of seven bands as shown in Table 8.1.

Band	SEDBUK efficiency
A	90 - 94%
B	86 - 90%
C	82 - 86%
D	78 - 82%
E	74 - 78%
F	70 - 74%
G	Less than 70%

Table 8.1 SEDBUK efficiency bands.
www.sedbuk.org.uk

Higher efficiency with multiple boilers

In non-domestic buildings one way of ensuring that boilers fire near their high load rating is to provide the required load with more than one boiler. This is known as a multiple system of boilers. As an illustration, a multiple system of boilers used to satisfy a 100kW load is shown in Figure 8.8. It can be seen that the 100kW load is provided by four 25kW boilers feeding heated water into a common flow pipe. A common return brings water back to the boilers from the heat emitters. The first benefit of this arrangement of boilers is that there is back up if one of the boilers fails. It can be isolated and heating can still be provided, albeit at a reduced capacity, by the other boilers. The second benefit is that the boilers are fired in a progressive manner to satisfy demand. So, for example,

in the morning when there is a high load situation all of the boilers will fire. Later in the day when the building has started to warm through, boilers 1 and 2 will fire continuously with boilers 3 and 4 shut down. At the end of the day, when heating is only required for topping up, boiler 1 will be firing on its own. The progressive mode of operation means that each boiler only fires near its full output rating. The system as a whole will therefore maintain a high efficiency, even though the load is decreasing.

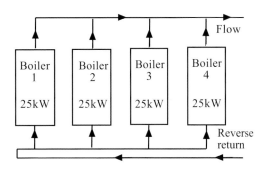

Figure 8.8. Multiple boilers for a 100kW load.

A further refinement to the process is the introduction of two stage burners. In our example this would mean that each boiler would be capable of firing at 25 or 12.5kW output, or would be turned off. The low setting would mean that heat could be input more gradually into the system and as a result there would be less cycling between the on and off states.

When a boiler is not firing heating system water will still be flowing through it. This means that the heat exchanger will be hot and so convective heat loss will take place as air currents move through the boiler. There are two ways of preventing this. The first is to close a valve on the return to the boiler heat exchanger. This, however, can upset the flows through the system. A better method is to allow the flow through the boiler to continue but to close a damper in the flue. This will stop convection currents through the boiler and does not upset the hydronic balance of the system. It is important, however, to have control interlocks to prevent the boiler firing with the flue damper closed.

Control of multiple boilers

Progressive operation of the boilers to match demand requires a control process known as boiler step control. It is based on boiler flow temperature. If this falls it is a sign that the water returning to the boiler is cooler having lost more heat to the spaces. This, in turn, indicates an increased demand for heating has occurred. As a result more boilers will be made to fire. Boiler 1 will be required to fire for more hours than any other boiler since it will operate during both high and low load situations. The boiler which is the first to fire up and last to switch off, in any heating period, is known as the lead boiler. To avoid unbalanced wear on the boilers the lead boiler will be cycled each week. So in week one, boiler 1 will lead, in week two, boiler 2 will lead and so on until after four weeks boiler 1 will once again be the lead boiler.

For optimum efficiency, with moderate costs, a typical arrangement is to have a condensing boiler as the lead. In this case the condensing boiler must always be the lead to achieve peak efficiency. The remaining boilers can still be cycled to reduce wear.✎

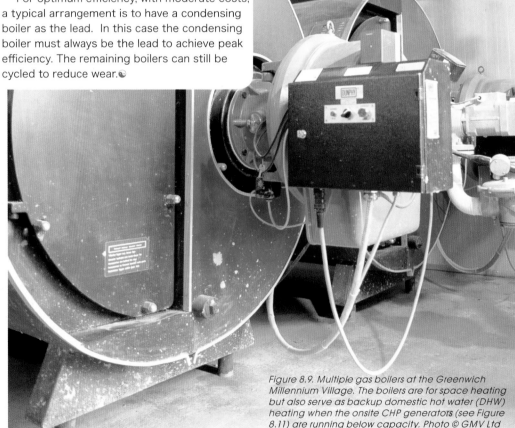

Figure 8.9. Multiple gas boilers at the Greenwich Millennium Village. The boilers are for space heating but also serve as backup domestic hot water (DHW) heating when the onsite CHP generators (see Figure 8.11) are running below capacity. Photo © GMV Ltd

Combined heat and power (CHP)

Gas or oil boilers are the primary source of heating in commercial buildings. However, in some buildings this may be supplemented by a combined heat and power (CHP) unit. These devices are based on internal combustion engines, similar to large vehicle engines (Figures 8.10 and 8.11). They have all of the components of a vehicle engine but the differences are that instead of running on petrol or diesel they run on gas (natural, biogas or bottled) and the drive rotates a generator rather than wheels. The generator produces the 'power' part of the output. Instead of a radiator to exhaust the waste heat from the engine to atmosphere, the CHP unit has a heat exchanger that transfers this heat into the heating system circulation. CHP units can also be based on gas turbine

technology which gives much greater heat and power outputs.

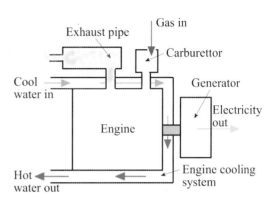

Figure 8.10 .Combined heat and power unit.

A typical non-domestic CHP unit would produce 120kW of heat and 70kW of electricity. CHP's are described in terms of their electrical (e) output and so this unit would be described as a 70kWe unit. The 60% efficiency

Figure 8.11. Combined heat and power unit at the Greenwich Millennium Village. The CHP gas powered engine is sized to meet the demand of the dhw load of the homes and the system is balanced by using thermal water stores and backup boilers located at energy centres around the site. This allows electricity to be generated at times when thermal demand is absent. Photo © GMV ltd

with which the CHP unit produces heat is lower than that of a gas boiler. The efficiency can be increased by 5% if an extra heat exchanger is used to recover additional low grade heat from the exhaust pipe and oil cooler. The overall efficiency would still be lower than that of a gas boiler. However, when the heat output is combined with the electrical output the efficiency is increased to approximately 85 to 90%. This is illustrated in the energy flow diagram of the CHP unit shown in Figure 8.12.

The economics of CHP units are complex and involve a balance between reductions in energy bills against capital and running costs. CHP units produce electricity at a unit cost that is much cheaper than can be purchased from the grid. But for the savings from this to pay back the capital cost of the installation the CHP unit must run for the maximum number of hours possible. Balanced against this is the fact that the CHP unit, like any engine, requires periodic routine maintenance. This involves changing oil, filters and spark plugs. CHP maintenance is regular and labour intensive and so costs are high. Economics is helping, as the energy delivered and used by good quality CHP systems is exempt from the climate change levy. Capital costs are also eligible for tax relief under the enhanced capital allowance scheme (see chapter 1).

to be installed. Specifically, its output must be sized to satisfy the base heating and electricity requirements of the building. If the CHP gives out more heat than the base demand, then at times of lower demand the system controls will switch it off to avoid over heating (Figure 8.13). If the CHP gives out more electricity than is required (Figure 8.14) by the building it will have to be used by other buildings on the site or exported to the grid.

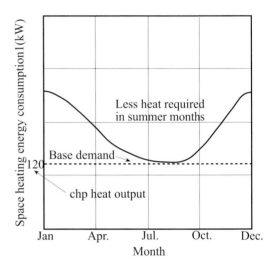

Figure 8.13. Heat demand profile showing sizing of CHP heat output to satisfy base demand.

The export of electricity requires the installation of extra meters, and unfortunately the price paid by the electricity companies for electricity deposited into the grid is low. The income it generates may not cover the hourly fuel and maintenance costs. It can be seen, therefore, that a high and consistent base demand is required for economic operation of the CHP unit. This tends to make them more suitable for buildings such as leisure centres and hotels with swimming pools and possibly, if demands indicate it is the case, nursing homes.

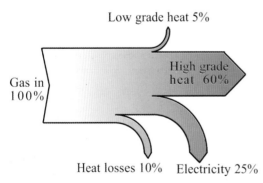

Figure 8.12. Energy flow diagram for a CHP unit.

Keeping the running hours of a CHP unit to a maximum requires a number of things. Firstly, the CHP energy output must be matched to the energy demand of the building into which it is

Secondly, the CHP unit will be part of a heating system incorporating gas boilers to provide the remainder of the heat requirement. To make sure the CHP has the maximum chance to run, the return water must run through it before passing to the boilers, i.e it must act as a lead boiler.

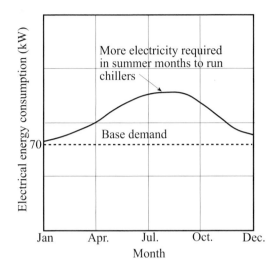

Figure 8.14. Electrical demand profile showing sizing of CHP electrical output.

Thirdly, the CHP unit must undergo routine maintenance at specified intervals. If a fault occurs between routine intervals, sensors, control devices and modems fitted to the unit allow it to auto-dial a maintenance company and give details of the nature of the fault. This will allow rapid attendance by a service engineer to rectify the fault.

Stirling engine based CHP units are available that have much lower heat and power outputs than the CHP units used to date. Because of this they are referred to as microCHP units. The outputs are 1kWe and 8kW. The lower outputs and much quieter operation make them suitable for small commercial buildings and housing. The estimated payback periods for these units, assuming an installed cost of £3000, is approximately 20 years at current fuel prices. This, however, falls to 3.5 years if bought instead of a boiler in new housing or as a replacement for a failed boiler.

The generation of electricity in power stations is extremely wasteful of energy. In recognition of this the government has set a target to achieve 10,000MWe of CHP generating capacity by 2010 as part of its climate change programme. Installed capacity in 2004 was 5606MWe, of which 40% are small scale CHP units with a capacity of 100kWe or less. ✆

Figure 8.15. Photo to right shows the community scale CHP station at Woking Borough Council, operated by Thamesway.
Figure 8.16. The schematic diagram of how the power is created at Woking's CHP plant.

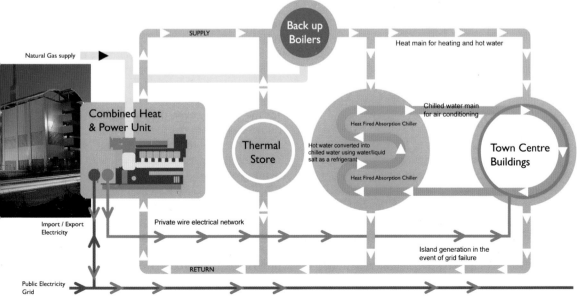

Fuel cells

The reaction between two chemicals can produce a range of effects, depending on the chemicals involved and the environment the reaction takes place in. The outcomes includes the production of new chemicals, output of light, colour changes, heat output and the release of electrons. It is the two latter outputs that are utilised in fuel cells. A fuel cell is a device in which two chemicals react, usually oxygen and hydrogen, to produce heat, electricity and waste by-products. In the case of hydrogen and oxygen, the waste by product is water. Fuel cells have been used to power space flights but they are now being tested as a source of heat and power for buildings.

A fuel cell is illustrated in Figure 8.17. It consists of two metal electrodes between which is an electrolyte. There are currently six types of electrolyte being investigated in fuel cells. The type of electrolyte gives the fuel cell its full name as in the 'proton exchange membrane' fuel cell (PEMFC) described here.

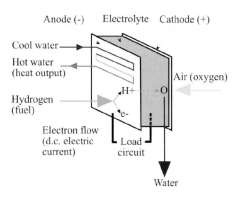

Figure 8.17. Fuel cell.

Hydrogen, whose atoms are composed of a single proton nucleus and a single orbiting electron, is passed over the anode. The electron splits from the hydrogen atom, helped by a platinum catalyst. The electrolyte, in this case a thin, solid polymer membrane, allows protons to flow through from anode to cathode but not electrons. As a result the electrons flow out of the unit to form the d.c. current. At the cathode the protons combine with oxygen and electrons returning from the load circuit to form water. Heat is released in the process, which is recovered by blowing air over the unit or by water cooling, giving a flow temperature of 70-80°C, which is compatible with building heating systems.

Individual cells are rated from a few to a few hundred watts. This is quite a low power output and so to be useful for buildings an array or 'stack' of fuel cells is required. A recent prototype array for a building had an electrical output rating of 4.5kWe and a heat output of 6.5kW. This demonstrates the similarity between heat and power output ratings typical of fuel cells. Typical energy conversion efficiency is 80%. At the other end of the output scale, a phosphoric acid fuel cell (PAFC), was used by Woking Borough Council for their district heating scheme, has a rating of 200kWe.

Fuel cells have advantages over internal combustion CHP units in that they are vibration free, silent, and low to zero CO_2 output if run off hydrogen supplied by renewable energy. Another advantage is that they have no moving parts. This reduces maintenance costs, but whilst it is estimated that the system will last 20 years, the internal cells in a stack may need replacing every 5 to 6 years. This is a cost that needs taking into account in any economic analysis. The main disadvatages of fuel cells is their high cost and the absence of hydrogen as a mains fuel. The hydrocarbon fuels; natural gas, lpg and methanol, contain hydrogen so they are often used as a source of hydrogen for the cell. However, the hydrogen needs to be released from the fuel in a device called a reformer. The reformer uses heat fed back from the fuel cell and so is a cause of reduced heating efficiency. It is also a source of some CO_2 emissions - released as a by-product of splitting the hydrocarbon fuel. Some types of fuel cell can be damaged by the presence of impurities in the hydrogen such as carbon monoxide. This is a potential problem with cells provided with hydrogen from a reformer. ☯

Heating system strategies & design

Having liberated heat from the fuel in the most efficient way, the next stage is to ensure that this heat is used effectively in the building. It is the role of the heat emitters, such as radiators, to release heat into a space to create comfort, without waste.

Heat emitters are available in a range of shapes and sizes, both of these variables have an effect on heat output. However, heat emitters can be categorised into two types - those that give out their heat mainly by convection and those that give out their heat mainly by radiation. Convective heaters warm the room air first, then the occupant. Radiant heaters warm the occupant and fabric of the room first, then the room air.

The choice of heat emitter/s should reflect the form, characteristics and low energy strategy of the building.

Form. The shape of a space affects how heat is distributed within it. Tall spaces, for example, are prone to stratification as described in *'Volume and ventilation heat loss'* in Chapter 4. As a consequence convective heat emitters should not be used in a tall space, as the warm air emitted by them will rise to the ceiling. A more appropriate heat emitter would be a radiant heat emitter or underfloor heating. If warm air heaters are used it is advisable to use them in conjunction with a destratification fan.

Characteristics. Modern buildings should not be draughty and existing buildings should be draught proofed to avoid ventilation heat losses. However, some buildings naturally have a high air change rate. One example is car workshops where regular door openings, as vehicles move into and out of the workshop, results in loss of heated air. Here again convective heating should be avoided and radiant heaters used to heat the occupants rather than the air.

A low energy heating strategy

Heat emitters should be compatible with the building's low energy strategy. Two generalised low energy strategies can be identified. Climate accepting or solar strategy, and climate rejecting or highly insulated strategy.

A climate accepting strategy requires large south facing windows to collect solar energy. As stated in Chapter 2, solar heat gains are unpredictable and so it is essential to have a heating system that can rapidly respond to changes in solar heat input. Therefore a heat emitter with a quick response time should be used, such as a low water content radiator. The radiator would also benefit from being made out of aluminium to reduce its thermal capacity further. Alternatively, fan convectors can rapidly vary their heat output by varying the speed or switching off the internal fan. Slow response systems such as storage heaters and under floor heating should be avoided in a solar house.

A climate rejecting strategy suggests small, highly insulated windows. As a consequence the solar gains are less important and less severe variations in solar energy input are obtained. Responsiveness of the heating system is, therefore, a lower concern than heating system efficiency. In this case it is beneficial if the heat emitters assist boiler efficiency. So, for example, over sized radiators or underfloor heating are recommended. Both of these use lower boiler flow and return temperatures that encourage condensing boilers to operate in condensing mode and therefore at a higher efficiency.

Zoning

Not all parts of a building need to be heated to the same degree at the same time. If the heating can be turned off in some spaces whilst being left on in others, savings can be made. Differing heating demands within a single building occur for two reasons. These are differences in heat gains and differences in occupancy patterns.

Heat gains

South facing rooms will experience solar gains and the heating effect may be sufficient to remove the need for mechanical heating. In this situation the heating on the south side of the building should be shut off. Heating may still be required in north facing rooms. It can be seen then that the building can be split along an east/west axis into two zones, one facing north and the other facing south. Further zones can be identified that are subject to other heat gains, for example, rooms with high occupancy levels or where extensive use of lighting or computers is being made.

Individual control of south facing rooms can be achieved using thermostatic radiator valves. An alternative method of zoning, which is more appropriate to larger buildings, is to install separate flow and return pipe work to each zone. A motorised valve, zone temperature sensors, pump, and an appropriate control system are required to control the flow of heat into each zone. As a result there is a capital cost associated with zoning a building. However, these additional costs will be recouped over time in the value of energy savings made. There are also non-energy benefits to zoning a building, such as greater degree of temperature control leading to improved thermal comfort and greater productivity of staff.

Occupancy patterns

Separate heating circuits can also be used to cater for differential occupancy of spaces within a building. One example is in the case of a school that holds night classes. Rather than heat the whole school for this event, the school should be zoned, and heating can then be supplied to the night school block only.

If the individual zones are being used on a commercial basis then heat meters can be fitted to the heating zone pipe work. These meters monitor how much heat is being taken by the zone from the central boiler plant. Knowledge of this allows accurate costing of out of hours use of spaces to be made. This information is also useful for energy management purposes (see Chapter 10).

Direct heaters are useful for creating small heating zones within an otherwise indirectly heated space, for example, to provide heating to a manned workstation within an unheated warehouse.

System components and controls

There are a number of components and controls in the heating system which can be optimised for energy efficiency.

Components

Pipework. The layout should be designed to be as simple as possible. Bends, reductions in bore and other components should be avoided where possible as these all add to flow resistance in the pipework. Resistance to flow must be overcome using energy in the form of electricity in a pump. The pipework must also be insulated. This is because the pipes are to carry the heat from one place to another and should not be a source of uncontrolled and unwanted heat input to rooms. Loss of heat from pipes can reduce the effectiveness of heat emitters and cause overheating in rooms through which the pipes run. Similar issues also apply to warm air heating systems that use warm air as the heat transfer medium and ducting to direct heat transfer. As with piping, the number of ductwork components should be minimised, ducts insulated where appropriate, and most importantly, be made airtight.

Pumps should be fitted with variable speed drives. This means that as zone valves close down and the demand for hot water in the building diminishes, the speed and hence flow rate of the pumps can be reduced. Reducing the speed of pumps and fans results in significant energy savings.

Controls

Controls are required to ensure that the heating system operates safely and efficiently and provides comfort for the building occupants. In terms of energy conservation, the control system should ensure that the heating system only operates when required and to the level required. The two basic forms of control for any heating system are time control and temperature control.

Controls for domestic heating systems

Figure 8.18 shows a typical arrangement of controls for a domestic central heating system. It comprises the following components.

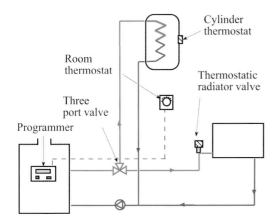

Figure 8.18. Domestic heating controls.

Room thermostat. This is a device that controls room temperatures. Control is made in relation to a preferred temperature setting made on the thermostat by the occupant. The thermostat is, in fact, a switch opened and closed as the room temperature rises above or falls below the temperature setting respectively.

The thermostat should be positioned in a representative room such as the living room at standing chest height, away from sources of heat such as direct sunlight. This means it will accurately sense the air temperature experienced by an occupant in the room. When the thermostat switch is closed, current can flow through it. This is interpreted by the control unit as a call for heat. The boiler will fire, the pump will run and the three way valve will direct hot water to the radiators. When the room temperature rises above the preferred temperature setting, changes within the thermostat cause the switch to open. As a result the control current will stop and the boiler and the pump will switch off. It can be seen, therefore, that room temperatures are controlled by stopping

and starting the flow of heat into the room as required. The room thermostat is central to controlling space heating energy use in buildings. This is because the temperature difference between inside and outside is one of the factors that directly affects the heat loss rate from the building. For an average outside air temperature of 6°C, increasing the internal air temperature setting from 20 to 21°C results in an increased heat loss rate of 7.1%.

Programmer. This is a time switch that determines the times within which the system will respond to a call for heat from the room thermostat. The start and stop times, between which the heating will be allowed to operate, are entered into the programmer. For example, heating may be required from 07:00 to 08:30 in the morning, then 17:00 to 23:30 in the evening. Modern microprocessor controlled programmers allow multiple daily heating periods and the ability to programme each day of the week with a different heating programme. An example is that the first 'on' period at the weekend may start at 8:00 and end at 12:00 to reflect the fact that the occupant is not in work on that day. Time spent setting up the programmer to accurately reflect occupancy times ensures that the building is not heated when it is unoccupied.

Cylinder thermostat. This is a temperature controlled switch similar to the room thermostat. The difference is that it is clamped on to the indirect domestic hot water (dhw) cylinder and therefore senses and controls the temperature of the dhw. When the switch is closed and therefore calling for heat, the three way valve will be instructed to divert boiler flow through the calorifier in the cylinder. This will cause the temperature of the water in the cylinder to rise. When the temperature reaches the setting on the thermostat the switch will open. The three way valve will then direct the flow away from the cylinder and back to the heating circuit.

Thermostatic radiator valve (TRV). This is a valve fitted to the inlet of the radiator. Gas in the TRV head (Figure 8.19) expands with temperature and pushes a gate downwards blocking the inlet flow. This will restrict or even stop the flow of heat into the radiator. The heat output will then be reduced causing the room to begin to cool. As it does, so the gas in the TRV head will contract and the valve will open up once more. TRV's allow room by room control of temperatures to be achieved. They are particularly useful in south facing rooms and rooms subject to casual heat gains. They give an extra layer of control in addition to the single room thermostat. At least one radiator should not have a TRV fitted to ensure that water flows through the boiler at all times.

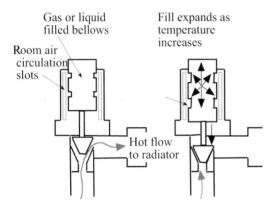

Figure 8.19. Thermostatic radiator valve.

The domestic controls described above treat the house as a single zone. The room thermostat senses the conditions in one room. The assumption is that the radiators have been accurately sized and balanced so that if any one room is satisfied, the others will also be satisfied. Low cost thermostatic radiator valves do give an extra layer of control and therefore energy saving. Controls for commercial buildings are more complex than those for domestic buildings. However, reductions in the cost of microprocessor based controls means that some of the ideas used in commercial controllers described below can be employed in domestic buildings. One example is the zoning of houses into two zones, one for the upstairs and one for the downstairs rooms.

Controls for commercial heating systems

Large buildings cannot be controlled effectively using domestic control systems. The components must be scaled up and certain refinements made to provide adequate control. The difficulties encountered in heating control in large buildings arise due to the buildings thermal inertia, different heat loads/gains, and differential occupancy of spaces. Both time and temperature control require more consideration than that given to domestic systems.

Time control in domestic buildings is adequately carried out using the fixed on/off time controller described previously. This is because, even on cold days, the time taken for the majority of domestic buildings to warm up to comfortable temperatures is unlikely to be more than twenty minutes. In this case the heating is simply set to come on 20 minutes before the start of occupancy. This period, when the building is warming up to the occupancy temperature setting, is known as the pre-heat period. Rapid pre-heating in domestic buildings is assisted by the fact that the boiler is often over sized. Whilst this rapidly heats the building, it does reduce system efficiency as the boiler will be more prone to thermal cycling. In large buildings the pre-heat period will be considerably longer due to the thermal inertia of the structure and the heating system itself. The pre-heat period is also variable. It is longer in winter than in spring and autumn because the building cools more during the night. This means a fixed start and stop time would be wasteful. This is illustrated in Figure 8.20. It can be seen that on a cold night the heating must come on at 1.00am to heat the building up to the required set-point by the start of occupancy at 8.00am. If this fixed 'on' time is retained on a mild night (dotted line), then the building is raised to the occupancy temperature at 5:30am because heating commenced with a higher internal temperature. This is two and a half hours of energy use prior to occupancy and so is wasteful.

To overcome this problem an optimum start controller is used. This is a device that calculates when the best time is to switch on the heating. The times of the beginning and end of occupancy are input to the device, say 8.00am and 5.00pm. The optimum start controller then monitors inside and outside temperatures, combines this with a knowledge of the thermal inertia of the building, and then determines at which time to activate the heating to achieve the desired internal temperatures by the start of occupancy. In the above example the optimum start controller would delay the onset of heating on a mild day until 3.30am (dashed line), thereby saving two and a half hours of heating which, for a large building, represents a significant saving in fuel costs and carbon emissions.

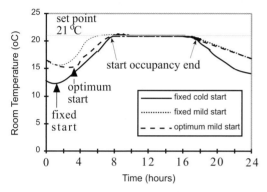

Figure 8.20. Graph of room temperature against time of day showing the benefits of optimum starting.

The optimiser can also use the thermal inertia of the building to switch the heating off mid to late afternoon. A slow decay in temperatures up to the end of the working day is unlikely to be noticed by the occupants and prevents the heating system from cycling.

The most difficult parameter to determine, for the effective operation of the device, is the thermal inertia of the building. Initial estimates of this may need to be modified during the commissioning stage to achieve accurate performance. Some devices monitor their own performance and carry out this adjustment automatically. They are known as self learning optimisers.

Temperature control is achieved in domestic buildings by simply switching on and off the flow of heat to the radiators. When the desired room temperature is achieved the boiler will be

switched off and after a short run on period, to dissipate residual heat, so will the pump. This is not practical in large buildings because of the thermal inertia of the large volume of water circulating in the heating system. Swings in temperature about the set point would be too great, as the water in the heating system was alternately heated and allowed to cool. Instead, systems in large buildings vary the amount of heat energy entering the space, as the demand for heating goes up or down. This process is achieved using a variable temperature (VT) compensated flow circuit.

The parameter used by the system to signal an increase in the demand for heating is a reduction in outside air temperature. Figure 8.21 illustrates the principle of operation.

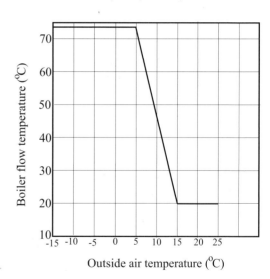

Figure 8.21. Compensation curves.

The graph is known as a compensated flow curve. Moving from left to right on the graph, it can be seen that as the outside temperature increases, the temperature of the boiler flow is progressively decreased. At 16°C outside air temperature, the boiler flow temperature is equal to ambient temperature, i.e. the heating is switched off. This temperature is known as the outside air cut off temperature. At this temperature no mechanical heating is required since 6°C worth of heating can typically be achieved from casual gains in the building such as passive solar energy, body heat, lighting and appliances.

The adjustment in flow temperature with outside air temperature is achieved using a variable temperature (VT) heating circuit. This circuit is illustrated in Figure 8.22. The boiler produces hot water for the constant temperature (CT) circuit at 80°C. Using a three way valve, a proportion of this hot water is allowed to pass into the heating circuit. When the demand for heat is high, such as on a cold day, more hot water will be allowed into the heating circuit. On a mild day less hot water would be allowed into the heating circuit. The radiator temperatures will therefore be hot on a cold day and luke warm on a mild day.

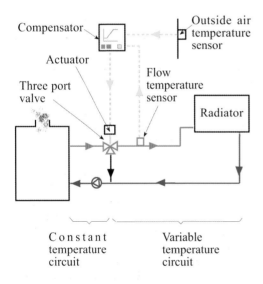

Figure 8.22. Variable temperature flow circuit.

Building management systems (BMS)

All of the control functions discussed previously for commercial buildings, including boiler step control, optimisation, compensation and zoning can be carried out using a building management system (BMS). A BMS is a computer based heating, ventilation and air conditioning control system which offers a great deal of flexibility in the way it is set up and operated. It also offers

the possibility of close interaction between the operator and the building services systems. The main components of a BMS are shown in Figure 8.23 and are described below.

Outstations

Unlike dedicated hard wired controllers that only control the functions for which they have been purchased, outstations can be programmed to perform a range of control functions. The outstation receives information from sensor about the status of the heating system and the building. The programme which decides what this information means and what to do as a consequence is called a control strategy. A simple example is if the room temperatures are below the required temperature set point. Temperature sensors will signal this to the outstation. Using the logic contained in the control strategy, the outstation will decide that heating is required and send signals to actuators to make the boiler fire and pumps operate to supply heat to the room. The control strategy refers to other rules before carrying this out. For example, heating will only be supplied if the time is within the occupancy or pre-heat period.

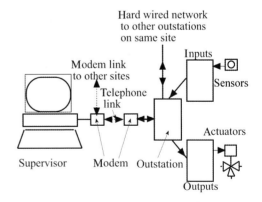

Figure 8.23. Building management system components.

Sensors are input devices for the outstation. They are transducers that convert a physical state into an electrical signal. There are two main types; analogue sensors and digital sensors. Analogue sensors return a varying signal to the outstation. For example, a signal in the range 0 to 5 volts from a temperature sensor can be set to represent the temperature range 0 to 25°C.

A digital signal can only take one of two values, for example 0 volts or 5 volts. Such a signal can be sent from a switch to represent it being opened or closed respectivly. So, for example, if a boiler was firing, a 5V signal would be returned. If it had failed then a 0V signal would be returned.

Actuators turn electrical signals into the physical actions required by the control strategy using motors or solenoids. An example of an analogue actuator is one which sets the position of a motorised valve. The electrical signal to it may vary between 0 and 5V. This corresponds to the fully shut and fully open positions. Hence a signal of 2.5V would cause the valve to be half open.

A digital signal can be used to open or close a solenoid. For example, changing the signal to a solenoid fitted to it from 0 to 5V causes a pump to operate. Changing the signal back to 0V causes it to stop.

The 'supervisor' is a standard personal computer which allows human operators to interface with the system. It is loaded with the necessary software to interact with the outstations. The supervisor can be used to programme the outstation with its control strategy. Once this is installed, it is possible to visualise all the information available to the outstation on screen. So, for example, room temperatures, the status of boilers, pumps and other equipment, such as the position of valves or dampers can all be displayed. Values are displayed graphically so that their interpretation is easily understood with only a small amount of training.

The system constantly upgrades the information it presents and also stores data at the outstation for later inspection. For example, room temperatures over the last 24 hours can be displayed graphically. This is a most useful

tool for diagnosing faults and commissioning the heating system following installation. The supervisor is also used to set variables. One example is the inputting of new room temperature set points.

Buildings fitted with a BMS have been found to have lower energy consumptions than comparable buildings with stand-alone controllers, provided that they are set up and operated effectively. There are a number of reasons for the savings that can be achieved. The first is the accuracy of control that can be achieved. The second is the ability of the system to signal heating system faults which may otherwise go undetected causing excessive energy usage. Finally, monitoring and management of energy consumptions is also facilitated by fitting sensors on to the utility meters. This allows logging of energy consumptions which can then be used to prepare reports and indicate excessive consumptions.

One supervisor can be used to control the operation of many outstations. The supervisor is typically located in the office of the energy or building manager. It can communicate with various outstations using modems and network cabling or via wireless links.

It is also possible for the BMS to communicate with other control systems in buildings. For example it is possible to integrate BMS systems with security systems. So, for example, access to spaces using key cards can be monitored. When it is known that all people have left a space, the heating can be turned off or down to a set back position, thus saving space heating energy.

One point of caution is that a BMS system can only save energy if it is designed and set up correctly in the first instance, and is then used in the manner described above. If there are inadequate resources in terms of training and staff time to operate the system, it has been found that a simple control system, that is used as it is intended, is better than a complex system that is used incorrectly. ❧

Domestic hot water (DHW)

Domestic hot water (DHW) provision requires that heat is input to cold mains water to raise its temperature. This heat can be taken from an indirect heating system or be provided by a direct water heater.

Methods of DHW heating for domestic buildings

Indirectly from a heating system

Using an indirect cylinder, some of the heated water flowing through the heating circuit is diverted, using a three way valve, through a calorifier (coil) within the hot water cylinder (Figure 8.24). The calorifier is a coil of copper tube, through which the heating system water flows. Heat transfer from the calorifier warms up the cold water held in the cylinder. The sizing of the calorifier coil is critical to achieving good efficiency. If it is undersized there will only be a small transfer of heat from it to the stored hot water. This will cause high temperature water to return to the boiler, causing it to cycle on and off, which is inefficient. It is preferable, therefore, to use cylinders with a large calorifier coil.

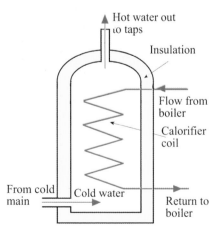

Figure 8.23. Indirect DHW cylinder.

The heated water rises to the top of the tank where it is drawn off to the taps. The cold feed, which enters at the base of the cylinder, is from a mains fed tank, which is sometimes built into the top of the cylinder to form an integral unit. Since the feed water tank is open to the air, the system is referred to as a vented or non sealed system. Unvented indirect cylinders are available which are similar to the system described above except that the cold feed is from a direct connection to the water main instead of from a tank. As a result hot water from the cylinder is fed to the taps at mains pressure. This gives a higher flow rate than a tank fed system.

The benefits of indirect water heating are that the central heating boiler performs two functions (space and water heating), and that there is a stored volume of hot water ready to meet peak demands. However, in summer, the low loads encountered by a central heating boiler required to generate hot water only lead to reduced boiler efficiency. It is therefore recommended that indirect cylinders are used in conjunction with a condensing boiler. The cylinder itself must be well insulated (at least 35mm of factory applied PU-foam insulation) to reduce heat loss from the stored hot water. These heat losses are known as standing heat losses.

There are a number of solar heating systems that utilise the indirect form of heating and these usually require a further coil to be installed in the dhw tank. Solar water heating is discussed in detail in Chapter 2.

Directly from a heating element

The most common example of direct water heating is via an electric immersion heater to heat water stored in a DHW cylinder. The immersion heater is a sealed resistive element through which electricity is passed, causing it to heat up. The immersion heater penetrates the storage cylinder making direct contact with the stored water. A typical domestic immersion heater would have a power rating of 3kW.

The immersion heater has an in-built thermostat to control the domestic hot water temperature. This switches the current on or off, as required, to maintain the pre set temperature, typically 60-65°C. The duration of operation of the heater can be controlled manually using a switch or automatically using a time switch. Electricity is costly and polluting but short duration use of an electric immersion heater in summer can be more efficient than an indirect heating system, due to its poor low load efficiency.

Combination boilers also create direct domestic hot water and these are discussed under *'Boilers'* earlier in this chapter.

DHW for commercial buildings

Hot water in commercial buildings can be provided by the methods used in housing discussed previously. The systems are, however, much bigger due to the increased demand for hot water experienced in larger buildings. Another method of indirect DHW production used in commercial buildings is to replace the indirect cylinder with a water to water plate heat exchanger. The source of heat is still the indirect heating system.

Water to water plate heat exchangers are built of a sandwich of convoluted thin plates (Figure 8.25). Alternate voids, created by the plates, carry heating circuit and DHW flows respectively. Heat is transferred from the heating circuit flow to the DHW flow by conduction across the thin metal separating the two flows. This process is fast enough to produce hot water instantaneously.

Plate heat exchangers have a number of advantages over storage systems;
- there are no standing heat losses since there is no stored volume of water to cool down overnight or at weekends
- legionnaires disease can arise where water is allowed to stand at the incubation temperature of the legionella bacteria. Since standing water is eliminated with plate heat exchangers the possibility of infection is avoided
- plate heat exchangers are physically much

smaller than indirect cylinders. This makes them useful where space is limited.

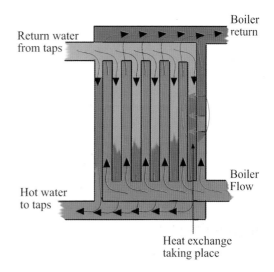

Figure 8.25. Diagram showing principle of operation of a water to water heat exchanger.

Since there is no stored hot water, which is used to satisfy demand at times of peak usage, the heat exchanger must be sized to satisfy the peak hot water demand of the building.

DHW loops

Until recently a significant difference between domestic and commercial DHW systems was the way in which the hot water is distributed to the taps. In domestic properties, a single pipe usually directs water from the cylinder to the tap. The length of pipe is known as a 'dead leg'. The length of the dead leg must be kept to a minimum. In large buildings the dead legs become over-long due to the large distances between hot water production and use. Heat losses from these long pipes would result in tepid water initially being drawn off from taps furthest from the hot water tank. Running off this tepid water until hot water was obtained coupled with the heat lost from the pipes themselves, results in a significant waste of energy. To provide a rapid response in buildings with long pipe runs, including some larger domestic homes, hot taps are therefore usually supplied from a secondary hot water loop (Figure 8.26).

A secondary DHW pump continually circulates hot water from the cylinder or heat exchanger around this circuit. As a result hot water is always available at the taps. This system provides a good hot water service but can lead to high heat losses from the secondary distribution pipework. To overcome this and to avoid uncontrolled heat entering spaces through which the secondary DHW pipes run, the pipes must be very well insulated.

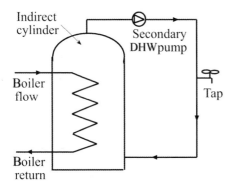

Figure 8.26. Secondary DHW circuit.

In commercial buildings that occupy a large site, it makes sense to decentralise the hot water system and to provide sources of hot water throughout the site corresponding to demand. This can avoid the need for long dead legs or a secondary DHW loop. Point of use or instantaneous heaters can be used for this purpose. For larger demands direct fired water heaters should be used. These devices are cylindrical in shape, containing a small volume of stored water (Figure 8.27).

The gas burner is sited at the bottom of the unit. The heat exchanger and flue run up through the centre of the stored water volume so excellent thermal contact is made between the source of heat and the water. Any heat losses from the flue also pass into the water. Since there is a stored volume, there will be standing heat losses. To reduce these, the exterior of the tank is well insulated and the volume of water stored is large enough to satisfy a surge in demand but small enough to reduce the standing losses. As a consequence of this and the other features described above,

direct fired water heaters operate at an efficiency of approximately 90%.

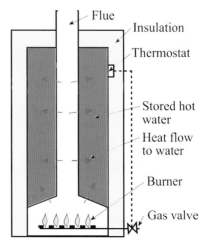

Figure 8.27. Direct fired gas water heater.

Building Regulations
It is a requirement of the Building Regulations part L2 that the DHW services make efficient use of energy.

Ways of achieving this requirement include;
* avoiding over-sizing of hot water systems
* avoiding low load operation of boilers
* not using mains electricity (unless demand for DHW is very low)
* using solar water heating panels
* reducing the length of secondary DHW loops and length and diameter of dead legs
* controlling the system so that hot water is provided only when required and to the temperature required. ☙

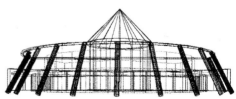

9 Cooling

Introduction

In winter, when indoor air temperatures are too cool for comfort, heat is added to the room air to increase its temperature. In summer the opposite can occur and air temperatures can become too warm for comfort. In this case energy must be removed from the room air to reduce its temperature. This is achieved using some form of cooling, commonly referred to as air conditioning.

The cause of high internal air temperatures is a combination of high outside air temperatures and high internal heat gains. Whilst the UK is not known for its hot climate, it is possible that in summer, daytime air temperatures can be in the high twenties for a number of consecutive days. This air enters the building and absorbs additional heat released from casual sources, such as sunlight, lighting, occupants and equipment. The largest contributor of heat is the sun, as shown in Table 9.1, which lists the average daily heat gain rate per square metre of floor area for different heat sources. The values in Table 9.1 are averages for the space over the year. Variations will occur depending on the time of year and closeness to windows.

Heat Source	Gain rate (W/m²)
Occupants	9
Lighting (typical)	20
Solar gains (south/east)	37
Equipment	25

Table 9.1. Sources of heat gain in a typical office building.

Closeness to windows. The figures for occupancy will be evenly distributed throughout the space. The solar energy gains will be greater near the windows than deeper parts of the space. Equipment gains will depend on where the equipment is positioned. Computers, for example, are usually fairly evenly spread out. Artificial lighting gains may be reduced near windows if an effective daylight utilisation strategy is adopted

Time of year. There may be greater gains from lighting in winter as a result of increased artificial lighting use on darker days. The gains from sunlight will be greatest in summer. However, sunlight is still present in winter and at this time of year it will penetrate more deeply into the building as the sun is lower in the sky.

Causal heat gains in office buildings can be sufficiently high that air conditioning is required all year round. The energy used by air conditioning systems is the prime concern but an additional concern is that mechanical cooling systems are filled with refrigerants. In the past CFC's were used but are now prohibited as they were found to damage the ozone layer. Modern alternatives are much less destructive and in many cases ozone benign. However, many of the alternatives are greenhouse gases which, if they escape, add to global warming. Some refrigerants such as ammonia and propane, are neither greenhouse gases nor ozone depleting gases. However, they do carry risks of toxicity and flammability respectively.

The proportion of the total energy used in a prestige office for refrigeration is 11%, with more added on for the fans and pumps used in distributing cold air or water around the building. In total, air conditioned buildings account for 2% of the UK's annual CO_2 output. It is likely in the future that the amount of energy used in air conditioning systems will increase due to two factors; global warming creating longer and warmer summers, and the move from an industrial economy to a service economy that makes greater use of information technology within office buildings.

Cooling a building using minimal energy requires the implementation of the following strategies;

- eliminate or reduce heat gains
- design the fabric and form of the building to promote natural ventilation, daylighting and passive cooling
- adopt passive cooling strategies that utilise ventilation and exposed thermal mass
- use low energy mechanical systems, such as air circulation fans and evaporative cooling
- restrict the area treated by air conditioning. The system should be constructed from energy efficient components and controlled to limit hours of use.

It is possible that the building will operate a mixed mode strategy to keep its occupants cool. This begins using passive techniques but may call upon mechanical systems to deal with cooling peaks during summer or when internal gains overwhelm the passive methods.

This chapter will begin by considering the range of casual heat gains in a building and how they can be reduced. It will then consider passive and low energy mechanical methods of cooling a building. ☯

Heat gains

This section will look at the various casual heat gains in descending order of size and consider ways of reducing them. This is particularly important, since passive and low energy mechanical cooling methods have a limited cooling capacity that would not be able to cope with unrestricted casual heat gains.

Solar heat gains

Solar heat gains were considered in Chapter 2 as a useful way of reducing the space heating energy consumption of houses and small commercial buildings. However, in buildings with large glazed areas or those with other substantial heat gains, the ingress of solar energy can cause overheating. Large glazed areas are the key risk factor for buildings, especially when these are facing south or west. South, because the solar intensity is at its greatest when the sun is in this direction. There are two problems when the sun is in the west. The first is that the sun is low in the sky and so is difficult to shade. The second is because the sun reaches the west in the afternoon and, the building fabric having heated up through the day, cannot absorb any more heat and so the air temperature will rise.

It follows from the above that the first two recommendations for reducing solar gains are to reduce glazed areas on the west and south faces of the building. Glass is a popular material with architects and so a number of contemporary commercial buildings have facades with glazed proportions approaching 80%. This contrasts with the guidance given for offices in the '*The lighting and thermal (LT) method of design*' in Chapter 4, which indicates that a glazing ratio of 40% should not be exceeded on a south facing facade.

Controlling solar heat gain with shading

There are various shading systems available for controlling the entry of sunlight through glazing. These include movable shading devices and fixed shading devices. The choice of sun control system depends on the orientation of the glazing, the performance required, the need to maintain daylight levels and the aesthetics of the building.

Movable shading devices, commonly referred to as blinds, can be moved into place when required and retracted when the sunlight has gone. Retraction on overcast days allows adequate daylight levels to be maintained. Three forms of blinds can be identified; roller blinds, horizontal or vertical louvre blinds and shutters. An additional benefit of blinds is their ability to reduce glare caused by a bright window. Blinds were discussed in Chapter 7, where they were considered as a method of alleviating overheating arising from adopting a daylighting strategy. This is added to below by describing a control strategy for the blinds.

Shutters, typically used in hot countries, are exclusively manual in operation. They can be solid and completly block out the sun, or have fixed louvre openings or perforations to let in some daylight.

Blinds can be deployed manually or automatically. Automatic control requires a control unit such as a building management system (BMS) connected to sunlight and internal temperature sensors and motorised actuators. The sensors detect a rise in temperature and if this occurs in conjunction with high sunlight levels, the blinds are made to descend. When internal temperatures decrease or the sunlight disappears the blinds can be retracted. This avoids the 'blinds down, lights on' problem that can itself be a cause of unnecessary lighting energy consumption.

A similar strategy can be adopted with horizontal louvre (venetian) blinds. In addition to the capability of full or partial retraction they also have the facility for rotation of the blades. So, for example, as internal temperature increases further, the blinds can descend down the glazing with blades in the horizontal position (Figure 9.1).

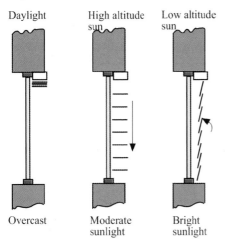

Figure 9.1. Automatic blind control strategy.

This allows some shading and maintains daylight entry. If the temperatures increase the blades can be rotated to the vertical position to totally obscure the sun. The reverse occurs as temperatures fall. Automatic control of blinds

is particularly useful when the glazing is out of reach, such as blinds, protecting the roof of a glazed atrium or within a double skin glazed walling system. Any changes in blind position must be carried out slowly to be less noticeable and avoid disturbing the occupants.

Fixed shading devices form part of the structure or an extension to the fabric of the building and, as the name implies, they are fixed in position. Since no adjustment is available the shading device must be appropriate for the range of sun altitude and azimuth experienced by the facade to which they are part. Generally speaking fixed shading devices fall into one of three categories; horizontal shading devices, vertical shading devices and combined horizontal and vertical shading devices. They differ from blinds in that they usually aim to cause little if any obstruction to the window, so views and daylighting are retained.

Horizontal shading devices are typically found as horizontal shelves projecting externally over the window head (Figure 9.2). They can be constructed out of lightweight materials, such as aluminium, timber or fabric. They are suitable for shading high altitude sun but not low altitude sun. This makes them useful for shading south facing glazing in summer but not for east or west facing glazing or south facing glazing in winter.

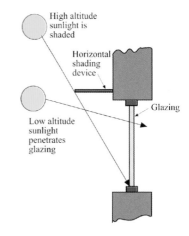

Figure 9.2 Vertical section through a window showing horizontal shading device.

Figure 9.3 is a shadow mask for a horizontal shading device over a south facing window. The grey area covers the parts of the sun path at the positions where the sun is obscured from the window. The upper semi-circle is fully obscured, indicating that the building itself, shades the window from all sun positions running from west to east, through north. The shaded area in the lower semi-circle covers the parts of the sun path with the highest altitude indicating that the sunlight from low altitude sun can pass under the horizontal shading device and hit the window.

each side of a south facing window. It shows that the shading system obscures low angled sun coming from the east to south east and west to south west.

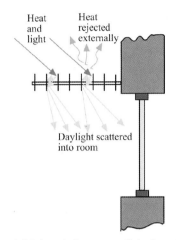

Figure 9.4 Brise solail over a south facing window.

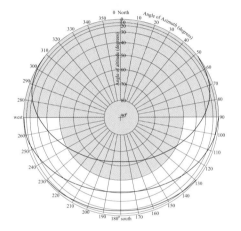

Figure 9.3 Shadow mask for a horizontal shading device over a south facing window.

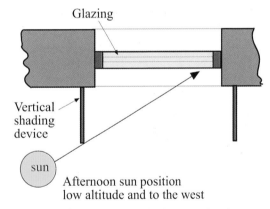

Figure 9.5. Plan section through a window showing vertical shading device.

Figure 9.4 shows a horizontal shading device composed of vertical plates. The purpose of this is to shade the sun but allow scattered daylight to enter the window.

Vertical shading devices are most commonly encountered as the vertical part of the window reveal, especially where the window is deeply recessed. Vertical panels are useful for shading low angled sunlight that strikes the window obliquely. For example Figure 9.5 shows a horizontal section through a south facing window that is protected from afternoon sunlight by a vertical projection.

Figure 9.6 shows the shadow mask associated with two vertical shading devices, one on

Combined vertical and horizontal shading devices are encountered as either the reveals of small windows or as egg crate shading devices as illustrated in Figure 9.7. Depending on the spacing of the elements, the shading device gives a good degree of shading for most sun positions, except for those where the sun is positioned on a line normal to the window i.e. is low altitude and opposite the window. However, views through the window are restricted in direction and the shading device is more noticeable, both externally and from within the building. This form of shading device is common in hot countries, appearing as perforated and carved timber screens placed over windows. The shadow mask for this device is the combination of both the horizontal and vertical shadow masks.

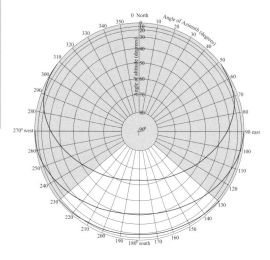

Figure 9.6. Shadow mask for a vertical shading device placed at both sides of a south facing window.

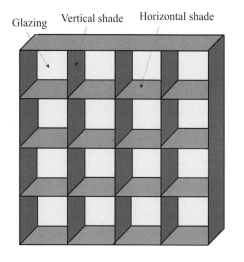

Figure 9.7. Combined vertical and horizontal shading device.

Controlling solar heat gain with special glazing

When sunlight hits a sheet of glass some of it is reflected, some absorbed and some transmitted (Figure 9.8).

The absorbed component raises the temperature of the glass and this energy is then re-released both internally and externally. More tends to leave the glass outwards than inwards, as it is usually cooler outside than inside. The quantities of incident solar energy that are reflected, absorbed or transmitted depend on the clarity and reflectivity of the glass and the angle of incidence of the sun's radiation striking it. For example, if the solar radiation hits the glass at an acute angle to its surface, more will be reflected. If the radiation hits the glass at 90° to its surface, then more will be transmitted.

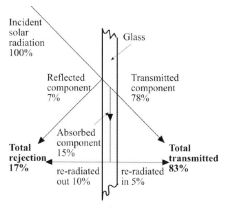

Figure 9.8. Reflection, absorption and transmission of solar heat through 6mm clear float glass.

Taken over a whole day, with varying solar angles, the components for clear 6mm float glass are transmitted 78%, reflected 7% and absorbed 15%. Of the 15% absorbed component, 10% is re-released externally and 5% enters the building. The total transmission is therefore 83%. By adding an extra sheet of glass to create double glazing, the total transmission is reduced to 72%. Once inside the building, the short wave solar radiation is absorbed and re-radiated at a longer wavelength. Glass is not transparent to long wavelength thermal radiation and so it cannot escape back out through the glass.

There are special types of glazing whose aim is to reduce the transmitted component and therefore reduce the solar cooling load. These two types are solar reflecting glass and solar absorbing glass.

Solar reflecting glass has a very fine metal coating applied to its outer surface to increase its reflectivity, like the silvering that is applied to glass to create a mirror (Figure 9.9). The amount of reflectivity can be varied depending on the thickness of the applied coat. It must be remembered that as the reflectivity of the glass increases the daylight transmission decreases. Table 9.2[1] shows that as sunlight transmission is reduced by increasing the reflected component, the daylight transmission is also reduced. Daylight is useful in that it allows artificial lighting to be turned off, thereby reducing the cooling load arising from lighting.

In existing buildings reflecting films are available that can be cut to size and applied to glazing to reduce solar gains.

Solar absorbing glass protects the building by absorbing the incident solar heat within the glass itself. It is created by mixing additives to the glass during manufacture that darkens its structure. This type of glass is also known as body tinted glass. Most of this trapped heat will be lost outwards rather than inwards, reducing the size of the overall transmitted component. Figure 9.10 illustrates the principle.

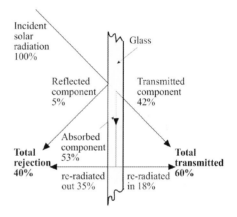

Figure 9.10. Reflection, absorption and transmission of solar heat through solar absorbing glass.

Table 9.3 gives details for four thicknesses of body tinted glass. It can be seen that increasing the thickness of glass, increases the absorbed component. A change from 6mm glass to 12mm glass reduces the solar heat transmission from 60 to 45%. However, this change also reduces the daylight transmission from 42 to 19%. >>>

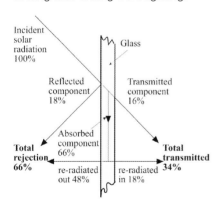

Figure 9.9. Reflection, absorption and transmission of solar heat through solar reflecting glass.

Type	Factor (%)		
	Heat		Light
	Trans.	Reflection	Trans.
10/23 silver	23	32	10
20/34 silver	34	18	20
30/42 silver	42	15	30

Table 9.2. Solar heat transmitance and reflectance and light transmission of solar reflecting glass.

Type	Factor (%)		
	Heat		Light
	Trans.	Absorbtion	Trans
4mm grey	68	40	55
6mm grey	60	53	42
10mm grey	49	71	25
12mm grey	45	77	19

Table 9.3. Solar heat transmitance and reflectance and light transmission of solar absorbing glass.

The absorption of solar heat increases the temperature of the glass. This can cause thermal discomfort to occupants working near to the glazing due to radiant heating. The use of solar absorbing glass is a less satisfactory solar control strategy than rejecting the solar energy immediately by reflection. One benefit of the reduced daylight transmission of both solar reflecting and solar absorbing glass is that it reduces glare from windows.

The above examples relate to single glazing. Both solar reflecting and solar absorbing glass performance is changed when it is incorporated into a double glazed unit. For example, 6mm 10/23 silver solar reflecting glass, when incorporated into a double glazed unit with a low emissivity inner leaf, has its total transmission reduced from 23% to 14%.

A variation on the above glazing systems is 'fritted' glass. This is glass that has been screen printed to produce a grid of opaque dots on its surface. If the dots are white, the glass becomes partially solar reflecting glass. If the dots are black, the glass becomes partially solar absorbing glass. Both types give a degree of internal shading that helps to reduce the effects of glare. The amount of shading and solar rejection can be increased or decreased by printing a closer or more spaced out arrangement of dots respectively.

Solar control glass should be used carefully as it permanently reduces daylight transmission. This may be acceptable on bright sunny days but unacceptable on overcast days.

Future systems

Research is continuing on special forms of glazing that change their solar characteristics in response to changing environmental conditions. There are three such types of glazing; photochromic glass that darkens as sunlight levels increase, thermochromic glass that darkens as its temperature increases and electrochromic glass that darkens in response to an electrical signal applied to the surface coating. All of these types of glazing have been produced in small scale test samples but as yet are too expensive to be used practically in mainstream buildings. As with other technologies, such as photovoltaics, mass production techniques may make these glazing systems viable in the future.

Lighting heat gains

Artificial lights are devices for converting electricity into light. Unfortunately this conversion process is not 100% efficient and heat is emitted as well as light. The heat output from lighting can be reduced by selecting energy efficient lamps and also limiting their operation using controls. This has been considered in Chapter 7. Virtually all of the electrical energy that goes in to a lamp to produce light makes its way into the building as heat. Therefore, reducing the amount of electricity used by artificial lighting, using efficient lamps, system design and control will reduce the cooling load. For example, the heat gain to a building from a typical lighting installation giving 500 lux on the working plane is 20W/m^2. An equivalent low energy lighting system would contribute a heat gain of 11W/m^2.

One system that was not considered in Chapter 7 is the use of remote lamps and fibre optics to convey the light to where it is needed, without conveying the heat. In this situation a powerful light source produces light in an environment where thermal comfort is not an issue, such as a plant room, or where cooling can be achieved by rapid ventilation. Fibre optic cables collect the light and convey it to rooms where it is needed. This allows light to be provided without the associated heat gains that may otherwise cause the room to overheat. This system can also be used in environmentally controlled display cabinets to reduce or eliminate the need for them to be mechanically cooled.

Occupancy heat gains

Building occupants are a source of heat. A person sitting at a desk will be giving out almost 100W of heat derived from metabolic activity. An active person gives out more heat depending on the amount of muscular exertion. Table

9.4 shows how metabolic heat output increases with increased activity.

When people congregate in large numbers, the combined heat gain can be substantial. Given that occupants are the reason for most buildings to exist, it is difficult to justify eliminating the occupants to reduce heat gains! In hot climates, rooms in which large numbers of people congregate are often adjacent to courtyards. If overheating is a concern, the doors connecting the room to the courtyard are opened and the gains can escape outside the building. This is difficult to achieve in modern, commercial buildings but the technique is partially adopted by increasing the volume of rooms in which lots of people congregate. Warm air will rise to the ceiling and the heat will be diluted in the large volume of room air (see Chapter 4).

Activity level	Heat Output (W)
Seated at desk	90
Walking in office	110
Light work	150
Heavy work	200

Table 9.4. Heat gains from occupants.

Office equipment gains

Office buildings house a large amount of equipment, such as personal computers, printers, fax machines, drinks machines and photocopiers. All of these pieces of equipment will give out heat whilst performing the function for which they are intended. Normally the equipment used by the building occupant is outside of the control of the building designer. However, if the elimination of mechanical cooling is part of the building's design strategy, then it is important that the building users are made aware of this and adopt methods that would reduce the cooling load arising from small power consumption. These are:

- choose efficient equipment that consumes the least amount of electricity to perform a given task. A good example of this is the choice of LCD computer visual display terminals (VDT) as opposed to cathode

ray VDT's. A typical cathode ray device consumes 200W of electricity whereas a LCD screen consumes 28W
- switch off the equipment when it is not being used. Much computer equipment now has this capability built in. In equipment where this is not built in the occupants should be encouraged to switch off unused devices themselves. Where this is not practical and the hours of non-usage are well known, simple time switches can be used (whilst ensuring essential supplies are maintained such as those for refrigerators or data storage devices).

These suggestions should form part of the 'user manual' to be supplied to the building management when a new building is handed over on completion (see Chapter 10).

Cooking gains

The heat liberated during cooking can be substantial. If this is released into the kitchen of a low energy house, overheating will quickly occur. Traditionally in hot climates cooking was undertaken outdoors and so no heat entered the building. Modern societies cook inside and so to emulate the traditional means of avoiding cooking gains, an extract fan should be used to remove the heat along with the cooking smells and moisture at source. This is best carried out using an extractor close to the source such as an over the hob extract unit. If this unit incorporates an air to air heat exchanger, it should be fitted with a by-pass for summer operation, so that it does not pre-heat incoming air. Commercial kitchens will incorporate extraction as the norm. Extract fans should be fitted with suitable controls to limit their operation to times of cooking, so that only excessively heated and polluted air is removed from the kitchen.

Summary

The techniques used to reduce the cooling load arising from casual heat gains in buildings are:
- prevent the entry of solar energy
- utilise daylight rather than artificial light
- choose energy efficient equipment

(including lighting)

- control the hours of use of the equipment
- extract the heat gains at source before they can raise room air temperatures, for example by fitting extract luminaires or cooker extracts
- increase the volume of the room so that the heat gains are absorbed by a larger volume of air and greater area of surface mass. This reduces air temperature rises
- do not compound cooling loads for example by placing computer rooms which generate heat on the south side of the building where solar gains also occur. ☯

Cooling the building

There are occasions when either the outside air temperature and/or the internal gains are so high that the internal air temperature becomes uncomfortably warm. When this occurs we have two options. The first is to make the occupants feel more comfortable, even though the air temperature remains the same. The second option is to take steps to reduce the temperature of air in the room and return it to a comfortable position.

Cooling the occupants

If higher temperatures can be accepted, then the need for cooling can be delayed or possibly avoided completely. This occurs naturally, to an extent, since higher internal temperatures are expected and tolerated to a greater degree in summer than winter. Acceptance of higher temperatures is most effective when the occupants are well informed and are aware that they occupy a building with a low energy strategy. They also need to have a degree of control over their environment. This typically requires access to openable windows. The building also needs to be shallow in plan so that more people are near to the windows. The use of vegetation and cool colours in a building has also been suggested as a way of psychologically creating a cooler environment without actually reducing air temperatures.

The most common method of improving comfort, whilst not reducing air temperatures, involves moving the room air over the occupants using a fan. Moving the air creates additional evaporative and convective cooling of the occupant's bodies. This acts to reduce core body temperature and helps in providing thermal comfort. This air movement can be achieved using desk or ceiling fans or a ducted ventilation system. This is not free cooling since electricity is being consumed by the fan. In addition, the heat liberated by the fan motor will create a small rise in air temperature. However, the fact that it is moving, will make it feel cooler to the occupants.

Passive cooling

Passive cooling is the process of reducing air temperatures without using refrigeration equipment. Three techniques can be identified: **free cooling**; **exposed mass and night time ventilation**; and **evaporative cooling**. Each of these will be discussed in the sections below. However, it must be stated at the outset that all passive methods have a limited cooling capacity and therefore it is essential to lower the cooling load by reducing casual heat gains first, as described at the beginning of this chapter.

Free cooling (not quite passive)

When overheating occurs as a result of internal heat gains, it is usual for the outside air temperature to be cooler than inside. If this is the case an amount of free cooling can be achieved by simply replacing hot internal air with cool fresh outside air. At its simplest this is achieved using openable windows. Free cooling can be enhanced using mechanical window actuators, controlled in response to increasing internal air temperatures. Air based air conditioning systems can also be used. The heater and chiller batteries must be switched off and any heat recovery system by-passed. This can form part of a staged cooling strategy where gains are controlled first by causing blinds to descend. Then, if temperatures continue to increase, the ventilation system is activated. If temperatures continue to rise, the chiller plant is activated to reduce ventilation air temperatures. Free cooling by ventilation is only possible when outside air temperatures are lower than inside temperatures. A comparison of these temperatures should be built into the building management system control strategy. If outside temperatures are higher than inside, then ventilation should be restricted to that required for good air quality, and alternative cooling methods sought.

Exposed mass and night-time ventilation

Reference was made in Chapter 2 to the thermal mass of a room. It was stated that exposed dense structural elements such as concrete floors, blockwork walls and concrete ceilings improve the utilisation of solar energy by acting as a short term energy store. This mass can also be used as a passive cooling method to reduce air temperatures during the day. The principle is illustrated in Figures 9.11 and 9.12.

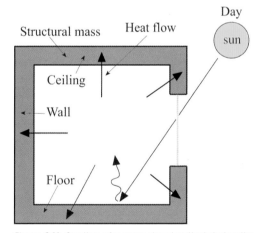

Figure 9.11. Section of a room showing that during the day exposed mass absorbs heat from the room air.

During the day heat gains cause the room air temperature to be higher than the structural temperature. Because of this heat flows from the room air into the structure raising its temperature whilst at the same time reducing the air temperature. It is estimated that if sufficient exposed mass is available, air temperatures can be reduced by 2 to 3°C. On a daily basis it is only the first 100mm depth of mass

that is involved in this process.

If nothing further is done the system will not work again the next day because the structure will still retain heat from the previous day. To re-cool the mass the room must be ventilated at night with cool outside air as shown in Figure 9.12. The structure is warmer than the night-time ventiation air and so heat moves from the structure into the ventilation air. This then leaves the building. This then leaves the building, thereby cooling the structure so that next day it is cooler than the daytime room air and is once again ready to absorb excess heat and reduce air temperatures.

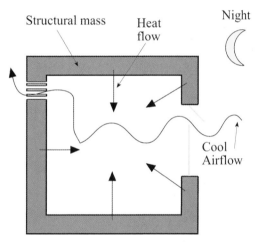

Figure 9.12. Section of a room showing that during the night, exposed mass loses heat to the ventilation air.

There are a number of issues that must be addressed for the exposed mass and night time ventilation strategy to cool effectively:

Admittance. Materials have a property known as admittance (Y). This is a description of the material's ability to exchange heat with the surrounding air as air temperatures change. The value of admittance, measured in W/m²K, is dependant on a combination of thermal conductivity (how well heat moves into and out of the material) and thermal capacity (the ability of the material to store heat). Dense materials, such as concrete, ceramics and marble, have a high value of admittance. Low density materials, such as plaster, carpets and insulation, have a low admittance value.

To be effective, the surfaces in a room being passively cooled, should have as high a value of admittance as possible. The movement of heat into the mass depends on the size of the variation in air temperature from the average air temperature. A positive temperature difference moves heat into the mass, a negative temperature difference causes heat to move out of the mass. Movement of heat into and out of the mass is restricted by the internal surface resistance (see *'Thermal properties of construction materials'* in Chapter 5). It can also be restricted by surface coatings, such as lightweight plaster.

Control. With a mechanical cooling system the chiller can be operated as and when required to satisfy changing cooling loads within the building. With exposed mass the cooling capacity is continuous at a low level, but gradually decreases towards the end of the day as the mass warms up. The overall capacity for cooling depends on the size of the temperature difference between the mass and the room air, and the area of material exposed and therefore available to absorb heat. Control of the passive system is achieved by varying the degree to which the mass is cooled overnight. This is brought about by monitoring outside air temperatures, the trend in this temperature, and the temperature of the exposed mass.

The basic control strategy is that, at night, openings in the envelope are opened or fans are operated to increase the ventilation rate of the building and so cool the mass. For example, if the daytime ventilation rate is 4ac/h, then at night this may be increased to 8ac/h. If the trend in outside temperatures is for a prolonged hot spell, the ventilation is allowed to continue longer to give deeper cooling of the fabric. If cooler days are predicted then the ventilation will be restricted to a shorter period. In either case temperature sensors, which can be embedded in the fabric, indicate the degree of structural cooling achieved, and if it is considered sufficient (usually based on operating experience) then the night time ventilation is

terminated. This is necessary to avoid overcooling the structure which may result in the need for space heating at the start of the next working day.

Exposing the mass. One of the problems with mass in office buildings is that it is traditionally covered up[2]. Overhead the mass is covered by suspended ceilings, the walls by lightweight plaster and the floor by a raised floor system. Figure 9.13 shows how the mass can be exposed to the room air. The suspended ceiling can be omitted. This requires high quality in the creation of the concrete work that forms the ceiling so that it can be painted and left exposed without being unsightly. Service runs also become exposed and again should be boxed in neatly. It is possible to distract attention from the exposed ceiling by using a suspended ceiling with lattice type ceiling panels.

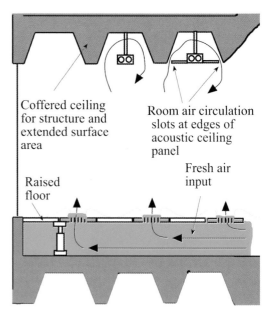

Figure 9.13. Exposing structural mass.

This forms a visual barrier but allows air to circulate easily through the panel. Internal walls should be formed from dense blockwork. These should be fair faced and joints finished neatly before painting. In office buildings, with the necessity for flexibility in the distribution of computer networks, communication and power cabling, it is difficult to omit the raised floor that normally covers these items. However, the mass in the floor can be utilised in mechanically ventilated spaces by supplying air to the space via the void beneath the raised floor (Figure 9.13). This brings it into contact with the thermal mass of the floor. The cooled air then enters the room via floor outlet diffusers.

Acoustic environment. One of the problems with exposed structural mass is that it is dense and therefore will not absorb the ambient sound that is naturally present, especially in open plan offices. This can lead to high background sound levels that interfere with work by masking telephone and other conversations. One way of overcoming this is to reintroduce some absorbent surfaces into the room. This could take the form of sound absorbent screens between workstations, or the use of suspended ceiling tiles that have ventilation slots created in them so room air can move behind them to come into contact with the ceiling mass. Sound passes through perforations in the underside of the panel and is absorbed by a layer of fibrous sound absorbing material above. This is illustrated on the right hand ceiling coffer in Figure 9.13.

Security. Night-time ventilation requires that ventilation devices are opened when the building is unoccupied. In many cases the ventilation openings are motorised windows. The opening of these can be a security risk unless smaller sections of larger windows are used, and the open panels are above normal access heights.

Pollution. A barrier to passive cooling that was raised as a siting consideration in *'Passive ventilation and cooling'* in Chapter 6, is that it necessitates the opening of windows. Many offices are in urban areas that suffer from noise and air pollution. This can be a serious disincentive to open windows. Consideration should be given to creating openings on faces of the building away from areas of traffic. The creation of internal courtyards in the building can be a useful way of achieving this.

High level openings experience less air pollution as they are above the traffic but require fans and ducting to deliver the air to where it is required. The problem of noise ingress can be reduced by creating purpose built openings that contain an amount of sound absorbent material. Air can pass through the short length of ducting but the traffic noise and other external sounds are absorbed.

As was stated earlier, the cooling capacity of exposed thermal mass and night time ventilation is limited. The capacity can be increased by cooling the mass to a greater degree overnight, or by increasing the area of exposed mass. A number of systems have now been utilised in various buildings throughout the UK to achieve this.

Cooling the mass using water. It is possible to cool the exposed mass by means other than air brought in during night ventilation. The BRE Environmental Office Building utilises an embedded underfloor cooling system. This is formed from a network of plastic piping built into the floor slab during construction. Passing cold water through the pipes cools the slab. This system also allows the mass to be cooled during the day as well as during the night. In the case of the BRE office, cool water is obtained from a borehole in the ground. It could also be obtained from an evaporative cooler (see *'Evaporative cooling'* later in this chapter).

Increasing the area of exposed mass for night time cooling. There are a number of ways in which the area of mass available for cooling can be increased. These include the use of earth tubes, hollow floor slabs and basement cooling.

Earth tubes. In this system a series of ducts are buried in the ground. One end is open to the outside air, the other terminates at an air handling unit inside the building (Figure 9.14).

At night fans are operated that draw air through the earth tube into the building. This cools the lining of the earth tube and any exposed mass in the building. During the day the building is once again mechanically ventilated by drawing air in via the earth tube. Contact of the daytime air with the walls of the earth tube cools it before it enters the building. There is a risk of condensation occurring on the surfaces of the earth tube. This could lead to mould growth and ill health amongst the building occupants. Monitoring of intake air temperature and moisture content, and earth tube wall temperature, can alert the building management system when the walls of the earth tube are at or below the dew point temperature.

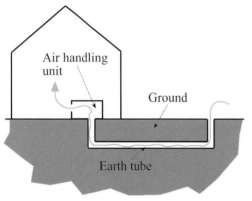

Figure 9.14. Earth tube.

Cellar labyrinth. This system utilises the exposed mass of a basement in addition to that exposed in the rooms themselves. For example, a basement room with walls composed of concrete, is constructed with a number of concrete partition walls. Within the walls are mechanically operated doors (Figure 9.15). Outside air is brought in at the far end of the basement and as it makes its way into the building it is cooled by contact with the basement walls, floor and roof. By opening or closing various doors within the labyrinth the path length, and hence degree of cooling experienced by the incoming air, can be varied.

'Thermodeck' system. This method of increasing the area of exposed mass utilises concrete floor slabs containing hollow bores (Figure 9.16). The bores are opened at each end to give an entry and exit point for the ventilation air. Intermediate bores are connected at

the ends to give a continuous air flow path. The slab is cooled overnight using night time ventilation. The next day air is brought into the building via the bores in the slab. Contact between the warm incoming air and the walls of the bores causes it to become cooler. It has been found that the more turbulent the airflow across the surface of the concrete, the greater is the heat transfer. It is for this reason that the greatest cooling effect occurs at the ends of the bores where there is a change of direction and turbulence occurs.

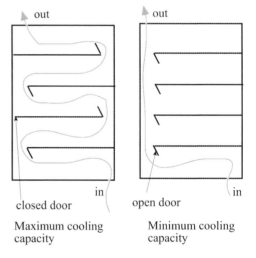

Figure 9.15. Plan of a typical cellar labyrinth layout.

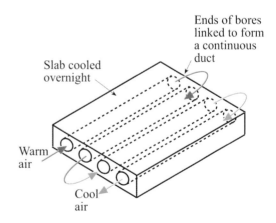

Figure 9.16. Thermodeck system.

Evaporative cooling

When water evaporates it changes from a

visible liquid to invisible vapour. For this to happen the water must absorb energy. It takes this energy from its surroundings and therefore the surroundings, having lost energy, become cooler. The amount of energy absorbed during evaporation of water is substantial. To illustrate this, the amount of energy required to raise the temperature of 1 litre of water from 0°C to 100°C is 0.42 megajoules (MJ). The amount of energy required to change 1 litre of water at · 100°C to vapour at 100°C is 2.26MJ.

The evaporation of water can be used for direct or indirect cooling. Direct cooling involves evaporating water in the space that is to be cooled. Traditional systems in hot countries use fountains, water trickling down ornate stonework or terracotta pots filled with water. Evaporation occurs more readily in a dry environment than a humid one and so these techniques work more effectively in hot dry climates. The reduced evaporation rate in hot humid climates means that evaporative cooling is of limited use there.

Direct evaporative cooling is seen in the UK within air handling units. Here the incoming airstream is passed through a water spray. Evaporation of the spray droplets occurs and this cools the airstream. The airstream will also be humidified in the process. Care needs to be taken with direct systems that bacteria and algae are not allowed to thrive within them, otherwise the organic matter can become airborne in water droplets, and if inhaled cause infections and allergies within the building occupants.

Indirect evaporative cooling involves the production of chilled water by evaporation. This water is then pumped through a cooling coil in an air handling unit through which incoming air is passing. The water is chilled in a cooling tower as shown in Figure 9.17.

The device shown is a forced draught cooling tower. Water is sprayed into the top of the device and droplets tumble downwards, while at the same time air is forced upwards through the cascading water by a fan.

The tower enhances evaporative cooling by increasing the surface area of water exposed to air. Evaporation is a surface effect, so increasing the surface area of the water in contact with the air increases evaporation. This is achieved by firstly injecting the water into the tower as a spray. It then tumbles down splash bars or thinly coats a PVC matrix. Not all of the water evaporates. That which collects in the base of the tower will have been cooled. The cooled water can then be pumped through a cooling coil in an air handling unit, or used within a chilled beam or chilled ceiling static cooling system.

It is important that the cooling tower is designed to minimise the escape of spray droplets and is regularly cleaned and treated to avoid the danger of the bacteria that causes legionnaires disease thriving in the water and escaping into the local environment.

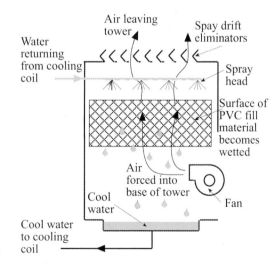

Figure 9.17. Forced draught cooling tower.

Mechanical cooling

Refrigeration plant is equipment that uses electricity to cool air or chill water. The majority of refrigeration systems are based on the vapour compression cycle. This system was described in Chapter 2 *'Geothermal energy'* and in Chapter 6 'Heat pumps', in relation to heat pump technology. In that section the heat pump was used to remove geothermal heat from the ground and place it into a building for space heating purposes. The ground becomes cooler and the building becomes warmer. In refrigeration, heat is removed from an air or water stream, causing it to cool. The heat that is extracted is rejected outside the building as waste. It is the chilled air or water that is used within the building for cooling purposes.

The energy consumed by a cooling system is taken up by two components. The first is the compressor that is the electric pump used to circulate the refrigerant around the system. The second are the fans and pumps used to move the cold air or chilled water away from the system and into the building. Figure 9.18 shows a diagram of a split air conditioning system, a simple method of providing direct cooling of room air. The compressor consumes the majority, approximately 95%, of the electricity used by simple refrigeration equipment.

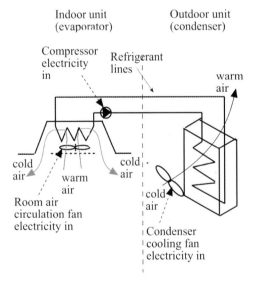

Figure 9.18. Split air conditioning system.

Coefficiency of performance (COP)

The efficiency of a cooling system is normally called the coefficient of performance or COP. The COP of an actual cooling system is given by a comparison between the energy value of the electricity put into the equipment and the energy value of the cooling got out of it. Mathematically this is:

$$COP = \frac{Cooling\ Capacity\ (kW)}{Total\ Power\ Input\ (kW)}$$

Typical COP's for cooling are between 1.5 to 2.0 which indicates that you can achieve 2kW of cooling for the consumption of 1kW of electricity. This compares with a COP of 2.5 to 3.0 if the refrigeration equipment is being used as a heat pump. To study factors affecting performance more clearly it is useful to look at the formula for the theoretical COP. This is given by;

$$COP = T_1 / (T_1 - T_2)$$

where;
T_1 = Evaporator ambient air temperature (K)
T_2 = Condenser ambient air temperature (K)

From this it can be seen that for the COP to be high, the difference between T_1 and T_2 should be small. Since T_1 is set by system requirements, the variable is T_2, the ambient temperature surrounding the condenser. Taking a split cooling system as an example, what this means in practice is that when the outside air temperature increases, the efficiency of the system will fall. This is unfortunate since most cooling is required in summer when high ambient condenser temperatures prevail. However, there are a number of things that can be done to reduce the condenser coil temperature. The first is to increase the size of the air-cooled condenser and ensure that there is good airflow through the device. The next is to consider the use of evaporative condensers. These spray the condenser with water to use latent heat removal, during evaporation of the water, to reduce ambient temperatures. Finally, the condenser can be immersed in water and therefore water-cooled. The water should be obtained from a large body of cool water such as a canal, river, lake or groundwater.

Ice storage

The COP of refrigeration equipment varies with the amount of work it is required to do. At low loads the efficiency will be reduced. One way of overcoming this problem is to use an ice storage system. Ice storage involves using an undersized chiller to produce ice slurry during the night. The ice is formed and stored in an insulated tank (Figure 9.19). During the day, the chiller would not have enough cooling capacity on its own to satisfy the cooling demands of the building. However, by operating the chiller at full load and drawing additional cooling capacity from the ice store, the building cooling demand can be satisfied.

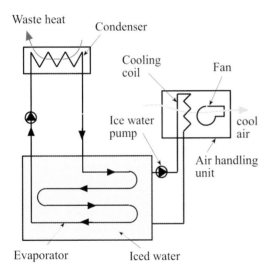

Figure 9.19. Ice storage cooling system.

The advantages of the system are that the chiller operates most of the time at full load and hence peak efficiency, it also provides a good proportion of the cooling requirement of the building using cheaper night time electricity tariffs. Both of these contribute to reducing operating costs.

Absorption chilling

There is growing interest in a method of cooling buildings that uses gas as a fuel instead of electricity. The technology is known as absorption cooling. The biggest difference between this and vapour compression cooling is that the compressor and refrigerant are replaced by a gas fired generator and a refrigerant/absorber mixture respectively. A diagram of an absorption chiller is shown in Figure 9.20.

The generator is filled with a mixture of refrigerant and absorber (solvent), which can be either water/lithium bromide (>100kW cooling capacity) or ammonia/water (30-800kW cooling capacity). The way the system works can be illustrated using the ammonia/water pairing as an example. In this case water is the absorber and ammonia is the refrigerant. The water is the absorber, giving the process its name, as it is so chemically attracted to ammonia vapour that it absorbs it out of the atmosphere.

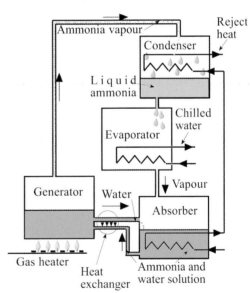

Figure 9.20. Absorption chiller.

A concentrated solution of ammonia in water is heated in the generator using a gas burner. The ammonia component vaporises first, as it has a lower boiling point than water, and passes into the condenser. The water that is left behind passes back to the absorber. The ammonia vapour condenses back to liquid ammonia in the condenser giving out heat, this is taken away for rejection outside the building by a water filled condenser cooling system. The ammonia now passes from the condenser into the evaporator via an expansion valve. In doing so its pressure drops and so it can evaporate once more. It does this by absorbing heat from the chilled water circuit. Chilling has therefore been achieved. The ammonia vapour now passes into the absorber where it is absorbed by the water from the generator to create a concentrated ammonia solution. Heat is given out when the two chemicals combine. This waste heat is removed by the condenser cooling coil circuit. The ammonia solution is pumped back to the generator where the cycle continues once more.

The above device is known as a single effect absorption chiller. Double effect units are also available which pre-heat the ammonia solution on its way back to the generator by passing it through a heat exchanger. This improves the efficiency of the unit. Double effect units require a higher temperature heat source (>140°C) usually derived from direct gas fired burners or pressurised hot water.

Absorption chillers are less efficient than vapour compression chillers with a COP of approximately 0.7-1.2. It follows that more gas energy will be required than an equivalent electric chiller (COP = 1.5 to 2.0). However the gas chiller will be less costly to run and emit less pollution per unit of cooling than an electrically driven chiller due to the high cost and pollution output arising from the use of electricity.

As well as direct gas firing some absorption chillers can be operated using waste heat. One form of surplus heat is that generated by combined heat and power units. In winter their heat output is used for space heating. In summer this heat is surplus to requirements and so can be used to drive the absorption chiller. This is known as trigeneration or combined cooling and power. When heat which would normally be wasted is used, absorption chillers emit much less CO_2 into the atmosphere than a vapour compression chiller for a given cooling effect. Research is currently underway which is investigating the linking of absorption chillers with solar panels as a source of generator heat. It is an advantage that the appearance of large amounts of solar energy coincides with the increased need for cooling.

Cooling distribution systems

Various systems are available to transfer the cooling effect of refrigeration equipment to the spaces that require cooling. Systems fall into two categories, direct expansion systems and indirect systems.

Direct expansion systems cool the room air by passing it directly over an evaporator coil.

Split systems, as illustrated in Figure 9.18, are the simplest cooling system and the most common type of device currently being installed in the UK. Manufacturers data should be considered along with a knowledge of the ambient operating conditions to select a device with the highest operating efficiency. Multi-split systems are also available that use one outdoor unit connected to multiple indoor units. The use of electrical re-heaters on individual indoor units, to provide heating alongside cooling, should be avoided.

Variable refrigerant flow system. A type of multi-split system using reverse cycle heat pumps so indoor units can operate in either heating or cooling mode. Heat recovery is possible if some units are operating in heating mode whilst others are operating in cooling mode. This is achieved by the re-direction of hot and cold refrigerant fluids.

Versatemp systems. These systems use room based water to air heat pumps to either extract heat from or deposit heat into a water loop circulating around the building. When simultaneous heating and cooling of rooms is required, e.g. cooling on the south side of the building and heating on the north, the system acts as a heat recovery and redistribution system (Figure 9.21).

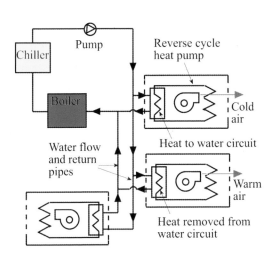

Figure 9.21. Versatemp cooling system.

Indirect, air based systems where air is cooled in an air handling unit and then sent to the rooms via ducting include;

Dual duct system. Two air handling units are used; one to produce cold air, the other to produce heated air. Both air streams are mixed on entry to the room to create the desired temperature with constant air supply volume. Uses a great deal of energy due to the need to both cool and heat air at the same time and so should be avoided.

Variable air volume system. Chilled air at a constant temperature is sent in varying amounts to the room depending on room temperature. The hotter the room the greater the volume of cooled air that is supplied. As lower volumes of air are required the fan speed should be reduced to significantly reduce fan energy consumption. Some systems use electrical heaters on the cold air terminals in case there is a joint need for cooling and heating. This should be avoided.

Indirect, water based systems include;

Fan coil units. This system chills water using a chiller and then circulates it to room based fan coil units. Warm air is circulated through the fan coil and becomes cooled. Some units can also be supplied with ventilation air.

Radiant cooling. This is where surfaces are cooled and comfort is achieved by radiant heat losses from the occupants of the room.

Chilled ceilings. These are composed of an array of purpose built suspended ceiling panels. The panels are of a standard size and made out of perforated aluminium sheet (Figure 9.22). A coil of copper pipe is fixed, in close contact, to the back of this panel. When chilled water is circulated through this pipe, the ceiling panel becomes chilled. Any occupants in the room below the panels will feel cooler because their bodies will radiate heat to the chilled ceiling, the opposite effect to being stood next to a hot radiator. In addition to the radiant cooling effect, air in contact with the ceiling will become cooled and descend into the room.

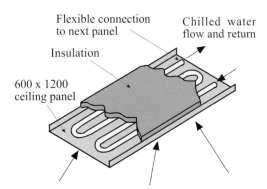

Figure 9.22. Chilled ceiling panel.

There is a risk that condensation will form on the chilled ceiling. To avoid this the chilled ceiling control system must monitor humidity levels within the space. If the humidity levels indicate a risk of condensation occurring then either the incoming air must be dehumidified or the chilled ceiling surface temperature must be raised. Chilled ceilings have a smaller cooling capacity than the cooling systems described earlier.

Chilled beams. These are an alternative to chilled ceilings. A passive chilled beam is shown in Figure 9.23.

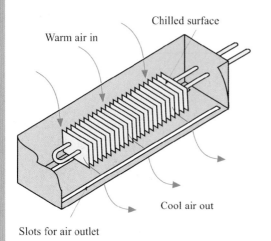

Chilled surface

Warm air in

Cool air out

Slots for air outlet

Figure 9.23. Passive chilled beam.

It can be seen that the chilled surface is formed into a linear finned coil. This coil is then surrounded by a pressed steel casing and is suspended from the ceiling. Warm room air rises to the ceiling and enters the top of the beam. It is then cooled by contact with the cold coil. The cool air descends into the room through outlet slots on the underside of the beam. It can be seen that chilled beams cool a room entirely by convection and provide comfort by bringing the occupants into contact with cold air.

As the cooling output of a chilled beam increases by reducing the water flow temperature through the device, there is a possibility that the beam will create uncomfortable cold down draughts. One way of overcoming this problem is to use active chilled beams. In these devices tempered ventilation air is supplied through ducting within the beam itself. The air leaves the supply ducting through slots or nozzles, with sufficient velocity that it drags warm room air into the beam and through the cooling coil reducing its temperature. The supply and chilled room air mix and enter the room via outlet slots on the underside of the beam. The outlet slots direct the cool air in such a way that it avoids draughts in the occupied zone.

The benefit of systems incorporating chilled

ceilings and chilled beams or active chilled beams alone, is that they are an energy efficient method of cooling. This arises due to the operating parameters of the system. The chilled ceiling and beams operate at a relatively high chilled water flow temperature. This means that the chiller has less work to do and therefore will consume less electricity. The coefficient of performance of the chiller is also improved by approximately 20% due to the higher evaporator temperature. When external conditions allow, the relatively high flow temperature water can be provided using the cooling effect of an evaporative cooling tower.

Chilled ceilings and chilled beams are often used in conjunction with a displacement ventilation system. This is a low energy mechanical ventilation system that was previously described in *'Fan energy consumption'* in Chapter 6. ❧

References for Chapter 9

1. Pilkington United Kingdom Ltd. Solar control glass data sheet. Cl/SfB (31) Ro6 (M5), May 1997

2. BRE Digest 454 Thermal mass in Office Buildings: Part 1 An introduction

Further reading

General Information Report 31. Avoiding or Minimising the Use of Air-Conditioning - a research report from the EnREI Programme (1995)

Good Practice Guide 280. Energy Efficient Refrigeration Technology - the fundamentals

Good Practice Guide 279. Running refrigeration Plant efficiently - a cost saving guide for owners

Good Practice Guide 248. Strategy for Major Cooling Plant Replacement

10 Energy management

Introduction

Having designed a low energy building there is no guarantee that on occupation, and without further intervention, its energy consumption in use will remain low. Some of the low energy aspects are more robust than others. For example, insulation will carry out its role of reducing the heat loss rate from the building without any kind of interaction or adjustment for many years. On the other hand, sensors may malfunction and controls may lose their adjustment, causing services to operate when not required and/or to inappropriate levels.

One example is when heating systems operate in unoccupied buildings at night-time. Another significant factor in excess energy use are the building occupants themselves. For example, windows may be opened to reduce temperatures rather than switching the heating off. It is for these reasons that the energy consumption of buildings should be continually monitored. This ensures that it is consistent with pre-set targets and past performance. Any divergence from target energy consumptions must be investigated and remedial actions taken to return the building to acceptable levels of performance.

Energy management involves gathering data on the size and destination of energy flows and then taking steps to minimise these flows. Most large organisations, such as local authorities, hospitals, universities and industry, employ energy managers to carry out this function. It is also possible to contract out this work to outside energy consultants. This is known as contract energy management (CEM). The staff in these businesses have responsibility for managing the energy consumption in a wide range of organisations. They work on the basis of a fixed fee or alternatively take a percentage of the estimated savings in energy costs that they achieve.

This chapter will investigate the various aspects of energy management by considering the range of duties that are part of the energy manager's job description. These are;

- energy purchasing
- operation of the Building Management System (BMS), (if one is installed)
- troubleshooting of energy consuming system faults
- running energy awareness schemes
- setting targets for energy consumption
- monitoring energy consumption
- making investments in devices that save energy
- preparation of reports on energy and environmental issues.

It has been found that, for the effective management of energy in a large organisation, it is necessary to have a key member of staff who has responsibility for and is the focus of energy issues. This is because energy can be overlooked when the focus is on completing the main activities of the organisation such as making and selling products and services. As well as the energy manager the duties may also be undertaken by a general manager with responsibility for energy issues, a facilities manager or building services engineer.

Energy purchasing

This role of the energy manager is often a financial one. It involves reducing the cost of fuel used by the buildings under the energy manager's control. With competition on the fuel supply market, there is great scope for negotiating lower unit energy costs from energy suppliers by competitive tendering. However, care should be taken that the lower fuel costs are not cancelled out by the additional energy usage that usually accompanies lower fuel prices. One way of avoiding this is to earmark savings arising from any reductions in fuel and power costs towards energy efficiency investments. In this way cost reductions, due to both reduced unit costs and due to energy savings, can be utilised for further investment in energy saving items. In this way the energy management department can become self supporting.

Reducing costs is the traditional role of the energy manager. However, it has now also become one of reducing the environmental impact of the organisation. As such the energy manager should now be giving consideration to the purchase of electricity from renewable sources such as 'green tariff' electricity (discussed in more detail in Volume 1) or assessing the values and payback of installing renewable power or co-generation equipment on/in the building or within the grounds (see Chapters 2 and 8).

The unit cost of fuels will have an impact on energy efficiency investment decisions (see *'Targeting consumption'* later in this chapter). If fuel costs are high, then there are more valuable savings to be made by investing in energy saving equipment than when fuel costs are low.

Building management systems

Building management systems (BMS) were described in Chapter 9. They are flexible building services control systems that allow a high level of user interaction. This gives the energy manager the ability to:

Commission the system. Following installation, all building services systems require commissioning to ensure that they are providing the necessary environmental conditions, are operating efficiently and functioning within prescribed limits. Commissioning should be checked across a range of operating conditions to ensure that the operating characteristics are maintained when the requirements on the system change.

Fine tune the system. Following commissioning the initial settings may require fine tuning

in the light of operational experience. The BMS system logs environmental data, such as room temperatures so that, for example, set points can be refined and the effects of the changes closely monitored over time. It is also possible to modify the control strategy. This is a more technical process involving software changes. It can be carried out by appropriately trained energy managers or instructions given to the BMS installer to write the modifications.

Modify operating parameters. It is unlikely that the operating parameters of the system will be fixed 24 hours a day and 365 days a year. Make sure the building management system controls are compatible to the actual requirements of the building, by changing temperature set-points to set-back positions when rooms are unoccupied, for example in empty hotel rooms. A second example is varying the heating programme, so that heating is only provided when required, for example, restricting heating in schools during holiday periods and evening classes.

Monitor energy consumption. A large estate of buildings may have a small number of utility meters recording energy consumption for the entire site. There is a requirement in the Building Regulations to install sub meters to give more detail on where the energy consumption is going within the site. Examples are recording the consumptions of individual buildings and individual large loads within buildings e.g. catering or chiller energy use. However, these meters are no use unless they are read and the information obtained is acted upon. To aid this, sensors can be affixed to gas, water and electricity meters that allow remote reading by the BMS. The information obtained can then be exported to other spread sheet and word processing software installed on the energy management computer for analysis and report writing.

Troubleshooting faults

Faults in energy consuming equipment and their controls can lead to excess energy consumption in a building. Examples are over heating or cooling rooms and conditioning to occupancy standards when the rooms are empty. There may also be less noticeable faults, such as a variable speed fan unit causing the fan to operate at high speeds at all times rather than reducing fan speed as the need for ventilation falls.

The energy manager can be made aware of the presence of faults from the observations of staff. An effective reporting procedure is necessary to obtain this information and act on it otherwise they appear as complaints. A second source is the BMS system. The BMS software allows the setting up of routines that monitor operational parameters of the building services systems. These routines check the data and look for readings that are outside normal operating limits. One example is a threshold set on boiler flow temperatures of say 85°C. The software continually monitors boiler flow temperatures and if the flow temperature exceeds 85°C an alarm message is displayed on the BMS supervisor screen. This may be caused by failure in the control system which must then be investigated and corrected.

Energy awareness

One of the problems with non domestic buildings is that the occupants have no personal involvement with the energy bills levied on the organisation. This means that there is a tendency to be profligate with energy. Some examples are: lights left on in unoccupied rooms, lights left on when there is sufficient daylight, windows opened whilst the heating is on and computers left running overnight. These actions also occur in peoples' own homes but are likely to be prevented by higher personal energy costs. There are two ways in which the behaviour in the workplace can be modified. The first is to raise awareness of energy issues amongst the building occupants. The aim is to encourage them to adopt energy efficient behaviour such as turning off lights in unoccupied rooms. The second is to provide incentives for them to reduce energy consumption.

Raising energy awareness within and around the organisation can be achieved using at least two methods;

Training sessions. Small groups of staff can be gathered for instruction on the importance of saving energy and shown, by practical demonstration and theoretical payback/benefit scenarios, how energy can be saved in the workplace.

Reiteration. Various types of publicity material can be created such as posters, articles in in-house magazines and stickers suggesting that equipment should be turned off when not needed. Stickers should be placed near occupant operated equipment such as light switches.

It has been found, in practice, that staff who have been made aware of energy issues do adopt energy saving behaviour. Unfortunately, it has also been shown that the majority of these staff revert back to their original profligate behaviour within four months. It is for this reason that awareness schemes should be repeated throughout the year. The challenge is to raise awareness without creating over familiarity that could lead to an eventual disregard of the message. One way of overcoming this is to use a variety of awareness methods and continually be innovative in the way they are presented to staff.

Awareness through incentive

People are more likely to carry out an activity if there is an incentive for doing so. Whilst there are real incentives for cutting energy consumption to protect the environment and conserve fuel resources, this tends to be detached from commercial building occupants. As a consequence some organisations provide financial bonuses to staff in line with the size of energy savings made. This could be restricted to key staff involved in energy savings, such as caretakers or alternatively can be distributed amongst all staff, say in the form of a free staff outing or some other communal bonus. This latter form is the most preferable as it encourages the motivation of all staff within the organisation.

One example that illustrates that energy

consumption is reduced when people make the connection with use and costs is seen in multi-residential properties using district heating. In many dwellings such as these, the heating costs are included as a fixed sum in the rent. As a consequence there is no relationship between energy consumption and costs. This has led to high energy consumption and tempera-tures due to heating being uncontrolled. These temperatures may then be reduced by opening windows. This can be avoided by restoring the link between use and cost. For example, install-ing heat meters (Figure 10.1) that monitor the amount of heat taken by each property from the central or district heating scheme. Energy can then be charged for as used rather than as a fixed sum in the rent. In case studies, where heat meters have been installed, overall energy consumption falls and so does tenants' expendi-ture each month.

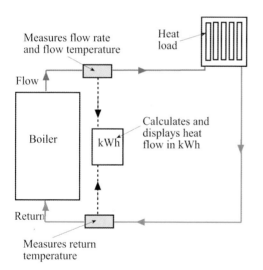

Figure 10.1. Heat meter components.

Targeting consumption

The energy manager needs to have a method of defining what represents a good energy consumption. This is necessary so that actual energy consumptions can be compared against the target to assess if the building is consuming energy at, above or below acceptable limits.

Target energy consumptions can be deter-mined in a number of ways. The first is to use historical energy consumption data for the building. This data is then normalised by dividing it by the treated floor area of the building and the number of degree days over the year. Treated floor area is the area of the building that has its environment changed using energy consuming services. This gives a normalised performance indicator (NPI) measured in kilowatt hours per square metre per year ($kWh/m^2/y$). Occasionally it is worth dividing the energy consumption by a different parameter if that would give a better indication of performance. For example, if school catering energy is being gathered for comparison with other schools, then annual energy consump-tion per pupil taking school meals may be a more appropriate indicator. Another way of setting a performance indicator is to predict it by calculation at the design stage (see *'Energy assessment methods'* later in this chapter). Another alternative is to obtain the energy performance indicators of comparable build-ings within the same area. For example, if you are setting energy targets for a primary school, data for other primary schools within the local authority should be consulted. If local data is not available then national figures can be used, such as those presented in the CIBSE applica-tion manual on energy auditing.[1]

Long term targets for energy reductions can then be set. Studies have shown that in existing buildings the potential for energy savings ranges from 10 to 60%. Typical average potential savings are of the order of 30%. Most organisations set modest targets, aiming to achieve 15% energy savings within the first 3 years of activity. The scope for savings will be less in a new low energy building. The key issue in energy management here is to maintain the initial low levels of consumption in the long term.

Monitoring energy consumption

The amount of energy consumed in a given period is determined from the difference between energy meter readings at the begin-ning and end of the period. For domestic customers meters are read quarterly, i.e. three monthly intervals. For commercial customers, monthly or possibly weekly readings should be taken.

Meters can be read manually and the data input into analysis software. Alternatively, it may be read using electronic readers with the facility for automatic data input. On a large site with many sub meters and short reading intervals, an automatic system will reduce the manpower required for data collection and storage. Some meters have transducers built into them so that an electrical signal, representing the rate of energy consumption, can be obtained. Other meters must have transducers attached to them. For example, optical pulse counters can be used to log the number of rotations per minute of the rotating disk or flashing LED that indicates current flow in an electricity meter. The electrical signals can be returned via radio links, the mains cables themselves or communications cabling such as the BMS network (Figure 10.2).

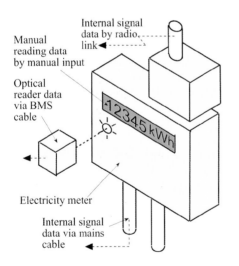

Figure 10.2. Alternative methods of collecting meter data.

Sub-metering
Sub meters should be used to measure the energy consumed by individual large loads within a building. However, if it is a large heat

load that is satisfied by a central boiler system, it is only possible to measure the gas input to the central boilers. To be able to determine where the thermal energy is going from the boiler's, heat meters are required (Figure 10.1). These measure the temperature of heated water entering the zone (°C), the rate of flow of heated water entering the zone (m³/h) and the temperature of water leaving the zone (°C).

From a knowledge of the thermal capacity of water and the volume that has flowed through the zone pipework over a given period, the amount of energy required to heat the volume of water and therefore that taken by the zone, can be determined. On some occasions it is not necessary to monitor the energy consumption if the equipment operates at a constant known load. In this case it is simply necessary to monitor the hours run by the piece of equipment and multiply this by its power rating in kilowatts. The outcome is an energy consumption in kilowatt hours.

It is a requirement of the Building Regulations that sufficent meters and sub meters are installed to provide the information to attribute energy consumption to end uses. A resonable provision is for 90% of the estimated annual energy consumption of each fuel (electricity, oil, gas, LPG and heating and cooling from district heating schemes) to be metered. Resonable provision of meters is to provide an incoming energy meter on all buildings greater than 500m² gross floor area, with sub meters for each separately tenanted area, for each piece of equipment with input powers shown in Table 10.1, and any process loads. This latter category is necessary to distinguish building energy consumption from that used to make products in the factory during industrial processes.

Energy monitoring software
Having taken the meter readings it is necessary to manage the data and analyse it to achieve some meaningful information. Software that has a database at its core, is available to assist with

this.

Plant item	Rated input power (kW)
Boiler installations or CHP plant feeding a common distribution circuit	50
Chiller installations feeding a common distribution circuit	20
Electric humidifiers	10
Motors for fans and pumps	10
Final electrical distribution boards	50

Table 10.1. Size of plant for which separate metering would be resonable.

Details about the locations of the meters are entered into it, such as building address and, if there is more than one meter, the location of further sub meters. The meter reading and time that the reading was taken can then be input to the database. Having stored the basic data, the software can then perform various analytical subroutines, such as:

Calculation of annual, monthly or weekly energy consumption. Note that the accuracy of this depends on the amount of energy consumed and the frequency of meter readings. The greater the rate of energy consumption, the more frequently the readings should be taken. Most software systems divide the energy consumption by the number of days between meter readings to give an average daily energy consumption. If the meter readings are taken at weekly intervals this gives a fairly accurate measure. If the meter readings are taken at quarterly intervals, the accuracy of energy consumption calculated for the quarter will be accurate but for any given week within this period will be low, unless the energy consumption is similar each day.

Analysis of usage patterns. The stored data can be output in graphical form. For example a bar chart of energy consumption per month across a year. This method allows the most rapid assessment of usage patterns. In its simplest form a visual check can be made to ensure expected patterns are occurring. One example is confirming a significant dip in space

heating energy consumption in summer. If the data is being continuously monitored by electronic means, the hourly energy consumption over the last seven days can be output. This will allow a check that energy is not being used when it is not required, such as in the evening or at weekends.

Normalisation of energy consumption using degree days (see Chapter 2). The space heating energy consumption of a building varies depending on the outside air temperature. The lower the outside air temperature, the higher the space heating energy consumption. This makes the comparison of successive annual energy consumptions difficult to make, as one year may have been particularly mild and the next particularly cold. Increased energy consumption in any particular year may be due to a faulty heating system or could simply be due to the lower outside temperatures. To eliminate this variable the energy consumption for each year must be divided by the number of degree days in that year to give an energy consumption per degree day (kWh/y/degree day). Degree day data for each year must be entered into the system.

Statistical analysis of the data can be carried out, such as regression analysis. This is where one variable is compared against another that is related to it to check if the relationship is as expected. One example is in the comparison between outside air temperatures and space heating energy consumption. It is known that heat loss is directly related to outside air temperature, so a graph of energy consumption against outside air temperature should be a straight line as shown in Figure 10.3.

It can be seen that as the outside temperature rises, energy consumption falls as expected. However, it can be seen that the predicted reduction in energy consumption to zero at 15°C outside air temperature is not realised. This could be base line energy consumption due to hot water usage or could indicate a control fault causing the heating system to run when not needed.

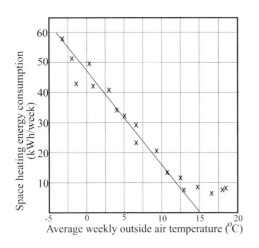

Figure 10.3. Regression graph of space heating energy consumption against outside temperature.

Another statistical technique is called the cumulative sum analysis (CUSUM). This method uses past energy consumption data as base line information and then sums any deviations from this on a weekly basis. The effect is to amplify changes in energy consumption so that they can easily be identified. An example of this is shown in Figure 10.4.

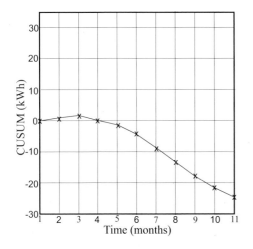

Figure 10.4. CUSUM plot.

The average space heating energy consumption is calculated on a weekly basis for the building over the previous year. This is then compared with each new week's energy consumption as it occurs. If the energy consumption has remained the same as last year there will be little or no change as indicated in weeks 1-4 of the graph. However, at the end of week 4 a new control unit was added to the heating system. This resulted in a small saving in energy in week 5, compared to the same week in the previous year. These savings continued in following weeks and each week's saving is added to the previous one, causing the line on the graph to descend. All energy consumptions were corrected by the software to take into account variations in outside temperature one year to the next. The cumulative savings can be converted into an amount of CO_2 which can be used as part of an environmental audit. It can also be converted into a cost saving and an accurate calculation of the payback period of the control device can be worked out.

Energy audits

Energy audits are a systematic method of identifying where and how much energy is being consumed in a building. It is usually carried out by analysing fuel invoices. This is useful information in itself but it can also be used to identify major sources of energy consumption so that they can be earmarked for the application of an energy saving measure. Another important aspect of energy auditing is the 'walk around'. This is where the energy manager tours the premises to visually identify sources of waste. Examples are seeing lights left on in well daylit spaces. It is recommended that energy audits are repeated at regular intervals, at least annually.

Energy saving investments

In large organisations the cost of implementing energy saving schemes can be high, especially where this involves the purchase of large items of equipment such as combined heat and power units. However, it is also possible to implement no or low cost measures, such as fine tuning of controls and energy awareness schemes.

Large schemes can often be funded under

a leasing arrangement where a contract energy management organisation pays the capital and installation costs of a device. It recovers its initial investment by taking a share of the value of energy savings until the costs and a profit are recovered. The value of energy savings to the business are much lower but at zero capital cost. However, the full value of reduced emissions of carbon dioxide belong to the organisation and so can appear as a positive element in an environmental audit.

The decision to invest in an energy saving feature is usually based on a comparison between financial costs and benefits. The costs are: the capital cost of the device, the installation costs and annual running costs (maintenance and any power input). The benefits are fuel cost savings. If installed at the outset there may also be cost savings available from reducing the size of the heating plant and lower maintenance costs as the plant has to run less often. There may also be non energy benefits, such as increased comfort and productivity of the building occupants.

Simple payback
The simple payback period is defined as the time taken for fuel cost savings to pay back the initial capital cost of the device. It is calculated by dividing the initial capital cost by the net annual running cost savings.

$$Payback\ Period\ (y) = \frac{Total\ capital\ cost\ of\ item\ (£)}{Net\ annual\ savings\ (£/y)}$$

The simple payback method is easily understood and is one of the most widely used methods of assessing financial viability. Most schemes that are approved have a payback period of less than three to five years. There are two main criticisms of the simple payback period. The first is that no account is taken of interest that you would have to pay on a loan taken out to fund the project or the value of other ways of making income from the initial capital sum, such as interest from simply investing the money.

It may be possible that investing the money

in shares could provide sufficient income that equalled or exceeded the value of energy savings made. To allow for this criticism various accounting methods are available that take into account aspects such as taxation, depreciation of equipment and interest payments. The second criticism is that the simple payback does not take into account savings that occur beyond the payback period.

Carbon payback
The decision on whether or not to expend money on installing an energy efficiency measure is still largely decided on financial grounds. It was stated in Chapter 1 that reduced energy costs and increased capital costs can make investments in energy saving devices difficult to justify on financial grounds. In any assessment of benefits arising from energy savings, strong consideration should be given to environmental benefits, such as reduced emission of pollutant gases. A carbon payback, for example, would compare the carbon dioxide emitted in the production of an energy saving device, known as the embodied carbon, with the net annual carbon savings made by having the device, i.e.

$$Carbon\ payback\ Period\ (y) = \frac{Embodied\ carbon\ (kgCO_2)}{net\ annual\ carbon\ reductions\ (kgCO_2/y)}$$

Reporting
Reporting begins when a new building is completed and handed over by providing a building log-book.

Building log book
The Building Regulations require that the owner and/or occupier of a building be presented with the log book which should include details on:
● whole building energy strategy
● description of services installed and their function on a zone by zone basis, illustrated by simple schematics
● installed capacities of the energy consuming plant
● copies of commissioning reports.
● operating instructions and maintenance

intervals
- a description of the location of each meter and sub meter, the fuel type it monitors, plant or space it monitors and the method for using the information as part of an energy management strategy
- copies of any measurements taken such as air permeability or thermographic studies
- copies of any energy calculations made, such as predicted energy consumption and carbon emissions.

It is essential that the log book is added to as necessary for example recording the activities of the energy manager in respect of any additions or adjustments that affect energy consumption.

On a day to day basis adjustments to controls, installation of new equipment and rectification of faults should all be logged. This good practice will ensure that new staff within the organisation have access to all the information that is necessary to ensure that the building and its services operate effectively.

Annual energy management reports give senior management the opportunity to judge the value of energy conservation work, as well as financial savings and energy usage reductions. The energy reductions should be converted into a carbon reduction figure. This can then be used in an overall environmental audit of the business. ☜

Environmental assessment methods

A number of methods exist for assessing either the energy consumption or environmental impact of a proposed building at the design stage. The methods and the information they supply is useful in a number of ways;
- they can be used as design tools by comparing the energy consumption or environmental impact of alternative designs. From this the effect of modifications can be determined
- the information related to the final design can be used as a standard against which the actual energy consumption of the finished building can be compared for monitoring and targeting purposes
- the information related to the final design can be used as evidence to obtain Building Regulations approval or satisfy the requirements of the Energy Performance of Buildings Directive
- the information can be used to promote good practice by highlighting exemplar designs
- the information, which is independently verified, can form part of a marketing strategy to promote the sale or letting of environmentally friendly buildings.

The energy calculation methods that now form the basis of the Building Regulations, i.e. SAP for domestic buildings and SBEM for non-domestic buildings, have been discussed previously in Chapter 5.

Environmental design software

Comprehensive building services design software, that is based on standard CIBSE calculation methods, is commercially available. Data, for example on wall/window dimensions, construction details, orientation of buildings and shading, are input manually on a room by room basis or can be imported from other software, such as computer aided design (CAD) packages. The in-built calculation routines will then calculate heating, cooling, lighting and domestic hot water energy loads. The software can then go on to assist in designing the services installation necessary to achieve the internal standards that were used within the energy calculations. The output is in terms of tabular quantities of energy and also graphical profiles. Most systems also convert the energy use into an emission of carbon dioxide, based on energy to CO_2 conversion factors. Modern systems use hourly weather data within their databases to carry out a dynamic calculation on an hourly basis. One example is determining how cooling load changes throughout the day as the sun's position and the external temperature changes.

Often this software is available as a series of modules that can be purchased individually or as a complete package. Modules may include heat loss and gain calculations, daylighting and artificial lighting design, ventilation calculations and electrical and mechanical design software.

Environmental assessment

Energy calculation methods have now been extended to cover a much wider range of environmental impacts. A number of ecological assessment methods exist, such as environmental footprinting but the main versions of this type of assessment used in the UK have been developed by the Building Research Establishment.

Building Research Establishment Environmental Assessment Method (BREEAM)

BREEAM is a comprehensive assessment tool for analysing and improving the environmental performance of buildings. Assessments are carried out by a network of registered assessors. The assessors consider the building design and allocate credits if it satisfies certain environmental criteria.

The range of building performance criteria that BREEAM assesses covers the following areas:

Management: overall management policy, commissioning of building services, good site management and procedural issues. Items include monitoring the number of waste skips used on the site.

Energy use: input of operational energy consumption from energy calculation software and also carbon dioxide (CO_2) output.

Health and well-being: inside and outside issues affecting health and well-being, such as proximity of workspaces to windows, air and water.

Pollution issues: one example is a consideration of the type of refrigerant gas used in air conditioning systems.

Transport: transport-related CO_2 and location-related factors. Issues considered include proximity to public transport and provision of bicycling facilities.

Land use: greenfield and brownfield sites, i.e. has the land been previously used or is it a new site?

Ecology: ecological value conservation and enhancement of the site. Involving an ecological impact assessment of the site.

Materials: environmental implication of building materials, including life-cycle impacts. Factors considered include recycling of existing materials and use of certified timber products.

Water: consumption and efficiency including provision of water metering and installation of devices to restrict water consumption.

Credits are awarded in each area according to performance related to set criteria. A set of environmental weightings then enables the credits to be added together to produce a single overall score. The building is then rated on a scale of pass, good, very good or excellent. A certificate is then awarded stating this which can then be used for promotional purposes. Having a BREEAM assessment carried out is costly. However, since the assessment begins at the design stage it can influence design and result in more efficient buildings that repay the cost of the assessment. BREEAM is a voluntary scheme but some charitable, local authority and environmental organisations require a BREEAM assessment of designs to be carried out in order to secure funding. www.breeam.org

Versions exist for a range of building types including:
- industrial buildings
- offices
- prisons
- retail premises
- schools
- for buildings that do not fit into those categories there is a bespoke BREEAM.

Ecohomes

A domestic version of BREEAM also exists called EcoHomes. This assessment method covers both new and renovated houses and apartment buildings. It is very similar to BREEAM covering the same assessment criteria but related to domestic scale buildings and the end result is once again a rating of pass, good, very good or excellent. www.breeam.org/ecohomes.html

Other schemes that may be introduced before the next update of this book could include LEED, AECB Silver and Gold Standard, Passivhaus and an EST advanced standard. There is a brief survey of most of these potential schemes in Volume 1. ☯

References for Chapter 10

1.CIBSE (1991) *Applications Manual AM5:Energy Audits and Surveys.*

Further reading

GPG165: Financial Aspects of Energy Management in Buildings.

GIL65: Sub Metering New Build Non-Domestic Buildings. 2001.

GIL 65: Metering Energy Use in Non-Domestic Buildings. 2002

Don't build your dream on someone else's nightmare.

Help prevent habitat destruction—ask for FSC certified wood. Learn more at www.fsc-uk.org

FSC

11 Water conservation

Introduction

The conservation of water is often linked with the conservation of energy. The most direct link with energy is seen in the saving in energy consumption arising from reduced use of hot water. Heat can also be recovered from waste water streams but this is most economical in non-domestic buildings with large volume, high temperature waste streams. In large organisations the conservation of water is a role that is usually carried out by the energy manager.

The availability of water in a country depends on the degree of rainfall, the catchment of this rainfall, the population density and finally, the quality and extent of the treatment and distribution infrastructure. If the availability exceeds demand then there will be no shortage of water. However, if any of the factors involved in determining the availability is deficient or demand exceeds supply, then shortages will occur. In hot - dry countries water has long been regarded as a most important and valuable resource. The availability of clean water means the difference between life and death. Temperate countries, such as the UK, have historically had good rainfall and collection, storage and distribution systems where supply normally exceeds demand. However, this may not always be the case if;

- the amount of rainfall declines due to global warming
- the quality of catchment and distribution is inadequate, for example, due to the utilities failing to stem leakage from their distribution networks
- demand increases due to the construction of more houses and existing houses using a greater number of water consuming appliances, such as dishwashers.

The potential effects of the imbalance between supply and demand were demonstrated in the summer of 2006 when poor rainfall rates led to supply restrictions in areas of southeast England. These shortages, combined with increases in water prices following privatisation of the water utilities, have led to a growing interest in water conservation.

By reducing water consumption in buildings, water and sewerage charges will be reduced and the following additional benefits can also be achieved;

- environmental protection by conservation of water resources and a reduction in the amount of chemicals used to treat water
- in non domestic premises, reduced standing charges, if the meter diameter can be reduced as a result of water conservation
- reduced hot water consumption results in energy savings
- reduced energy used to treat and pump water supplies and sewerage
- reduced stress on the water supply infrastructure.

This chapter will look at demand side reductions by considering the technologies available to reduce water consumption, the use of reclaimed water and also the management of water use.

Taps, toilets and urinals

Figure 11.1 shows a breakdown of the water usage in a typical home. It can be seen that the two largest uses are personal washing (taps) and toilet flushing. In non-domestic buildings, these two uses remain high in staff washrooms, with the additional consumption by urinal flushing systems. This section will look at methods of reducing the amount of water used by toilet and urinal flushing and that discharged from taps. It will consider this by looking at mainstream methods for water reduction and also by considering novel systems that are now available.

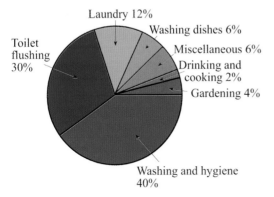

Figure 11.1. Pie chart showing the breakdown of water usage in a yypical household.

Taps

In housing, simple good practice can usually bring about optimum usage of water simply by turning off dripping or running taps when not needed, using a plug instead of using a running tap, repairing dripping taps and not over filling baths and basins. A dripping tap can lose a litre of water per hour. In the home a tap left running or dripping is often noticed by the noise and is turned off. The main area of concern is in public washrooms where the lack of personal involvement with the bills or appliances can result in taps being left running. In this situation there are three ways in which the output of these taps can be minimised. These are;
● using taps which are self closing
● using taps which have a reduced flow rate
● isolating the entire water supply to the washroom when it is vacant.

Self closing taps take two forms. Firstly, there are mechanical push systems, also known as percussion taps, where depressing the tap head opens the valve allowing water to flow. As the water flows out, a spring gradually closes the valve, resulting in a controlled volume of water leaving the tap on each depression. The second type of self closing tap uses a detector within the sink or built into the base of the tap. The detector is usually a passive infra-red (PIR) detector, which registers body heat from the hands. When heat is detected a signal is sent to a control unit that opens an electrically operated valve, known as a solenoid valve. This allows water to flow when hands are detected in the sink area. On removing the hands from the sink the valve is closed. This technology and percussion taps are also used to control the flow of water out of shower heads in changing rooms.

Reducing the flow rate. The speed at which water flows from a tap is known as the flow rate. It depends on water pressure and tap configuration. It is measured in units of litres per second (l/s) and can be determined by placing a measuring jug under the tap and timing how many seconds it takes to fill up to the five litre mark. This time must then be divided by 5 to get the flow rate in l/s. Smaller vessels can be used but they will fill up more quickly and so timing becomes more difficult. A typical open tap with a 5mm stream has a flow rate of approximately 0.3 litres per second. Multiplying the flow rate by the time the tap is left open (in seconds) determines the volume of water in litres discharged from the tap. This volume can be reduced by reducing the flow rate of the tap. This is, of course, a basic function of taps, by turning the tap anticlockwise the bore is slowly opened and the flow rate increases. If there is potential for taps to be left running in the open position some method of permanently reducing the bore is required.

Tap restriction is achieved by placing a restricting device in one of three locations. Firstly, flow restriction can take place by fitting a ball type valve into the pipe supplying the tap. The benefit of this is that the valve remains accessible and adjustable so that the flow rate through the tap can be varied to give a reasonable but not excessive flow. Secondly, restriction can take place within the body of the tap itself by removing the top of the tap and inserting a plastic restrictor. The final method is to reduce the tap outlet by inserting a spray nozzle into the outlet of the tap. This grid-like insert converts the tap discharge from a flow to a spray. Tap restrictors can reduce the flow rate of a tap by up to 70% when compared to a standard unrestricted tap. Care should be taken to avoid fitting tap restrictors to slow flowing taps as this could reduce the flow rate to unacceptable levels, create annoyance and compromise hygiene. Care should also be taken when fitting outlet reducers to keep the new outlet above the full sink water level to avoid back syphoning up the tap which is a potential cause of contamination for water supplies.

Since tap restrictors reduce the flow rate from taps they should not be used where rapid filling is required, for example on bath taps or, in the non-domestic situation, on taps used to fill cleaner's buckets.

Washroom isolation. The use of presence detectors and solenoid valves can be extended from the isolation of individual taps to the entire washroom. A PIR or ultrasonic detector is fitted in the washroom to detect presence in the main area. When no presence is detected for 15 minutes two solenoid valves shut off the hot and cold supplies to the washroom. This instantly prevents the loss of water from taps left running. It also prevents water loss if a toilet cistern is overflowing and has gone undetected. BREEAM points are available from the specification of washroom isolation. Care should however be taken that the isolation does not conflict with the filling strategy of automatic urinals (see later).

One factor that can lead to water waste is the running of taps until the desired water temperature is obtained. In commercial buildings a secondary hot water loop can avoid this (see *'DHW loops'* in Chapter 8). Another solution would be to examine the design of pipe layouts as described below.

Pipe layout. Care must be taken in the layout and length of pipe runs to both hot and cold taps. If the pipe runs are long, cold water contained in a pipe can become heated and may be run off to waste until the stream runs cold. The opposite is the case for hot pipework. The water may lose heat and tepid water then

will be run off until hot water leaves the tap. Insulating pipes, keeping runs short and separating hot and cold flows helps to avoid this problem.

Toilets
The flush of a modern toilet discharges 6 litres of water. This is a relatively small amount of water when compared with the 9 or 13 litre flush of an older toilet. There is no prescribed lower limit for the volume of a flush but reducing the volume of water further must be carried out with care as the prime function of the toilet must be retained - which is removal of the waste in one flush.

In older toilets there are a number of remedial measures which can be used to reduce the volume of water discharged with each flush. Water displacement devices can be inserted into the cistern such as rubber blocks. The block displaces an amount of water equivalent to its own volume. Each flush will save a volume of water equivalent to this volume. Another method is to insert a hippo bag into the cistern. This is a plastic bag containing crystals that absorb water and expand, displacing up to 3 litres of flush water as it does so. Hippo bags can usually be ordered free from your local water authority. An alternative method is to use cistern dams. These are rubber sheets which are inserted into and across the cistern isolating part of the flush water, which is therefore not discharged on flushing. Care must be taken with each of these devices that sufficient water is discharged on flushing to clear the toilet bowl. Inadequate clearance will result in hygiene problems and the necessity of a second flush would result in waste.

Dual flush cisterns are also available that use a lower volume of water to remove urine than that to remove faecal matter. Instructions should be visible on the cistern as to how the dual flush operates. As with all mechanical devices it should be checked periodically to ensure it is working correctly. Reducing the amount of water used in toilet flushing could reduce domestic water consumption by 10%.

Urinals

In the UK urinals operate using an automatic flushing cistern as opposed to a manual flush which is more common overseas. The mode of operation is that water is allowed to enter them at a very slow rate. When the water gets to the top of a siphon, the cistern discharges its contents into the urinals. The entry of water into the cistern is regulated to give a flush not exceeding 4.5 litres[1] every twenty minutes. The system is effective and requires little maintenance. However, two problems arise. Firstly, the urinals flush during occupancy hours even if no one is using them and secondly the urinals continue to flush outside occupancy hours during the night, weekend and holiday periods, again when they are unused.

Two types of system are available which restrict flushing of the urinals to within occupancy hours; both are based on a form of occupancy detection;
● hydraulic systems
● detector/solenoid valve systems.

Hydraulic valves are installed in the supply pipe to the cistern. The valve within them is normally closed, preventing water from entering the cistern. However, turning on a tap or flushing a WC in the toilet area results in a reduction of water pressure in the pipe. The pressure reduction causes a valve to open in the device allowing a small volume of water to enter the cistern. This process is repeated as each person visits the urinals and washes their hands until the cistern is filled and subsequently flushes. It can be seen therefore that frequency of urinal flushing is linked to tap usage or toilet flushing within the washroom area. As with all water saving devices, careful commissioning is required to ensure the devices operate as designed. A major benefit of the system is that they require no power supply for their operation.

Detector/solenoid valve systems do require either a mains or battery power supply. The units comprise an occupancy detector such as a passive infra-red (PIR) detector or an ultrasonic detector which is linked via a control

unit to a solenoid valve (Figure 11.2). There are various control strategies, one of which is that when occupancy of the washroom is detected a timer is initiated. Twenty minutes later the control unit opens the solenoid valve in the pipe work for a sufficient time to allowing enough water to flow to cause a flush. The unit is de-activated during the waiting period so that if the washroom is used regularly flushes will still only occur every twenty minutes. If the washroom is not visited for example, at weekends, then no flushes occur. Some units are programmed to give one flush in each twenty four hour period in the absence of occupancy to fill traps and enhance hygiene.

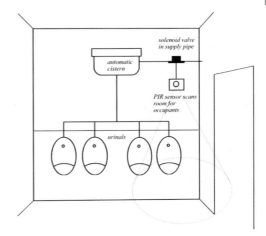

Figure 11.2. Diagram of an occupancy based flushing control system.

Novel systems

The sections above describe how traditional sanitary ware can be modified to save water. This section details some of the innovative products that have been developed to reduce to a minimum the volume of water consumed by sanitary appliances. The devices described are;
● waterless urinals
● vacuum toilets
● composting toilets.

Each of these systems have been used more frequently overseas but are now being introduced to a greater degree in UK buildings.

Waterless urinals

The basic principle of waterless urinals, as the name implies, is to eliminate the use of water for flushing. Waterless urinals are available in two main forms; barrier systems and contact disinfecting systems. Both systems require that existing traps are replaced by waterless alternatives. A saving in capital costs can be made in new buildings because a water supply to the urinals is not required. Savings will be made in terms of zero water use but there will be running costs involved in the provision of chemical consumables.

Barrier systems use a low density fluid inserted into the trap (Figure 11.3). This fluid is a mixture of oil and disinfectant and will float on any urine in the trap. Additional urine descends through the barrier liquid, through the trap and is discharged to the drain. The trap requires topping up each day, a task that is usually carried out by the cleaners. Complete replacement of the barrier liquid is recommended between two and six times a year, depending on frequency of urinal use.

Contact disinfecting systems deodorise and disinfect the urine as it leaves the urinal. A disc or rod of material, impregnated with disinfectant, is inserted into the upper part of the trap.

The insert must be replaced on a weekly basis. Urine flows over the material releasing disinfectant and a deodorant.

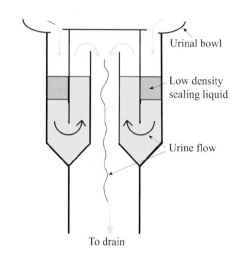

Figure 11.3. Cross sectional diagram through a waterless urinal trap.

As with anything novel, there is a degree of reticence for specifiers to use the systems due to lack of performance information. It is important to note that installations are now being made in the UK and performance is being monitored. This will give confidence in the system's

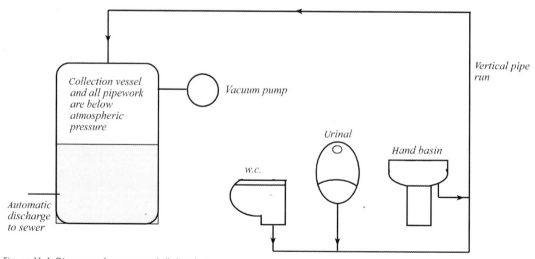

Figure 11.4. Diagram of a vacuum toilet system.

ability to deal with odours, hygiene concerns and the effects of discharging of concentrated urine to the sewerage network.

Vacuum toilets

Traditional sanitary systems rely on the carrying away of waste by relatively large volumes of water. The driving force for this is the fall of water by gravity in continuously downward sloping pipes from the toilet itself to the main sewer. Vacuum sanitary systems, on the other hand, are driven by air pressure (Figure 11.4). Commonly used on ships and in some locations on the continent, a number of systems are now being installed in UK buildings. The system operates as follows. The toilet bowls contain a small volume of water, approximately 1.2 litres, into which the waste is deposited. This is, however, isolated from the discharge pipe work by a valve. The pipe work beyond is maintained at a pressure 0.5 bar below atmospheric pressure by pumps in the plant room. Depressing the toilet handle results in the valve being opened. External air pressure then forces the contents of the toilet along the pipe work to a collecting vessel in the plant room. A fresh volume of rinse water is then added to the bowl resulting in a saving of 4.8 litres of water per flush.

As well as the water conserving benefits of vacuum toilets, a number of additional advantages of the system can be highlighted;

- standard diameters of gravity sanitary pipe work are 100mm. Vacuum systems use 50mm pipe work. This is less expensive and more simple to accommodate in the building
- no extract ventilation pipes are required in the toilet area as a volume of room air (60 litres) is drawn into the toilet with each flushing. Replacement air is drawn into the toilet cubicle from the washroom area
- each flush uses 1.2 litres of water, compared with a standard flush of 6.0 litres
- system design is more flexible, since vertical pipe runs can be used
- large objects inserted into the toilet cannot get past the discharge valve and so are easily removed, preventing serious blocking of pipes.

One of the first large scale installations to be installed in the UK was at Birchanger green service area and 60 room motel[2]. The system serves 127 toilets. At the time of installation the predicted running cost savings were £8200 per annum, compared against additional system costs of £16400, giving a simple pay back period of two years.

As with most systems, there are issues to consider as well as the benefits. The first is that the sound characteristic of flushing is changed. A standard flush lasts 12 seconds and achieves a sound level of 80 dBA, a vacuum flush lasts 3 seconds and reaches a sound level of 78 dBA. However, the character of the sound makes it more 'surprising'. The other issues to consider are that the system must be installed by specialists and that electricity is needed to operate the vacuum pumps and also to discharge waste from the collection vessel to the main sewer when it is full. The cost and environmental impact of electricity use must be considered when determining the overall environmental impact of the system. The cost element is relatively simple to consider. But the environment is more complicated as you are comparing water savings with CO_2 emissions arising from electricity usage.

Composting toilets

Composting toilets do not use water to flush away the contents of the toilet bowl. Instead the waste simply falls into a composting chamber where it is broken down into harmless matter by the action of aerobic bacteria. Figure 11.5 is a cross sectional diagram of a typical composting toilet. Sitting on the seat, the internal cover falls to reveal the compost chamber. The waste falls into this chamber, which is well ventilated to encourage aerobic digestion. The waste is mixed either manually or by motor to mix the fresh material with old material containing active bacteria. The process of digestion by the bacteria converts the waste into compost or humus which falls into the humus tray for storage.

On emptying the tray, which is slid out to the front of the unit, the contents can be used as a soil fertiliser. The smallest toilets require a small electric heater to encourage aerobic digestion and to evaporate excess liquids. A fan is needed to ventilate the unit (Figure 11.5) which draws in room air, passes it through the composting chamber and discharges odours outside. The cost and CO_2 output due to the electrical consumption of this fan and heater must be considered when looking at overall environmental benefits.

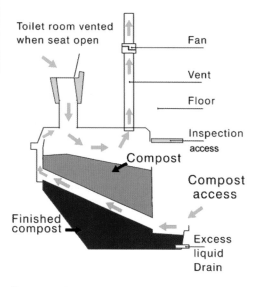

Figure 11.5. Cross sectional diagram of a composting toilet.

Some composting toilets have a relatively small bowl in the bathroom but this is connected via a vertical pipe to a composting chamber on a lower floor, possibly the cellar. The larger size of the composting chamber makes it suitable for a family and the heat generated by the composting process may make it unnecessary to have a heater to drive off excess liquid and a fan to cause air movement as there is sufficient buoyancy in the warm air created during digestion.

Accommodation of composting toilets needs some thought in existing housing since they are physically larger than conventional flush toilets. In small households or holiday homes the humus tray needs emptying once per year.

This period will be shorter in households with a greater number of occupants or more continuous occupation.

Reclaimed water systems

Each UK citizen uses, on average, 150 litres of water per day. Of this only 2.5 litres are used for drinking. This means that 147.5 litres of potable water are used for purposes for which non potable water could be used. It is too costly to provide dual mains systems to buildings so all delivered water is potable. However, there are two local sources of non potable water that could be reclaimed and utilised. These are rainwater and grey water. Greywater is water originally from the potable mains supply that has been used for washing, bathing, washing dishes or washing clothes. Greywater will contain chemicals, organic suspended solids and contaminants, such as fat and grease. These can all cause maintenance problems if greywater is collected for re-use.

Foul water is that derived from toilet flushing. Its use cannot be contemplated, unless it is passed through an effective sewage treatment plant to remove suspended organic matter, pathogens and reduce its biochemical oxygen demand. Even then it must be subjected to continuous monitoring for water quality, especially contamination by faecal bacteria. The use of a small scale sewage treatment plant and a reed bed system for final cleaning of the effluent is a possible solution to on-site reuse of grey and foul water.

Because of the problems of using greywater and foul water this section will concentrate on the use of rainwater to reduce the intake of water from the mains.

Collection and utilisation of rainwater

Rainwater has traditionally been collected by gardeners for watering plants. Their systems collect rainwater from a down spout draining the roof. For internal uses this rainwater must be diverted, filtered and stored in a large collection vessel or an underground storage tank (Figure 11.6). Since there is often a lack of space in domestic buildings this storage tank is most likely to be installed externally below ground, accessible via a manhole cover. Overflow pipework from the storage tank allows excess water to flow to the normal surface water drain. In non-domestic buildings there may be sufficient room and structural strength within the roofspace to accommodate the storage tank. This is useful as a flow of water to the tank and from it to appliances could be by gravity. However it loses the benefit that a subterranean tank has of being in a cool, dark environment which discourages the growth of algae and bacteria.

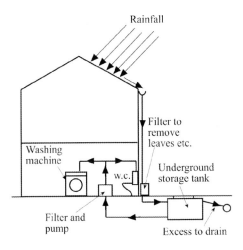

Figure 11.6. Diagram of a rainwater collection and utilisation system.

Rainwater is relatively clean when it is falling through the sky, although it will pick up some air pollution. However, it has the potential to become seriously polluted as it falls on the roof and runs through the gutters. Here it can come into contact with bird droppings. It is for this reason that collected and filtered rainwater is considered non-potable and is usually restricted to toilet flushing or possibly as a supply for washing machines. Rainwater can be used for drinking but it must first be thoroughly filtered and then sterilised using an ultra violet light. The filtration is necessary to remove suspended

particulates from the water. If they are not removed pathogens could be shaded from the ultra violet light by a particle of dirt and so would not be killed. The ultra-violet steralisation unit consists of a length of quartz glass pipe, through which the water to be treated flows. Alongside this pipe is a powerful lamp that emits ultra violet light. Just as UV radiation can cause skin damage in humans, it also kills bacteria and other pathogens in the water.

When using rainwater in a building, the pipes in the system must be clearly marked. This avoids the risk of cross contamination occurring at a later date when others may occupy the building and carry out work on the water system, possibly installing new sinks by tapping into the pipework. All water bylaws, testing and fitting regulations must be complied with to ensure that the system is safe and does not pose a health risk.

Rainwater harvesting design calculations
(With thanks to Rainharvesting Systems Ltd for provision of the following collection data)

It is important that a rainwater system and storage tank be sized correctly. This can be done using this simple calculation:

    Roof area (plan view m²)
    x annual rainfall (mm)
    x filter collection efficiency
    x co-efficient of collection of the roof
    = total annual rainwater collection (ltrs).

The roof materials and pitch will affect the collection co-efficient. For instance, pitched slate would transfer the water to the gutters quickly and be good - 80% (0.8), a flat roof would suffer more from evaporation and wind blown losses - 50% (0.5).

Most pre-filters are very efficient ,80 (0.8) to 95% (0.95) when clean, but time reduces this, so a regular cleaning programme should be followed in order to keep to these collection levels (about 4 to 6 times a year). This is probably the only regular maintenance a system will need.

Example rainwater calculation

A terraced house with a pitched tiled roof of area 70m² (co-efficient of collection about (0.75) and a rainwater pre-filter (efficiency 0.9) in a region that has 900mm of rainfall :

$70 \times 0.75 \times 0.9 \times 900 = 42,525 ltrs$

This would yield 42.5m³ of rainwater each year.

Tank size. From this figure a proven and reliable calculation, that gives an optimum tank size to give about 18 days of storage, would be to install a tank that will hold 5% of the annual yield (2126 ltrs). We also need to take into account three factors;

- the desired rainwater volume (2126 ltrs)
- 10% "wet" volume at the bottom
- 10% dead space at the top.

So from this we can conclude that we need to chose the next standard size tank above this, say 2600 ltrs (or nearest). Choosing too large a tank can give a longer number of day's storage but can increase the cost significantly and perhaps risk a decrease in water quality if the tank failed to overflow. The tank does need to overflow occasionally, as this is part of the cleaning process. (For more detailed information on this see *'Rainwater harvesting'* in Volume 1).

Water demand. Using the same terraced house occupied by two people using say 150 ltrs/day each, with about 46% (69 ltrs/person/day) being used for toilet flushing, washing machine and gardening would result in an estimated annual consumption of:-

$69 \times 2 \times 365 = 50,370 ltrs (50.37m^3)$

This figure works out to be of the same order as the rainwater supply potential, so from this we can conclude that a significant part of the total water consumption of the house could be met from rainwater harvesting.

Commercial. In a commercial situation the roof areas and potential uses for non-drinking water are higher so the volume of water saved could be much greater.

A commercial example might be: a factory

with a roof area of 1000m² and 900mm of rainfall employing 40 people, using rainwater only for toilets. 1000 x 0.6 x 0.85 x 900 = 459,000 ltrs potentially to collect. 40 x 3 (visits to the loo) x 6 ltrs x 5 days x 52 weeks = 187,000 ltrs required.

This example illustrates that more than enough water can be collected off only half the available roof area. Rainwater harvesting needs to be considered as a part of a long term and overall environmental plan towards more sustainable development. The advantages to us and the wider environment of preventing flooding and erosion of all the water courses, are incalculable.

Water management

Following the design and installation of any water consuming system, incorporating water conserving technologies or not, the system should be monitored and managed to ensure that consumption remains within acceptable limits. Any deviations from predicted consumption should be investigated and action taken to bring water usage back to normal levels.

Monitoring and targeting

It is known that metering of domestic supplies results in water consumption savings as shown by trial installations in the Isle of Wight. This, in part, is for punitive reasons, i.e. fear of higher bills and in part, due to increased awareness of consumption.

Consumption must be related to some kind of baseline to determine if it is at acceptable levels or not. As with energy, initial consumption targets can be set, based on system design consumption or comparison with similar installations. For example, a local authority can log the water consumption of all its schools and devise a water performance indicator (WPI). A useful figure is annual consumption of water per pupil per year (litres/pupil/y). By comparison of the figures for each school, those schools with high WPI values could be identified. The highlighted schools should then be investigated to identify and eliminate the cause of the excessive consumption. This procedure is only possible in those buildings where the water is metered. However rising water and sewerage charges justify installation of main and additional sub meters in order to monitor the whole or parts of buildings. BREEAM points are available in new non-domestic buildings for the installation of meters with an electronic reader and output that can be integrated into the building energy management system.

In the absence of a large comparative body of information, monitoring is still useful to identify sudden increases in consumption above the norm, such as results from leakage.

Identification and avoidance of leaks

Regular inspection of sanitary appliances can identify dripping taps and running overflows which can then be repaired. Leaks in hidden pipe work and especially those underground can only be identified by monitoring water consumption and noting a sudden unexplained increase in consumption. Taking water meter readings at the beginning and end of a period during which little or no consumption should occur, can confirm the presence of a leak. One example is taking meter readings at the end of the working day on Friday and before the start of work on Monday. Any consumption above background levels, for example for flushing urinals, would indicate a leak.

When a leak is suspected, a number of techniques are available for leak detection. Visual inspection, looking for damp patches, can be useful but many leaks occur underground. In this situation acoustic leak detection can be used. These systems use sensitive microphones to detect the sounds of leakage and can pin point a leak to within one metre.

Water fuses are available, which are a flow valve fitted into the supply pipework. If an excessive flow takes place through the water fuse it automatically shuts, closing off the water supply to the premises. The main function of these devices is to avoid major damage from a burst pipe system. However, they will also stop the excessive loss of water arising from a burst main pipe.

Water conservation awareness

In 1996 the government placed water companies under the statutory duty to promote the efficient use of water by its customers. This, in practice, has taken the form of water supply companies taking out advertisements in newspapers and including leaflets in bills informing customers about the ways in which water consumption can be reduced. Companies also offer advice on methods of water reduction to individuals and companies. Within industry, the efficient use of water by staff should be promoted by management, usually by the energy manager. Methods include the use of educational seminars, reports in internal newsletters, poster campaigns and information stickers in washrooms. Schemes such as these should be repeated at regular intervals as it is known that awareness schemes can result in significant water savings but these tail off quickly with time as water consuming behaviour returns to normal.

References for Chapter 11

1. BS 6465 part 1, p17, HMSO, 1984
2. Brister, A. Are You Throwing Money Down The Pan. Building Services. pp24-25, August 1995

Useful websites

Rainharvesting Systems Ltd
    www.rainharvesting.co.uk
UK Rainharvesting Association (UKRHA)
    www.ukrha.org
Water Regulations Advisory Scheme (WRAS)
    www.wras.co.uk

Appendix A
Guide to the properties of most commonly available building insulation materials

Many people wish to understand more about the properties of insulation products. John Garbutt, with the assistance of members of the Thermal Insulation Manufacturers Association (TIMSA) and others have compiled the following checklist.

Cellular glass

Cellular glass is manufactured using glass, which is ground into a fine powder and mixed with carbon. It is then placed in trays and passes through a cellulating oven. The reaction of oxygen in the glass and the carbon results in an inert mass of hermetically sealed glass cells which contain 2/3rd vacuum and 1/3rd CO_2. It is inorganic and contains no binders. It is suitable for roofs, walls and floors.

- Manufactured from 66% post consumer recycled glass.
- Thermal conductivity typically ranges from 0.040 to 0.050W/m.K depending on compressive strength.
- Relies on CO_2 and a partial vacuum in cells for its thermal properties.
- Non-toxic, non-irritant, HFA blowing agent, formaldehyde and fibre free.
- Non-combustible and Euroclass A1, no contribution to fire.
- When used with combustible products it will retard the spread of fire.
- Non-corrosive and fungus/insect resistant.
- Impervious to water vapour diffusion and does not require a vapour barrier to protect it.
- Impervious to liquid water.
- Impermeable to air and manufacturers recommend that all board joints are sealed to give a completely air-tight layer.
- Dimensionally stable, with high compressive strength - 500 to 1600kPa.
- Does not settle.
- Can be recycled.
- As an inert product it has no

effect on the water table and in time it is assumed that it would return eventually to be sand from which it originated.

Cellulose fibre

Cellulose fibre insulation is typically manufactured from recycled newspaper. The addition of a non-hazardous, inorganic salt fire retardant provides excellent protection against fire, well above the Building Regulations' requirements. It is also protected against biological and fungal attack, treated against insects and is unattractive to vermin.

It is designed for use in timber frame walls or other constructions protected against exposure to liquid water, e.g. lofts, pitched roofs, steel framed structures and floors. It is installed by registered specialist installers, employing one of three recommended installation techniques: damp spray, open blown or dry injection. Correctly installed, cellulose fibre completely fills the inner wall cavity, eliminating all gaps, which prevents convection currents. No cutting is required. It is harmless to other common building components, such as copper pipes, electric cabling and nail plate fasteners.

- Content is over 80% by weight recycled paper; balance comprises inorganic salt fire retardant.
- Thermal conductivity typically ranges from 0.035 to 0.036W/m.K.
- Relies on entrapped air and the insulation properties of paper for its thermal performance.
- Non-toxic and non-irritant, no added formaldehyde and free from VOCs.
- Flame retardant; Class 1 flame spread rating.
- Non-corrosive and fungus/insect/vermin resistant.
- Its hygroscopic nature means that it absorbs water vapour at times of high humidity and releases it when conditions allow. This prevents any problems of excessive moisture build up within a wall or other insulated structure.
- Should not be used in applications exposed to liquid water.

- Air movement will not disturb the product in a loft because of the friction bonding between adjacent fibres.
- Dimensionally stable.
- Low compressive strength.
- When installed in lofts and floors at densities between 25-30kg/m³ it may settle (due to vibration or other reasons), but an allowance is made for this during installation.
- When installed in walls, at densities between 45-60kg/m³, the installation method ensures no settlement.
- Can be recycled or reused at end of life.
- The paper content is biodegradable.

Expanded polystyrene (EPS)

Polystyrene is an organic, thermoplastic polymer. The manufacturing process of EPS uses expandable beads. The beads incorporate a hydrocarbon blowing agent (pentane) so that, when heated with steam, they expand to more than 30 times their original size. The expanded beads are subsequently fused together in a mould to produce a shaped product or a large block, which can be sliced into boards.

The tiny amount of pentane used in the product is released to atmosphere immediately on manufacture and is replaced by air. The released pentane is quickly broken down in the atmosphere but can also be recovered in processing plants.

- All waste EPS produced during the course of manufacture is recycled back into the manufacturing process.
- Waste packaging is collected and incorporated in insulation products to provide a second long term use of the raw material.
- Thermal conductivity typically 0.038W/m.K.
- Some modified types of EPS can achieve values as low as 0.030W/m.K.
- Relies on entrapped air for its thermal properties.
- Non-toxic and non-irritant, HFA blowing agent-free, formaldehyde and fibre free.

- Styrene monomer present in minute amounts.

- Fire performance when installed as recommended meets all the requirements of the Building Regulations.

- Non-corrosive and fungus/insect resistant.

- Water repellent - moisture has a minimal effect on thermal performance.

- Virtually impenetrable to air flow through the product.

- Dimensionally stable in use.

- A wide range of compressive strengths available up to 500kPa / does not settle in use.

- Can be recycled by a variety of processes at end of life.

- Non-biodegradable.

Extruded polystyrene (XPS)

Polystyrene is an organic, thermoplastic polymer. XPS is manufactured via a continuous extrusion process. Polystyrene granules are melted, mixed together with additives and a blowing agent, and then extruded under pressure through a die to form rigid foamed polystyrene which is then cut and trimmed to form insulation boards. The flexibility of the process allows XPS to be produced with a wide range of physical properties and board dimensions.

Blowing agents used today include HFCs, carbon dioxide and pentane. Of these, HFCs provide the best (i.e. lowest) thermal conductivity. The blowing agent migrates out of the cell structure over a very long period of time and is replaced by air, thereby increasing the product's thermal conductivity. This, however, is accounted for in the 'declared' thermal conductivity values used for design.

- All waste XPS produced during the course of manufacture is recycled back into the manufacturing process, as can be customers' scrap.

- Thermal conductivity typically ranges from 0.029 to 0.038W/m.K, depending upon the blowing agent.

- Has a closed cell structure and relies on the entrapped blowing agent for its thermal properties.

- Non-toxic, non-irritant, formal-dehyde and fibre free / no health risks associated with the use of XPS.

- Styrene monomer present in minute amounts.

- Fire performance: reaction to fire - Euroclass E.

- Non-corrosive and fungus/insect resistant.

- Resistant to rain, snow, frost and water vapour / very low water absorption.

- Unaffected by air movement as it is a rigid closed cell foamed plastic.

- Excellent thermal dimensional stability - note though that maximum working service temperature is 75 degrees C.

- Range of compressive strengths available, including high strength products for load bearing applications / does not settle.

- Can be recycled at end of life.

- Non-biodegradable / prolonged exposure to intense sunlight will cause surface to degrade into fine dust.

Mineral wool (glass wool and rock wool)

Glass wool and rock wool insulation are manufactured by spinning a molten inorganic material at high temperature to form a matrix of fibres, which are bonded with a thermosetting organic resin binder. The fibres are stable and durable and are typically available in the form of mats, rolls, slabs, pipe sections and loose wool.

UK and EU legislation confirms that mineral wool Insulation is safe to work with. Mineral wool has been cleared of any suspicion of being a possible carcinogen by IARC (the International Agency for Research on Cancer), which is part of the World Health Organisation (WHO).

- In the UK, glass wool typically contains from 50% recycled glass, both from manufacturing waste and post-consumer glass (cullet).

- Rock wool contains varying amounts of recycled material, including post-consumer waste and by-products from other industries diverted from the waste stream.

- Thermal conductivity typically

ranges from 0.031 to 0.044W/m.K depending upon product.

- Relies on entrapped air for its thermal properties.

- Non-toxic & free from pentane or other VOCs.

- Non-combustible in accordance with ISO 1182 and typically rated Euroclass A1 or A2.

- Non-corrosive and fungus/insect resistant.

- Water repellent and non-hygroscopic.

- Air and vapour permeable in unfaced forms, allowing constructions to 'breathe' and providing suitability for acoustic applications.

- Dimensionally stable.

- Compressive strength varies depending upon product. Resists settlement.

- Can be recycled at end-of-life - availability of facilities varies by manufacturer.

- Non-biodegradable but any waste sent to landfill is classified non-hazardous.

Multi-foils

This comprises multiple layers of a metalised material interleaved with wadding and foam, with a nominal thickness of 25-30mm. An R-value equivalent to 5.00-5.25m².K/W is typically claimed by most manufacturers of this type of product (giving a thermal performance equivalent to 200-210mm of mineral fibre).

These claims are based on performance tests devised by the manufacturers themselves, because they argue that the internationally established tests (hot box, hot plate and heat flow meter) are inappropriate for their product, a position ridiculed by almost all experts in the field. They are able to make these claims as there is no harmonised standard for them to use and they have chosen to ignore the European wide agreed process for the evaluation of the thermal performance of products in such a position. However, natural concern in the industry about the validity of the claimed R-value has led to a number of independent tests being carried out, with sobering results.

A hot box test of a leading multi foil insulation product by the National Physical Laboratory (NPL) in accordance with BS EN ISO 8990 yielded an R-value of 1.71m².K/W, including air spaces. These results were backed up by some in-situ tests described by T.I.Ward and S.M.Doran in a report by BRE, which demonstrated U-values up to four times worse than they should have been, based on the claimed performance data. The measured U-values were in much closer agreement with the 1.71m².K/W R-value found by NPL than with the 5m².K/W value claimed by manufacturers.

This leads to the worrying conclusion that buildings constructed using multi foil insulation could fall massively short of complying with approved documents L, if the calculations were based on the manufacturer's performance claims. These shortcomings will become even more apparent as the Energy Performance of Buildings Directive (EPBD) lays bare the actual energy efficiency (or lack of!) for each building.

This mess is currently in the process of being resolved by the government through the provisions of the new approved documents L and its supporting text "Conventions for U-value calculations, 2006 Edition" from the BRE (BR443). It has given multi-foil insulation manufacturers until the end of 2006 to gain CE marking for their products which would include an EU agreed method for thermal performance claims, and after that it has stated that either this CE marking data or the methods allowed by BR443 (hot box, hot plate or heat flow meter) should be used.

- Some products may contain some recycled content.
- Thermal conductivity – debated (see above).
- Relies largely on blocking radiative heat transfer for its thermal properties.
- Insulation is non-toxic & non-irritant.
- No relevant fire test data is provided so one can assume its performance is very poor.
- Fungus/insect resistant and no more corrosive than other common insulation materials.
- Moisture resistant.
- Virtually impenetrable to air flow through the product.
- Dimensionally stable in use.

- Compressible.
- Can be recycled or reused at end of life.
- Non-biodegradable.

Phenolic foam (PF)

Phenolic insulation is manufactured by a continuous process in which a liquid insulation mixture is laid down between two flexible facing layers. The mixture contains two components which, under the action of a catalyst, create an exothermic reaction. This heat evaporates a volatile liquid blowing agent contained in the mixture which forms a matrix of small bubbles or cells. When the reaction in the mixture stops, a rigid cellular board is created which is then cut and trimmed to size.

The main blowing agent used today by far is pentane, though some other blowing agents are still used. The blowing agent will remain in the cells if they are left intact by the manufacturing process but, over time, air will diffuse into the cells diluting the blowing agent and the product's thermal conductivity. This, however, takes many years and is accounted for in 'declared' thermal conductivity values. The cellular structure of phenolic insulation is much finer than rigid urethane. This inhibits gas diffusion and hence these products have very low thermal conductivity values, regardless of facing material.

These products are suitable for virtually any thermal insulation application. The main exceptions are applications where extremely high compressive strength is required and inverted roofs. They are commonly used in applications where fire and smoke performance is critical, e.g. in applications where the insulation is exposed on the inside of buildings (pipe and duct insulation / wall and ceiling lining products).

- Little or no recycled content.
- Thermal conductivity – 0.021 to 0.024W/m.K depending upon thickness.
- Relies largely on entrapped blowing agent for its thermal properties.
- Insulation is non-toxic, non-irritant, fibre-free & styrene-free.
- Independent measurements on installed phenolic insulation have revealed atmospheric formaldehyde concentrations

of around 0.02ppm (well within the limits of the natural background level of 0.00-0.05ppm) - exposure to levels below 0.05ppm is normally classified as unexposed.

- Results of fire tests to BS476: Parts 6 and 7 give the insulation a rating of Class 'O' to the Building Regulations – products are available that achieve a Euroclass B rating – insulation carries a best possible smoke obscuration rating of <5% to BS 5111: Part 1 - products are available that achieve an s1 'SMOGRA' rating.
- Fungus/insect resistant and no more corrosive than other common insulation materials.
- Moisture has a minimal effect on thermal performance.
- Virtually impenetrable to air flow through the product.
- Dimensionally stable in use.
- High compressive strength – up to 150kPa / does not settle in use.
- Can be reclaimed and reused as an insulation material or in a variety of other non-original applications / if not reclaimable then incineration for useful heat is the recommended end-of-life option.
- Non-biodegradable.

Rigid urethane (PIR/PUR)

Rigid urethane is a term that covers a spectrum of products incorporating polyurethane and polyisocyanurate insulation. Rigid urethane insulation is manufactured by a continuous process in which a liquid insulation mixture is laid down between two flexible facing layers. The mixture contains two components which, under the action of a catalyst, creates an exothermic reaction. This heat evaporates a volatile liquid blowing agent contained in the mixture which forms a matrix of small bubbles or cells. When the reaction in the mixture stops a rigid cellular board is created ,which is then cut and trimmed to size.

The main blowing agent used today by far is pentane. The blowing agent will remain in the cells if they are left intact by the manufacturing process but, over time, air will diffuse into the cells diluting the blowing agent and the product's thermal conductivity. This, however, takes many years and is accounted for in 'declared' thermal conductivity values. The process is much slower and much less marked in products faced with gas-tight foil based facing materials, hence these products have very low thermal conductivity values.

These products are suitable for virtually any thermal insulation application. The main exceptions are applications where extremely high compressive strength is required and inverted roofs. Rigid urethane products are even available for injection into cavity walls (NOT to be confused with UF foam).

- Some manufacturers use raw materials from recycled plastic (PET) drinks bottles and x-ray film / some facing materials contain recycled paper and glass.
- Thermal conductivity – 0.022 to 0.028W/m.K, depending upon thickness and facing material.
- Relies largely on entrapped blowing agent for its thermal properties.
- Insulation is non-toxic, non-irritant, fibre-free, formaldehyde-free & styrene-free.
- Results of fire tests to BS476: Parts 6 and 7 depend upon the product and the manufacturer but data is generally available - fire performance when installed as recommended meets all the requirements of the Building Regulations – products are available with LPCB and FM approval and half hour fire resistance certification to BS 476: part 21 – products are available that achieve a Euroclass B in application.
- Non-corrosive and fungus/insect resistant.
- Moisture has a minimal effect on thermal performance.
- Virtually impenetrable to air flow through the product.
- Dimensionally stable in use.
- High compressive strength – up to 150kPa / does not settle in use.
- Can be reclaimed and reused as an insulation material or in a variety of other non-original applications / if not reclaimable then incineration for useful heat is the recommended end-

of-life option.
- Non-biodegradable

Sheep's wool

Sheep's wool insulation can contain up to 15% polyester within its blend as a necessary lofting agent. Wool Insulation will adapt to the shape of rafters, joists and studs to provide a permanently tight fit. It is suitable for use in roofs, walls and floors and ideal for breathing wall constructions.

- No recycled content but wool is a fully renewable resource.
- Thermal conductivity is typically 0.039W/m.K.
- Relies on entrapped air for its thermal properties.
- Cost can be higher than other insulants.
- Non-toxic, non-irritant & formaldehyde free.
- Wool does not burn but rather melts away from an ignition source and extinguishes itself. It is treated with a natural fire-proofing agent to improve its intrinsic fire resistance and complies with BS 5803-4 (spread of fire) achieving results of zero for ignitability, spread of flame and heat evolved.
- Non-corrosive and fungus/insect resistant.
- Allows the migration of water vapour throughout the material – it is naturally breathable.
- Will absorb up to 40% of its own weight in moisture, which will subsequently re-evaporate when conditions change - insulation will maintain its thermal performance during this process.
- Any external water ingress into the product will subsequently re-evaporate out.
- Still air does not affect the product.
- Dimensionally stable.
- Compressible.
- End-of-life - can be reclaimed and reused.
- Biodegradable (it is assumed that the polyester content is so negligible that biodegradation would take place).

Editor's note: other less common insulations (eg hemp flax, cork etc.) are covered in some detail within particular stories in Volume 1. Volume 1 is available direct from the publisher at www.newbuilder.co.uk or from wherever you purchased this book.

Appendix B

Glossary of terms

Acoustics: concerned with the properties of sound

Active: characterized by energetic activity or the use of energy

Admittance: a measure of conduction, numerically equal to the reciprocal of the impedance

Biomass: organic matter used as fuel

Calorific value: the energy contained in a fuel, determined by measuring the heat produced by complete combustion of a specified quantity of it, usually expressed in joules per kilogram

Combustion: rapid chemical combination of a substance with oxygen, involving the production of heat and light

Convection: the movement caused within a fluid by the tendency of hotter and therefore less dense material to rise, and colder, more dense material to sink under the influence of gravity, which consequently results in heat transfer

Daylighting: the illumination of buildings with natural light

Efficacy: the ability tp produce a desired or intended result

Efficiency: the ratio of the useful work performed by a machine or in a process to the total energy expended or the heat taken in

Emissivity: having the power to radiate something, especially heat or light

Evaporation: to turn from a liquid into a vapour

Fuel cell: a cell producing electric current directly from a chemical reaction

Geothermal: of, relating to, or produced by the internal heat of the earth

Global warming: the gradual increase in the overall temperature of the Earth's atmosphere due to the greenhouse effect, caused by the increased levels of greenhouse gases

Greenhouse effect: the trapping of the Sun's warmth in the lower atmosphere, due to the greater transparency of the atmosphere to visible radiation from the sun, than

to infrared radiation emitted from the planet

Greenhouse gas: a gas that contributes to the greenhouse effect by absorbing infrared radiation, e.g. carbon dioxide, methane and chloroflourocarbons

Heatpump: a device which transfers energy from a colder area to a hotter area by use of mechanical energy

Illuminance: the amount of luminous flux per unit area

Inertia: a property of matter by which it continues in its existing state, unless that state is changed by an external force

Insolation: the amount of solar radiation reaching a given area

Luminance: the intensity of light emitted from a surface per unit area in a given direction

Luminescent: the emission of light by a substance that has not been heated, as in fluorescence of phosphorescence

Ozone layer: a layer in the Earth's atmosphere at a height of about 10 kilometres, containing a high concentration of ozone, which absorbs most of the harmful ultraviolet light reaching the Earth from the Sun

Passive: relating to or denoting heating systems that make use of incident sunlight as an energy source

Permeability: the state or quality of a material or membrane that causes it to allow gasses or liquids to pass through it

Photovoltaics: the branch of technology concerned with the production of electric current at the junction of two substances

R-value: the capacity of a material to resist heat flow, the higher the value the greater the insulating power

Radiation: the emission of energy as electromagnetic waves or moving subatomic particles

Reflection: the throwing back by a body or surface of light, heat, or sound without absorbing it

Refraction: the phenomenon of

light, radio waves, etc., being deflected in passing obliquely through the interface between one medium and another

Renewables: a source of energy that is not depleted by use

Resistance: the impeding, slowing or stopping effect exerted by one material thing on another

Thermal conductivity: the rate at which heat passes through a specified material, expressed as the amount of heat that flows in a unit time through a unit area with a temperature gradient of one degree per unit distance

Thermography: the study of heat distribution in structures or regions

Transmittance: the ratio of light energy falling on a body to that transmitted through it

U-value: the capacity of a material to transmit heat flow, the higher the value, the greater the insulating power

Wavelength: the distance between two points on adjacent waves that have the same phase, for example, the distance between two consecutive peaks or troughs

Appendix C

List of advertisers

Appendix D Author profiles

Principal author - Richard Nicholls

Richard is an applied physicist who began his career in buildings as a research assistant engaged in field trials of low energy houses and condensing boiler heating systems. He then spent time in industry as an energy manager with the role of reducing the energy and water consumption of a large group of local authority buildings. He is currently a senior lecturer in the department of Architecture, Huddersfield University, where he teaches environment and services to all undergraduate and postgraduate pathways and is course leader for the MSc. in Sustainable Architecture. Writing credits include the book 'Heating, Ventilation and Air-Conditioning' and editor of the website **www.info4study.co.uk**

Derek Taylor

Derek is Principal of Altechnica, the Milton Keynes based renewable energy innovation, consulting, industrial design, ecological design and architectural practice - established in 1990 - which carries out renewable energy consultancy, zero energy design of buildings and technology innovation. Derek is a Director of the Milton Keynes Energy Agency and a Visiting Lecturer in Renewable Energy in Design in EERU at the Open University.

Mike George

Mike George has more than twenty years experience in the construction industry. He graduated as an Architectural Technologist from the School of Technology at the University of Glamorgan in 2004 and is currently lecturing part–time at the University.

John Garbutt

John has been in the insulation manufacturing industry for seventeen years and is currently Marketing Director at Kingspan Insulation Ltd. He has worked for manufacturers of mineral wool, extruded polystyrene, rigid urethane and phenolic insulation. He is widely respected in the field for his technical expertise and has played a major role in the UK government's consultation process for the next revision to Approved Document L of Building Regulations for England & Wales. With a BA Hons in Natural Science from Cambridge University, and a Masters in Earth Sciences from the University of Minnesota, he is also an avid environmentalist in his private life. He is professionally and personally interested in the topic of sustainability and believes with a passion that manufacturers need to be open and honest about what they do, and that they should be responsible about what they make and how they make it.

About the Green Building Press

The Green Building Press is an independent publishing business run by people who are committed to sustainable living. It was established in 1990 to encourage and promote sustainable and environmentally responsible construction with the aim of delivering this information to as wide an audience as possible. Its website (which includes masses of free information) and publications help people create healthy and ecological homes and buildings. Its publications include the quarterly magazine, 'Building for a Future', the Green Building Bible and GreenPro, the online eco building database. At the free web forum anyone can ask questions about any aspect of eco building. The information is presented in a user-friendly manner to appeal to both professionals and the general public. The business model also follows the same philosophy and all work is to a strict environmental policy. The offices are in a building renovated to high environmental standards on a farm managed for timber and wildlife. The majority of its energy requirements are from renewables (wind, sun and water).

Index